JODI BIEBER **SOWETO**

INTRODUCTION BY NIQ MHLONGO

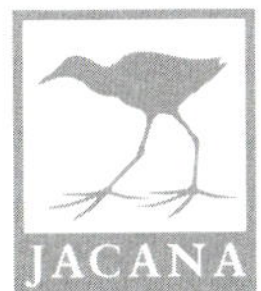

JACANA

First published by Jacana Media (Pty) Ltd in 2010

10 Orange Street
Sunnyside
Auckland Park 2092
South Africa
(+27 11) 628-3200
www.jacana.co.za

ISBN 978-1-77009-806-0

Cover design and layout by Francois Smit
Set in Berkeley
Printed by Craft Print, Singapore
Job no. 001184

See a complete list of Jacana titles at www.jacana.co.za

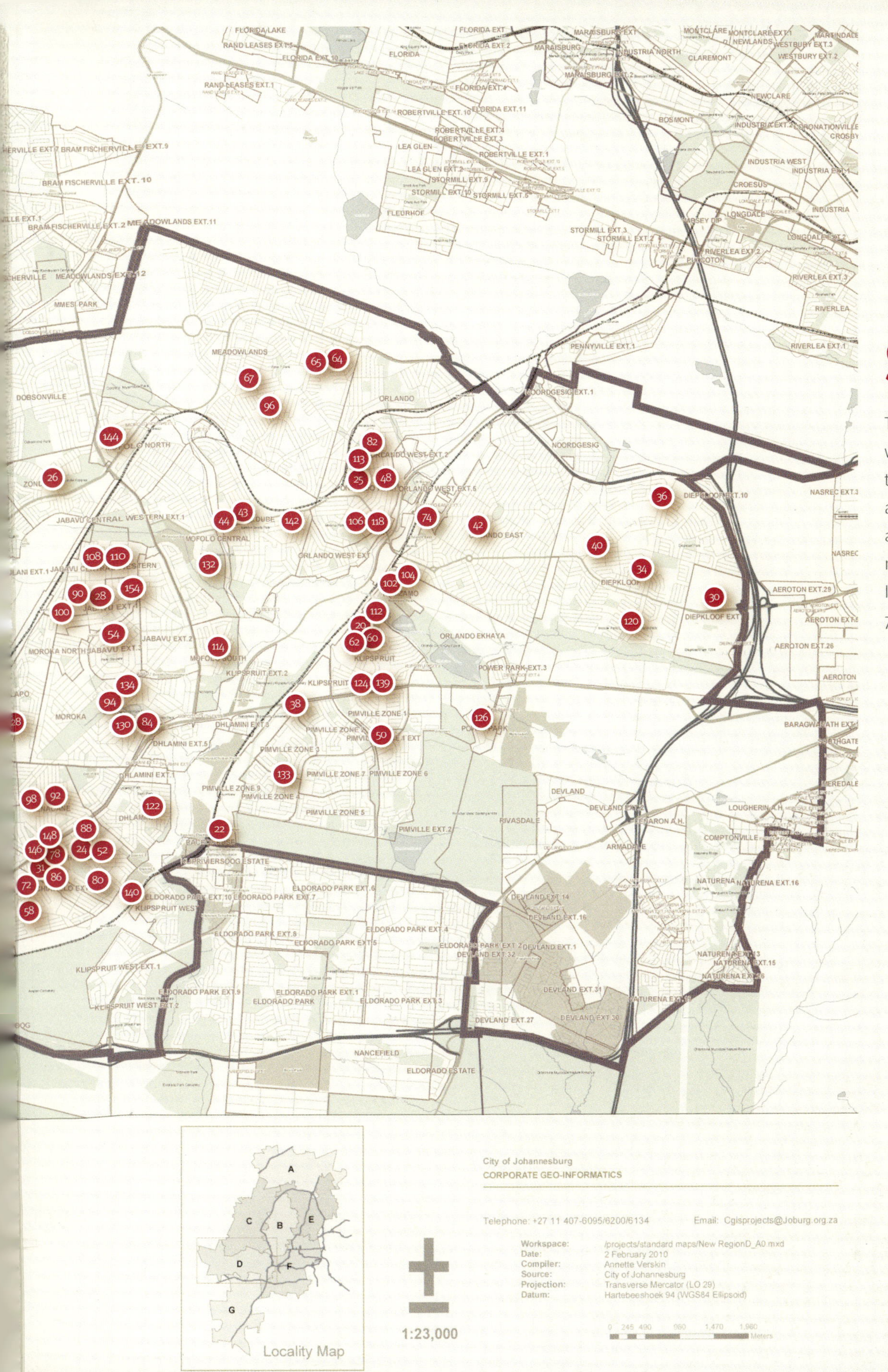

SOWETO
This is a rough indication of where each photograph in the book was taken. Some areas have been excluded as a few of the photographs did not make it into the book. I travelled approximately 7000 kilometres.
City of Johannesburg
CORPORATE GEO-INFORMATICS
Telephone: +27 11 407-6095/6200/6134
Email: Cgisprojects@Joburg.org.za
Workspace: /projects/standard maps/New RegionD_A0.mxd
Date: 2 February 2010
Compiler: Annette Verskin
Source: City of Johannesburg
Projection: Transverse Mercator (LO 29)
Datum: Hartebeeshoek 94 (WGS84 Ellipsoid)
1:23,000
Locality Map

FOREWORD

THE GOETHE-INSTITUT

The importance of Soweto in the collective consciousness is hard to overstate. It registers as a place born of resistance, perhaps even embodying the South African struggle for freedom.

Like the rest of Johannesburg, Soweto came into being as a consequence of the discovery of gold; the mines and resulting industrialisation needing workers.

Sections of the shanty town that grew up were gradually turned into formal structures of mortar and brick, and apartheid policies swiftly followed, with devastating result. Our combined image of Soweto is often overwhelmed by this meta-narrative, by its resultant socio-economic hangover, as much as by the struggle heroes and momentous events that defined it in the history books.

But the birth of Kwaito is attributed to Soweto too. And beyond the grand narratives, there is and always was lot of dancing – a lot of everything else too in a place defined by its energy and cosmopolitan nature. It seems timely in 2010, this year of the fist African FIFA Soccer Cup, to celebrate Soweto and Sowetans, and not just because of their love of the game.

This publication contemplates daily-lived realities, where here, as elsewhere, South Africans are continually reinventing themselves and their urban space. Labelling and unlabelling, claiming and discarding, Sowetans have created Soweto anew. We at the Goethe-Institut are proud to have been able to support both this book and the acclaimed home-grown photographer, Jodi Bieber, in the creation of an open-ended essay, a celebration and a partial portrait of life in Soweto today.

Peter Anders, Cara Snyman

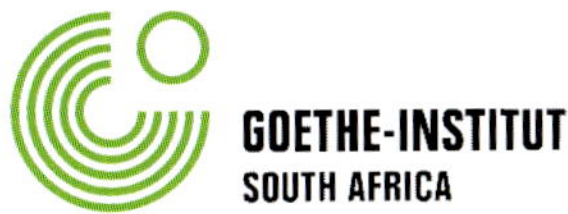

FROM WHICH COUNTRY ARE YOU?

J O D I   B I E B E R

*S*oweto came about when a French/Swedish friend, Axel Gylden, made me aware that there were very few contemporary photographic books on Soweto. Soweto is on our doorstep and sometimes we take significant things and places for granted. I have always loved photographing in Soweto. Early on in my photographic career, shortly after the 1994 elections, I would ask the then-picture editor of *The Star* newspaper, Robyn Comley, in a quiet moment if I could go and take my own photographs in Soweto. I remember as the light softened in the late afternoon, the *gogos* (grandmothers in Zulu) on the streets used to say: "Don't stay too long, the *tsotsis* (criminals) will be out after dark". Finally, they would ask me, "From which country are you?"

Fast forward a couple of years and on returning to Soweto with Axel I knew some things had certainly changed on my visit to the upmarket Maponya Mall on the Old Potchefstroom Road. As superficial as it might sound, the fact that an upmarket shopping centre existed in Soweto had symbolic connotations for me. In my mind it was a symbol of change, of normality. It was an image rarely portrayed in the international media on South Africa. This could be a scene from the upmarket shopping centres in the wealthy northern suburbs of Johannesburg or the USA, except the majority of people at Maponya Mall are black.

Fast forward to 2009. How would I approach my project, with a population of over 900 000 people (census of 2001) and approximately 32 areas within? This was a huge ground to cover.

I knew that one of the references to Soweto in the mind of the outsider would be of Hector Pieterson, who was killed in June 1976. Or perhaps it would be the famous Vilakazi Street, or Baragwanath Hospital, or poverty, HIV/Aids, or even the dusty crime-ridden streets of Soweto which I found to be not all true. I saw so much more to Soweto.

The project was built on instinct. I travelled 7 000 kilometres by car in a three-month period and these photographs are what I gathered along the way. The book is by no means the A-Z of Soweto.

Once you start spending time in Soweto you realise how diverse and different we are as a nation. Soweto operates in a completely different way to the suburbs of Johannesburg. I found myself feeling envious of how people embrace pubic living. Children play on the pavements, soccer matches are being refereed in the streets, and adults are chatting or gossiping or flirting with neighbours, friends or lovers. Music systems can be found on the stoeps of two homes next to each other pelting out different sounds. I always turned around to my assistant and said this would never happen in the suburbs. The police would be called in to put a stop to the loud music. Music is like breathing for Sowetans.

Another beautiful Soweto feature, which differs from the Johannesburg suburbs, is that when there is a wedding, funeral, or the birthday party of a one year old, it is okay to place a tent in the middle of your street as all your neighbours would be invited and everyone will be fed. The spirit of this for me was admirable. You have to remember though that nothing starts dead on time in Soweto. It is a standing joke amongst the people.

Weddings are generally on Saturdays. I failed dismally to get a photograph of a bride and bridesmaids hanging out of the window of a cool car, careering across both sides of the streets. Another Soweto fact of life is that from one o'clock in Thokoza Park, wedding photographs take place. The poses and the outfits are a feast for the eyes. But it is not so easy for the photographer, as it takes place in the harshness of the day's light.

One-year-old birthday parties are a big trend in Soweto. The parents have all the possibilites of playing with fantasy for this special day. It can range from a Barbie doll themed party, to inviting the Jo'burg Fire Department to show off their beaming red fire truck. Cynics would say Sowetans are buying into Western culture. For me, however, it put a smile on my face, it was nostalgic. It reminded me of the privileged birthday parties I enjoyed during apartheid. And it is also a good excuse for parents to have a good time.

Talk of parties leads me to food and drinks. One of my favourite meals in Soweto came from being fed at weddings or birthdays. Large pots of meat, pap and salad. Did you know green is 'in' and brown is 'out'? Here I refer to what beer is drunk.

Green bottles are more fashionable than brown in Soweto. I am not to sure if the brand is as important.

With all due respect to the popular resturaunt establishments. I loved the more low-key places like Tshidi's Place in Dube. It is run from home and you sit in the lounge eating your meal with other patrons. Another favourite for me was buying a T-bone, pap and salad take-away from Nomthandazo and Kgomotso Letsebe's house in Meadowlands, Zone 5 – and eating it at the Orlando West Regional Park where children from the neigbourhood played against the backdrop of the Orlando Football Stadium. I see a compromise has been reached between the City of Johannesburg and the people selling livestock next to the park. They are still there.

I loved Panyaza Butchery Chisa-Nyama (Braai or Barbeque) in White City Jabavu, where you buy meat that is braaied for you, and you listen to DJ's playing the best sounds. The coolest of the coolest in the trendiest of cars hang out here. Many of these people moved to the suburbs but return every weekend as they prefer the vibe.

A trend that is developing strongly in Soweto is wanting to be self-sufficient in the township and not having to go and find it in the suburbs. An impressive example is Thesis, a local clothing brand created by 5 young Sowetans, with a mixture of Western design and a Soweto touch. Their shop is in Mofolo village.

Vilakazi Street is another spin off from this. It doesn't only cater for the foreign tourist but locals alike who want to support Soweto and who do not want to drive off to the suburbs to spend their hard earned cash.

The number of sub-cultures amongst the youth is ever-growing. From rockers like Ree-Buurth, to vegetarians (yes, it is possible to get a tofu bunny chow in Soweto (The Kitchen Cafe, Rockville,

Moroka) to the Model Cs (the children who live in Soweto but go to school in the suburbs), to motorbikers like the The Soul Seekers Biking Club.

Fashion, bling and hair is big in Soweto. I decided to take photographs at the famous Hector Pieterson School because of its historical importance. The main issue at the beginning of term at assembly was not politics but about girls turning their school uniforms into fashionable clothing items. Ripped ties, short skirts and funky wigs. Girls wearing wigs were singled out that day. They were told to embrace their natural beauty and leave the wigs for later on in life. You could see some of the girls' faces drop, knowing what they had spent on their stylish wigs.

It doesn't matter if you are from Diepkloof Ext or from an informal settlement in Power Park, outward appearance is very important to a Sowetan.

We all fear the unknown and have preconceived ideas of what it might be. Informal settlements for instance. It is easy to have a preconceived notion what it might be like inside. On closer inspection, it is something quite different. It is admirable how many of the shacks are decorated with such a dignity, pride and creativity whilst the occupants wait, mostly patiently, for a new RDP home. At the same time, I met well-educated young women who had received flying colours in their final year at school, and their paths in life would play out somewhat differently from their parents.

Things are not all rosy and poverty makes it difficult for many to step out of the cycle they find themselves in, however great their potential.

The people I chose to photograph in the book all had something special that drew me to them. It was not something academic or something that one could research. It was a spontaneous feeling I had because of the person's character or the individualism they projected.Or sometimes it was a certain facet of Sowetan society I felt I needed to portray. I would meet people in the streets or malls or in their yard and stop and tell them about my project. Sowetans, I found, do like photographs and they were excited at the possibility of another side of Soweto being shown besides the stereotypical view.

Throughout my time in Soweto, nearly every single person I met (and there were many), asked me which country I was from. No one could believe I was South African. People told me only tourists come to Soweto. That made me a bit sad.

Sowetans are incredibly friendly and it takes only a greeting to get invited into someone's house. Their backdoors generally stand wide open when someone is at home.

I felt very safe in Soweto. I hear the cynics going "yeah, yeah". It is true, crime is on the decrease. Many people said to me that the community became tired of the crime in Soweto and now the police and community are working very close together. It was said that on every street there is a resident who is on the Community Policing Forum. I was more fearful of the taxis on the road going there than anything else.

Soweto is home to its people. Sowetans are made up of very different individuals with different values and beliefs. Sowetans believe they are at the cutting edge of the trends being set in the country.

When you go to Orlando West Regional Park at around 5 o'clock and see the children laughing and playing from neighbouring homes with the football stadium in the background, you realise that life can be pretty normal here, even with the major setbacks and tragedies that people encounter. The scene is similar to any other park in the world. It's just that sometimes we are not given the opportunity to see this normality in an African context. Children will continue to play with their friends in the park, as the media frenzy dies down after 2010 Football World Cup. They will still ask the white stranger entering their park "From which country are you?"

ZWAKAL'eMSAWAWA

NIQ MHLONGO

Mention the word 'Soweto' in any part of the world and people will probably understand that you're talking about the heartbeat of South Africa. But be warned, you are more likely to answer some nuisance questions about crime, unemployment, or how it is to live in a place of poor shanty dwellings where people die of violence and disease every day. Most of us are not offended by this misconception of our township because much of the struggle against apartheid happened here; hence we Sowetans boast that 'the road into democracy in South Africa runs between our small, grey, four-roomed matchbox houses'.

There is no doubt that the images of Soweto that dominate outsiders' minds are of the June 16th 1976 student uprising, when the township was virtually in a state of war against the apartheid regime. My great moments about my township, however, involve the events that occurred on a social level. In Chiawelo, where I spent the most time, we watched Chinese movies on Saturdays at the bioscope that was stationed at the nearby Gazankulu Primary School. These played during the day and at night, and the cost of each movie was fifty cents. Most of my childhood friends loved Chinese Karate movies by Bruce Lee, such as *Enter the Dragon*, and *The Dragon Fly*. Western movies like *The Good, The Bad and The Ugly* were normally shown at night and my parents wouldn't allow me out of the house at that time of the day. The person that owned the bioscope was the father of the popular fighter, Dingane Thobela. My parents preferred me to go to the closest bioscope, the one in Gazankulu School, rather than the Sansuzi in Kliptown which would have meant my having to catch the train.

In my street, the few families that were considered 'rich' were the one's that owned a television set. There were only two houses out of about twenty that had a TV set. Unlike my parents who preferred listening to the radio dramas from what was known then as *Zulu FM* and the former *Radio Tsonga*, I used to pay ten cents to watch the *A Team* TV series starring Mr T at the Mthombeni family house at the corner of our street. Since the dining rooms were very small, the family could only accommodate about twenty, and you had to make sure that you arrived very early to book yourself a piece of floor near the TV set. The only times I remember missing an episode was when the unreliable electricity was cut off. People used to think that the blackout was caused by the birds that often landed on the electricity pole, and it is the reason they encouraged us to kill them with our slings and then braai them. Although I had a bird-sling myself, I was not good at shooting.

Although the electricity was off quite often, the Mthombeni family made sure that they got their ten cents cover charge by using the car battery to connect the TV, but only for the *A Team* series. I guess they had analysed the influence of characters such as Mr T to the youth as we used to cut our hair like him. For a long time my group of friends and I shaved part of our hair completely off on the sides of our heads leaving a Mohican in the middle, as we imitated our favourite movie star.

On Sunday mornings and afternoons we waited for what we called the 'banana car' and the ice cream car to come, while playing with a kite, or marbles, or tennis, or driving our own toy cars made out of wire. Those who collected plenty of bottles would get extra packets of Simba chips from the 'banana car'. Ironically, we also looked forward to the coming of the police Hippo armoured car as they used to offer us some delicious ginger biscuits.

Sunday morning was also a day I was expected to beautify our small garden in the yard by cutting the lawn with shears. There was serious competition in the township to have the home that had a beautiful lawn and a well-polished stoep. The cutting of the lawn would take me about three to four hours, and when the sun was hot, I would use the umbrella to shield myself from it. My brothers would be polishing their shoes on the veranda while the jazz music of Mike Makhalemele; or the Mbaqanga music of Mahlathini and the Mahotela Queens blasted away from the speakers that would be put outside. That was the time before CDs, when we had only vinyl or tapes. My sister liked playing 'fahfee' or 'M'China' gambling games on Sundays, and at nine in the morning the 'Chinese Man', as we called him, would come to collect the bets.

Another important thing that I learned in our home, apart from cutting the lawn, was how to make a fire on the Welcome Dover coal stove. Every matchbox house had this particular stove, and at five o'clock every morning and then again in the evening, my two sisters and I would take turns to light the fire to boil water and cook the breakfast mealie porridge and the dinner. If you happened to come to Soweto at that time, you would think all the houses were on fire because of the coal smoke from the chimneys. My mother preferred the traditional *mbawula* coal stove as she considered it to be warmer than the Welcome Dover.

Our house had only two bedrooms, yet it accommodated all the eleven family members; my eight siblings and my parents. I used to sleep with my other four brothers in the small room and our parents occupied the other room. I became accustomed to sleeping with the lights on because two of my brothers who had jobs would switch the light on early in the morning as they prepared to go off to work. My three sisters slept in the kitchen or dining room, and the small toilet outside the house was used as a makeshift bathroom.

An unfortunate thing about my township though is that most places were 'no-go zones' because of the feared gangs such as the Ama-Sharks, or the Vikings of Mlamlankuzi, The Eagles of Phomolong, Ama-Damara from White City, The Dirty Dozen in Phiri, as well as the Black Power gang from Ndofaya, Meadowlands. It was difficult for us to go from one place to the other freely because we were frequently robbed. Although almost every Sowetan speaks all black South African languages, the issue of ethnicity was one of the biggest problems that we faced. For example, if you were Sotho from Tladi and happen to be in a Zulu-dominated territory like Zola, you were more likely to be robbed or assaulted by the gangs. That was the time when the infrastructure was not in place; the streets were dusty and without lights. It meant that we had to be very careful when going to the public swimming pool such as the one in Senoane, which was the closest to my home. My brother, who loved going to The Pelican nightclub in Orlando West, once was robbed of his money and his favourite two-tone coloured Florsheim shoes on his way there. The Pelican, which was just next to the Orlando train station, used to be one of the few decent and favourite chilling places where people could watch musicians like Sipho 'Hotstix' Mabuse play live music. It was a popular spot for international music bands, a place where both blacks and whites mixed in the heyday of apartheid.

Before the popularity of *shisanyamas* (braai/barbecue places), braais used to happen inside the yards of our matchbox houses on the occasion of *stokvel* social gatherings. Our house in Chiawelo hosted those interesting *stokvel* gigs on a monthly basis, and my brother's friends would come and drink beer and listen to the jazz music of Miles Davis or John Coltrane, or The Soul Brothers on his Tempest Hi-Fi. Every one of those guests would be 'dressed to kill'. My brother used to be a great dresser and he owned several pairs of trousers called Brentwood. He loved matching his trousers with Pringle shirts and a Dobbs hat, and he always had a yellow cloth on the pocket of his shirt to dust his shiny black C&J shoes after each dance move. The morning before the *stokvel*, which normally happened on Saturdays, my brother would send me to collect his trousers from the mobile dry cleaners in Chiawelo Train Station. The dry cleaning service only happened on weekends, and the woman who owned the business would park her brown VW combi at the station between 9 am and 12 pm on Saturdays and Sundays. My job during the week was on Tuesdays and it was to wait for the garbage truck with our plastic bag full of waste.

There was always a soccer match on weekends at the nearby dusty soccer grounds of either Joburg City, or Stars, and we used to watch live games there. The Stars team had professional soccer legends such as Mike Sporo Mangena, who ended up playing for Kaizer Chiefs and Moroka Swallows. My eldest brother Fanuel was also a well-known soccer player for Joburg City, and was nicknamed Seven. I don't know how the name came about, but I guess it was because of the position he used to play in the team.

The wall of our small bedroom was a contested space. My elder brother and I supported Orlando Pirates, while another was a Kaizer Chiefs fan, and the third brother loved the Moroka Swallows team. On one side of the wall there were Pirates pictures and on the other side my two other brothers put the Chiefs and Swallows photos. As a die-hard Pirates supporter, my elder brother would remove the Chiefs and Swallows pictures from the wall when his team lost. But when the team won, he always shouted the slogan, "Once a pirate, always a pirate". One of the reasons I also supported Pirates was that my brother would give me money to go to the bioscope if I listened to his stories about the team.

He would tell me the stories about his loyalty to the club even when Shintsha Guluva, Kaizer Motaung, an Orlando Pirates player decided to form his Kaizer XI in the seventies, after playing in the USA. Kaizer XI, later known as Kaizer Chiefs, became bitter rivals of Orlando Pirates and still today, the people of the township recall this history. Pirates fans think Motaung betrayed them and stole their players to start his successful club which is today an established brand.

My brother Herman who supported Swallows was also a referee in the National Soccer League. He would always take me to the Orlando Stadium to watch some of the games, and after each game he would recount to me legends about his team. According to him, one could see birds flying high over the stadium whenever Swallows scored or won and he would always say, *"zandiz' izinyoni"*, in praise of the team. But it is still Orlando Pirates, and their 'children', Kaizer Chiefs, that can still bring both the township and South Africa to a standstill when there is a match between the two clubs. The football encounter between the teams is known as the Soweto Derby. Speaking of nostalgia, everyone knows that in the past booze used to be free, or sold at half price in Soweto when Pirates won a game.

My elder brother, on the other hand, always boasted that former President Nelson Mandela was an ardent fan of Pirates. He argued that Kaizer Chiefs was formed way after Mandela was imprisoned on Robben Island, therefore there is no way that he could have been a fan. Like my brother, most older Pirates fans believed that the reason that their team was no longer winning the league, was because the players had stopped visiting James Sofasonke Mpanza's grave. Mpanza was at the heart of the development of Soweto and it was he who told

people in the forties to occupy vacant municipality land and to erect houses made from sacks that became known as Emasakeni. As a result, the Johannesburg municipality was eventually forced to buy more land and to build additional houses for African people in the area. During a competition in the early sixties to name the township that had mushroomed around Orlando East, one of the names that was entered was Mpanzaville, after Mpanza. The city authorities eventually decided to settle for SOWETO (short for South Western Township). Pirates are known as *ezikamagebhula, ezagebhula umhlaba kamasipala,* meaning 'those who took the vacant municipality lands by force', and this is a reference to the character of Mpanza, this leader of the people of Orlando.

A rumour circulated around Soweto, that before a game in the olden days, Pirates players and the coach used to go to Mpanza's grave to perform rituals and ask for luck. *Umuthi* (traditional medicine) was commonly used, and they would also make white players, like the goalkeeper and coach Anderson, undergo the same ritual. It is also said that during the 1976 student uprising, cars that had an Orlando Pirates sticker on them were not burnt, irrespective of who the owner was. Even today, you see immaculate, expensive German cars with Orlando Pirates sticker and it is said that this protects you from would-be car hijackers because they are likely to be supporters of this legendary Soweto football club.

While appreciating the township's significance in the struggle against apartheid, it was the advent of democracy in 1994 that made Msawawa or M'Southern, as we now affectionately call Soweto, the symbol of the New South Africa. Whether you drive in through the Soweto Highway, which used to be called Old Potchefstroom Road (now Chris Hani Road), you'll definitely realise that Msawawa is a township of contrasts, with a mixture of rich suburbs and poor shanty dwellings.

In Orlando West, for example, Soweto has its own up-market suburb called Beverley Hills, where I lived when my brother Elvis bought a house there in 1990. Here, life was different as there was hardly a common four-roomed red or grey brick house as there were in Chiawelo. In Orlando West, you found mansions with the toilets inside the house itself, similar to the ones found in Rosebank or Sandton, in the northern suburbs of Jozi. After 1994, which brought with it Black Economic Empowerment, I could spot a few Ferraris, Lamborghinis, and Audi A8s.

In drinking places, such as the Spanish Inn, Nambitha or Sakhumzi, one can see that Sowetans exude a sense of cosmopolitan sophistication, both in their speech, dress and gait. They compete with one another, wearing high-quality brand names such as Roberto Botticelli for shoes, Eduard Dressler and Giovanni Gentile for suits, Louis Vuitton and Gucci for bags and accessories. Women can tell a man's taste by smelling his Hugo Boss, or Dolce & Gabbana perfume. Huge plasma TV screens are likely to be broadcasting European football, cricket or golf while the patrons drink a magnum of Moet et Chandon, Hennessy Cognac or a shot of Johnny Walker Blue. This is a business meeting place where Soweto's high-class socialites meet to network and discuss government tenders and politics, whilst constantly making or taking calls.

Apart from soccer, Soweto is also the centre of South African culture, and has developed its own sub-culture. In popular relaxation joints like The Rock in Rockville, Panyaza in White City, Sedibeng in Meadowlands, Masakeng in Mofolo South, Herman's Place in Protea South, and the Backroom in Pimville, one can experience the friendliness and vibrancy of Soweto. Come here on a weekend, and you'll concur that the township is a trendsetter in language, fashion, music, dance and general social discourse. The Regina Mundi Church, situated on the Chris Hani Road, used to be the home to numerous anti-apartheid organisations, and hosted the funerals of most of political activists. Next to it is the popular Thokoza Park, where people go to braai under the branches of the willow trees. It is there that you are most likely to hear the new kwaito, house and hiphop sounds blasting away from the flash cars owned by the youth of Msawawa, as they show off their new-found wealth.

Indeed, you're welcome to Soweto. Even those who have moved out because of their financial success will tell you that "we sleep in our up-market suburb houses, but still live in Msawawa".

Niq Mhlongo is the author of two novels, (*Dog Eat Dog*, Kwela 2004, and *After Tears*, Kwela 2007) and two short stories (*The Dark Side of Our Street* published in German Anthology called Yizo Yizo, Verslag 2005, as *Auf der Schattenseite*, and *Golihood Drama* published by Jacana Media in 2006 in the anthology called *The Obituary Tango*. His first novel *Dog Eat Dog* won the Spanish award called Mar de Letras Intenecionale Prize in 2006. His works have been translated into several languages including Dutch, Spanish, French, German and Italian, and he has been featured in many International literary conferences, fellowships and residencies, including IWP in IOWA (USA). Niq has a BA (majoring in African Literature) from Wits University.

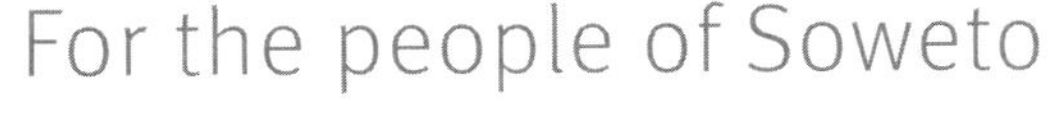
For the people of Soweto

"Soweto is like Hollywood to me.

Everything is here.

There is no longer a need to go to the other side of town."

Sibongile Mazibuko, *Jozi FM 105.8*

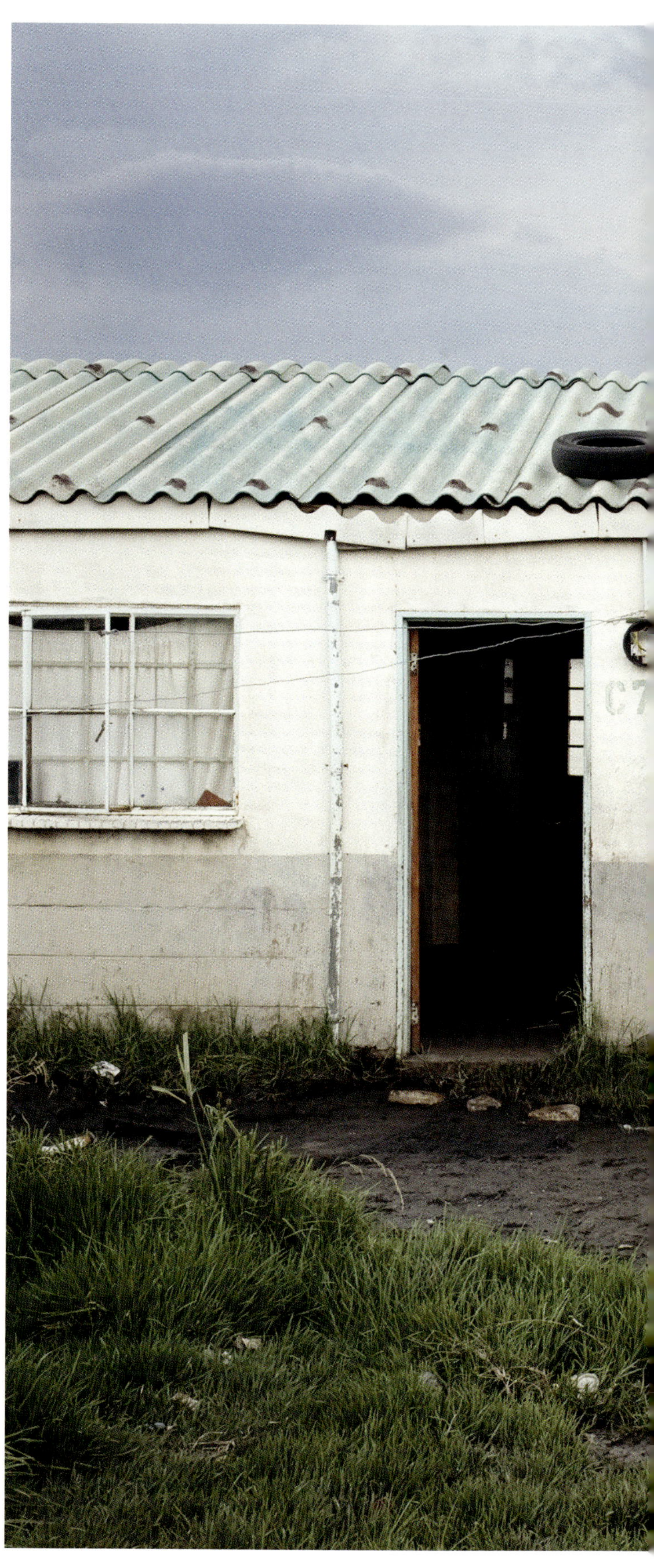

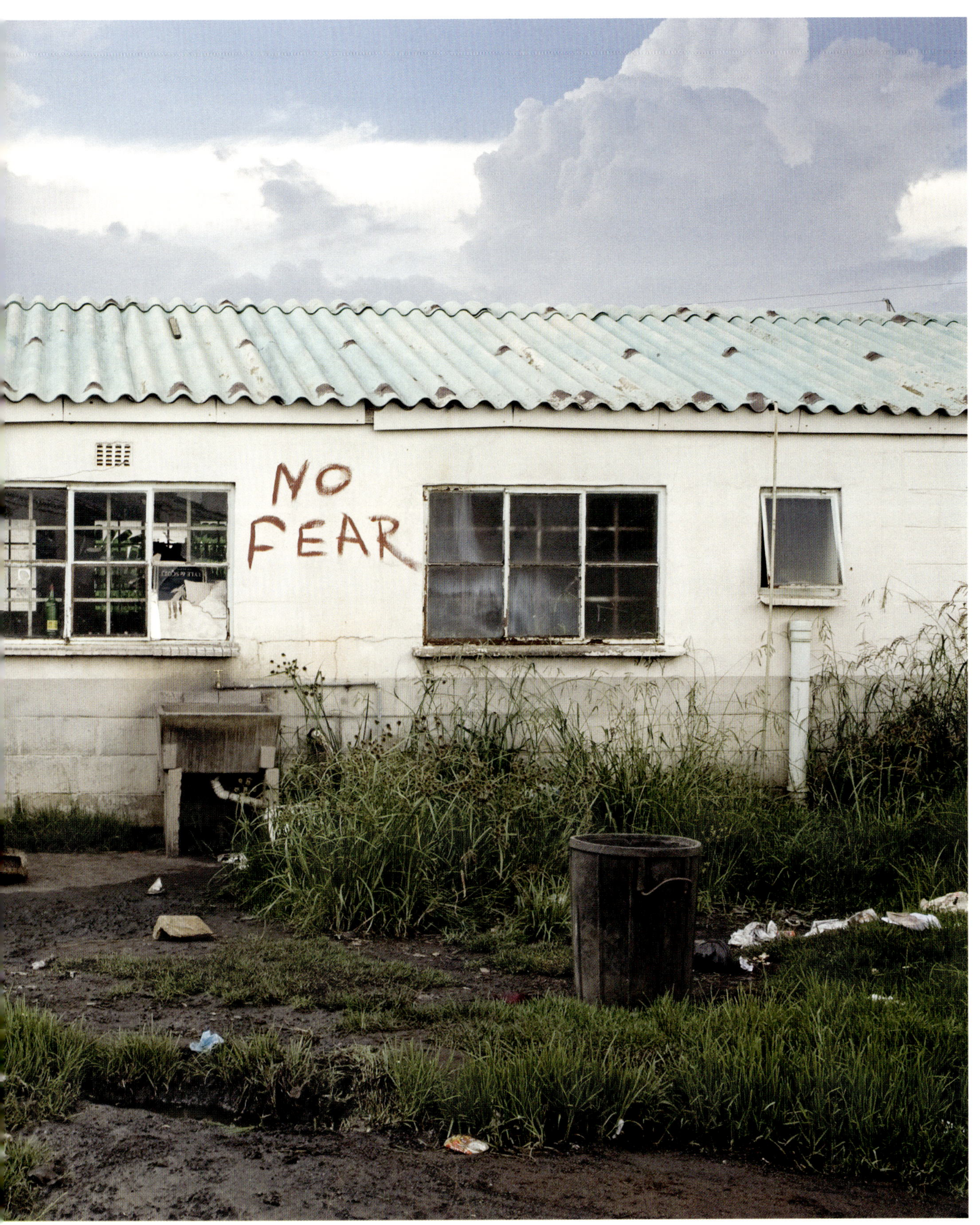

NO
FEAR

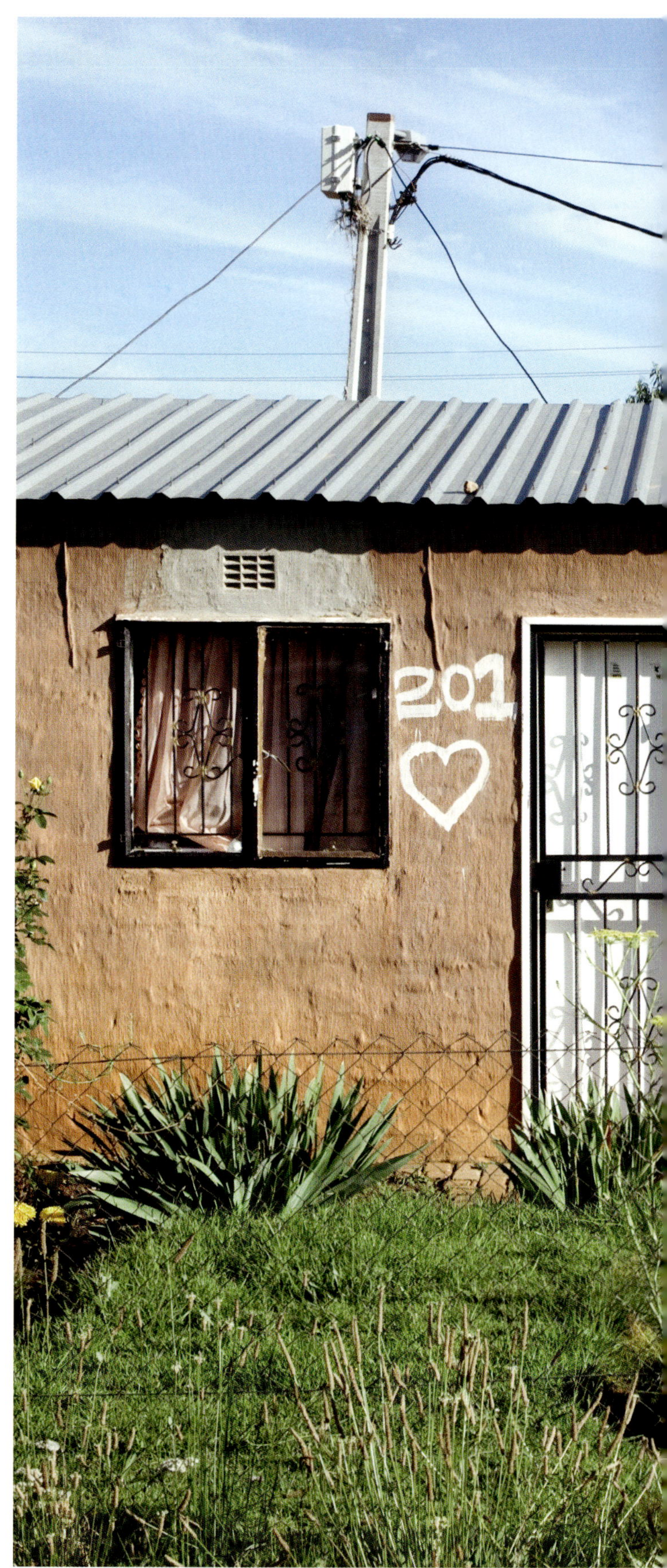

[next page left] Graduation party, Arise
and Shine Crèche, Chiawelo, 2009
[next page right] Phefeni Junior Secondary
School, opposite the Hector Pieterson
Museum, Orlando West, 2010

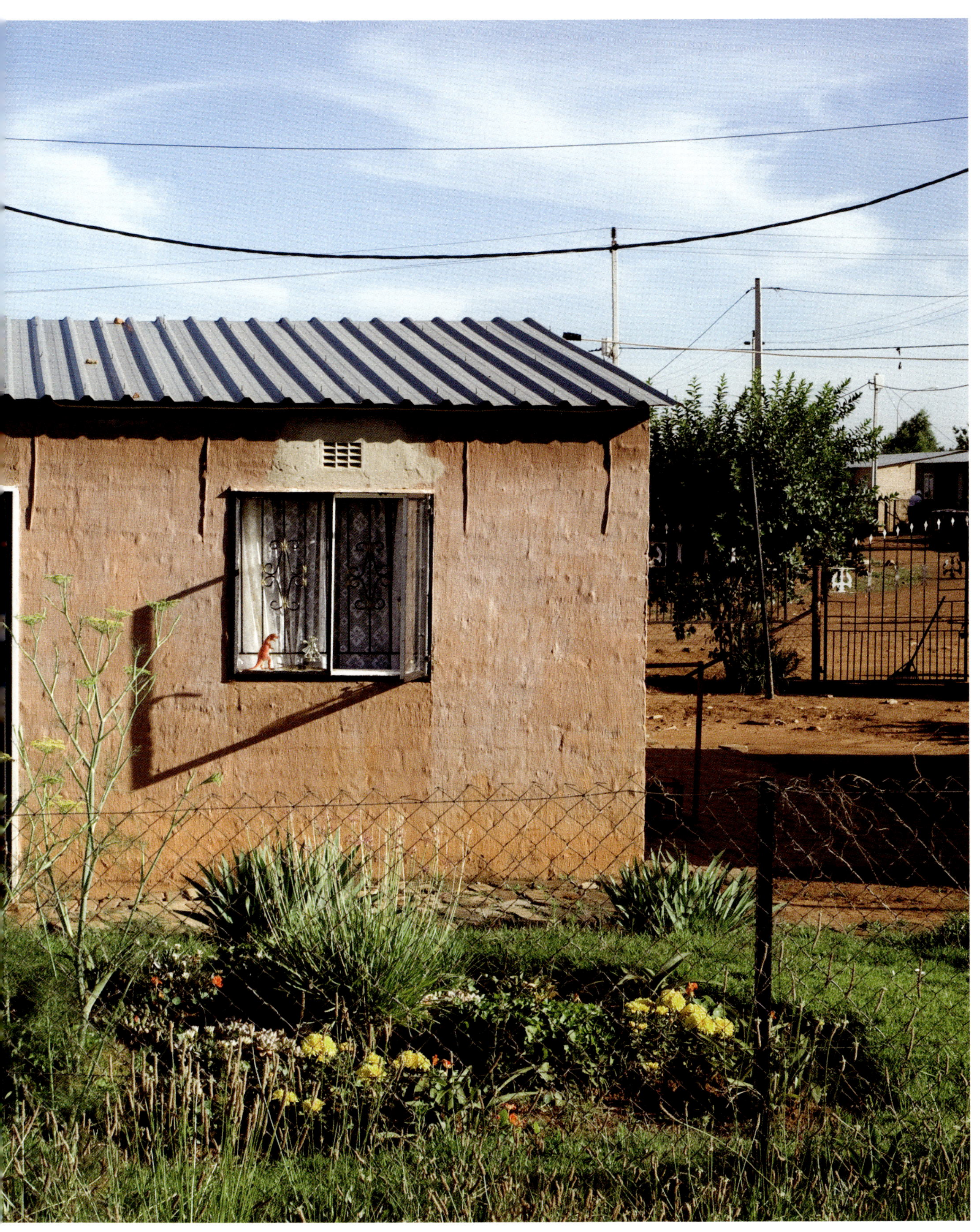

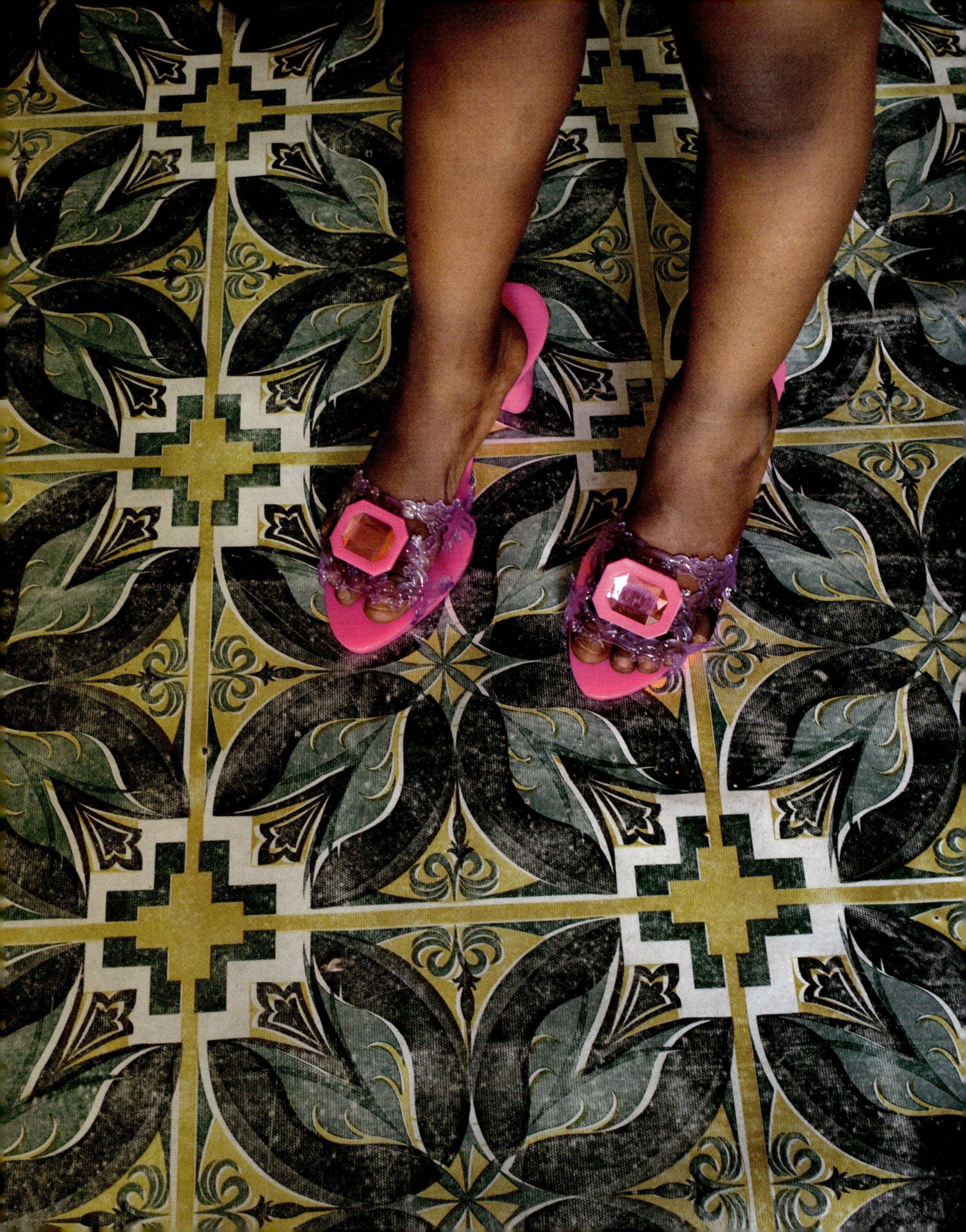

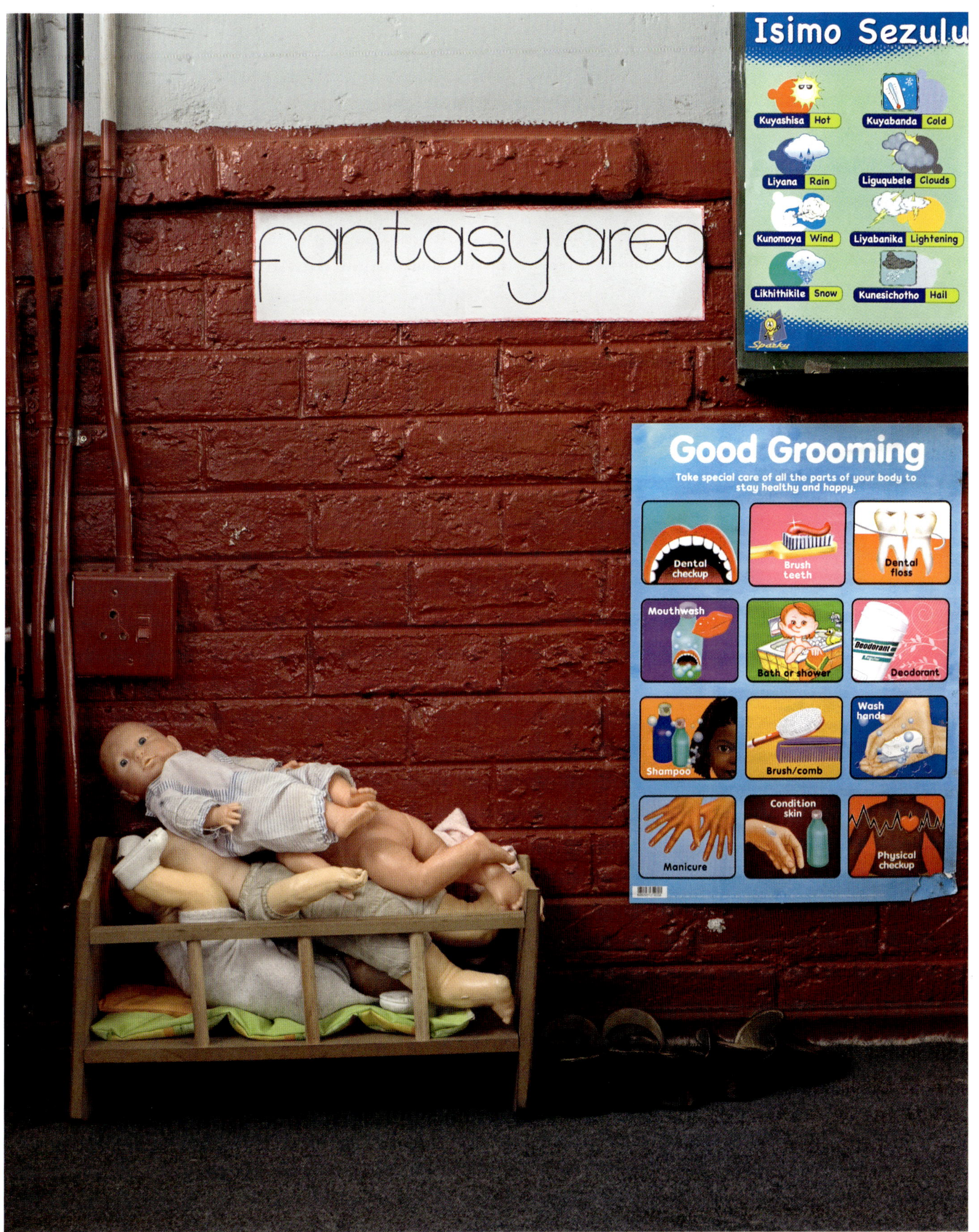

fantasy area
Isimo Sezulu
Kuyashisa Hot
Kuyabanda Cold
Liyana Rain
Liguqubele Clouds
Kunomoya Wind
Liyabanika Lightening
Likhithikile Snow
Kunesichotho Hail
Sparky
Good Grooming
Take special care of all the parts of your body to stay healthy and happy.
Dental checkup
Brush teeth
Dental floss
Mouthwash
Bath or shower
Deodorant
Shampoo
Brush/comb
Wash hands
Manicure
Condition skin
Physical checkup

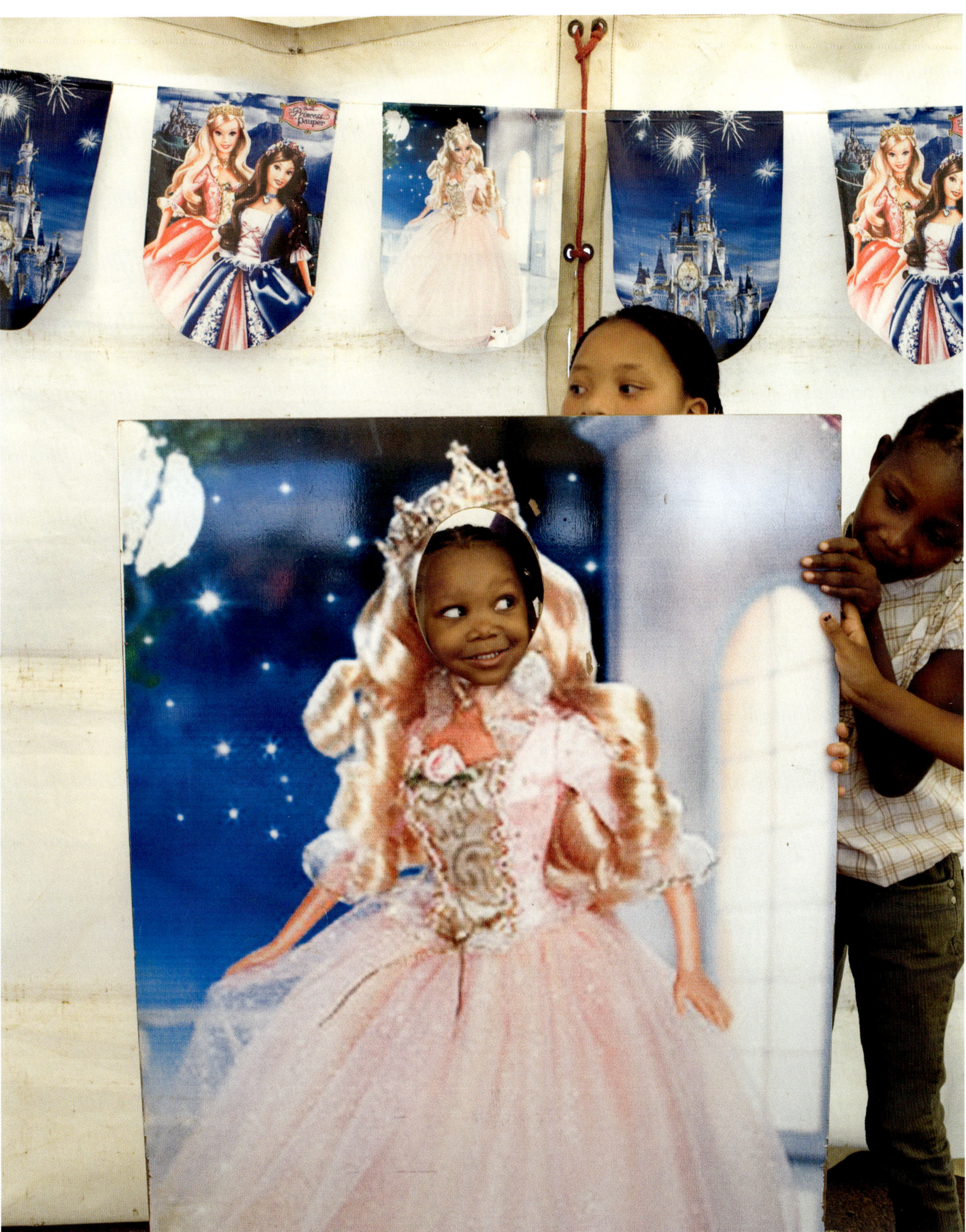

28 | Bongani Mashego and Sabelo Dlamini at a birthday party, White City Jabavu, 2009

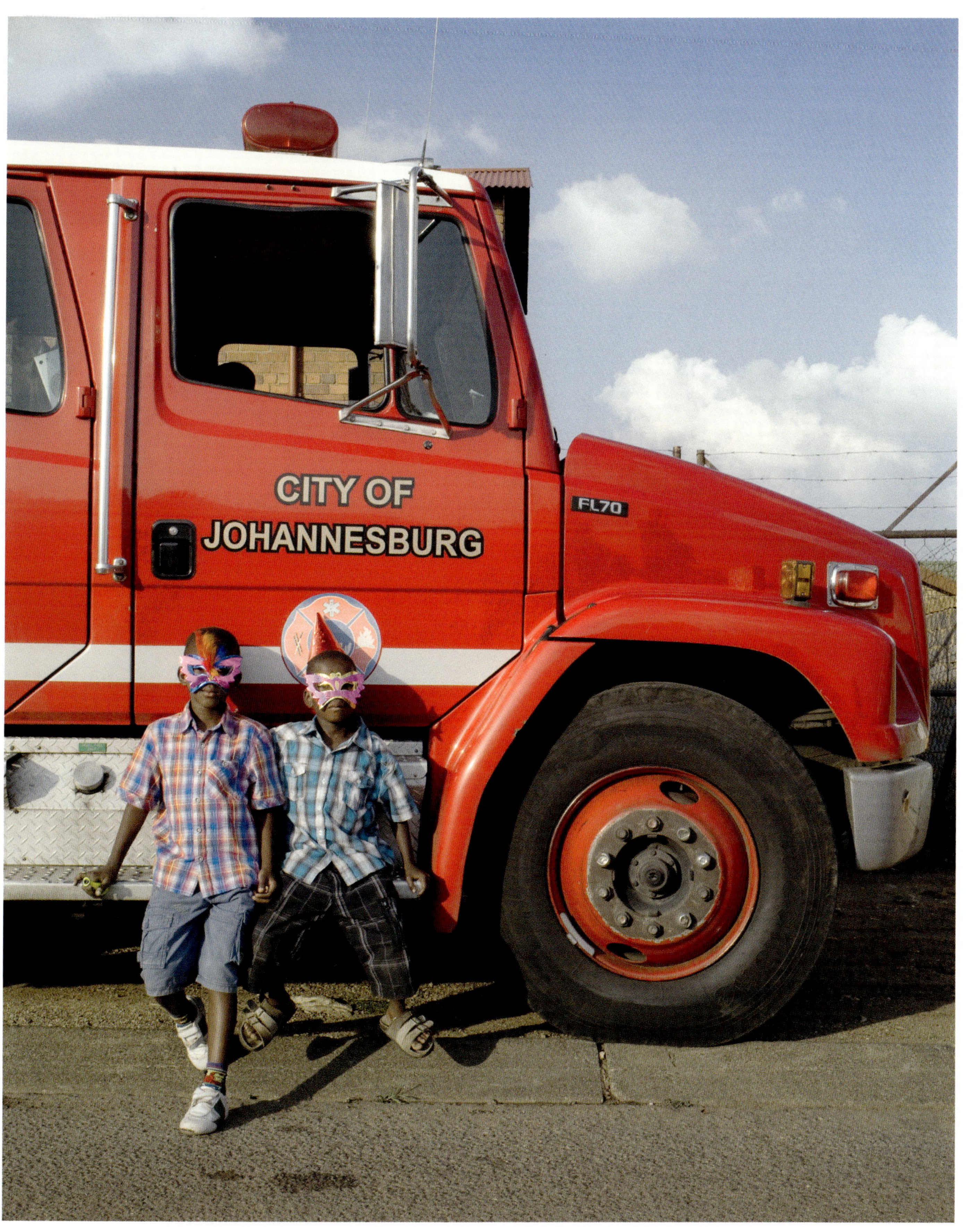

CITY OF
JOHANNESBURG
FL70

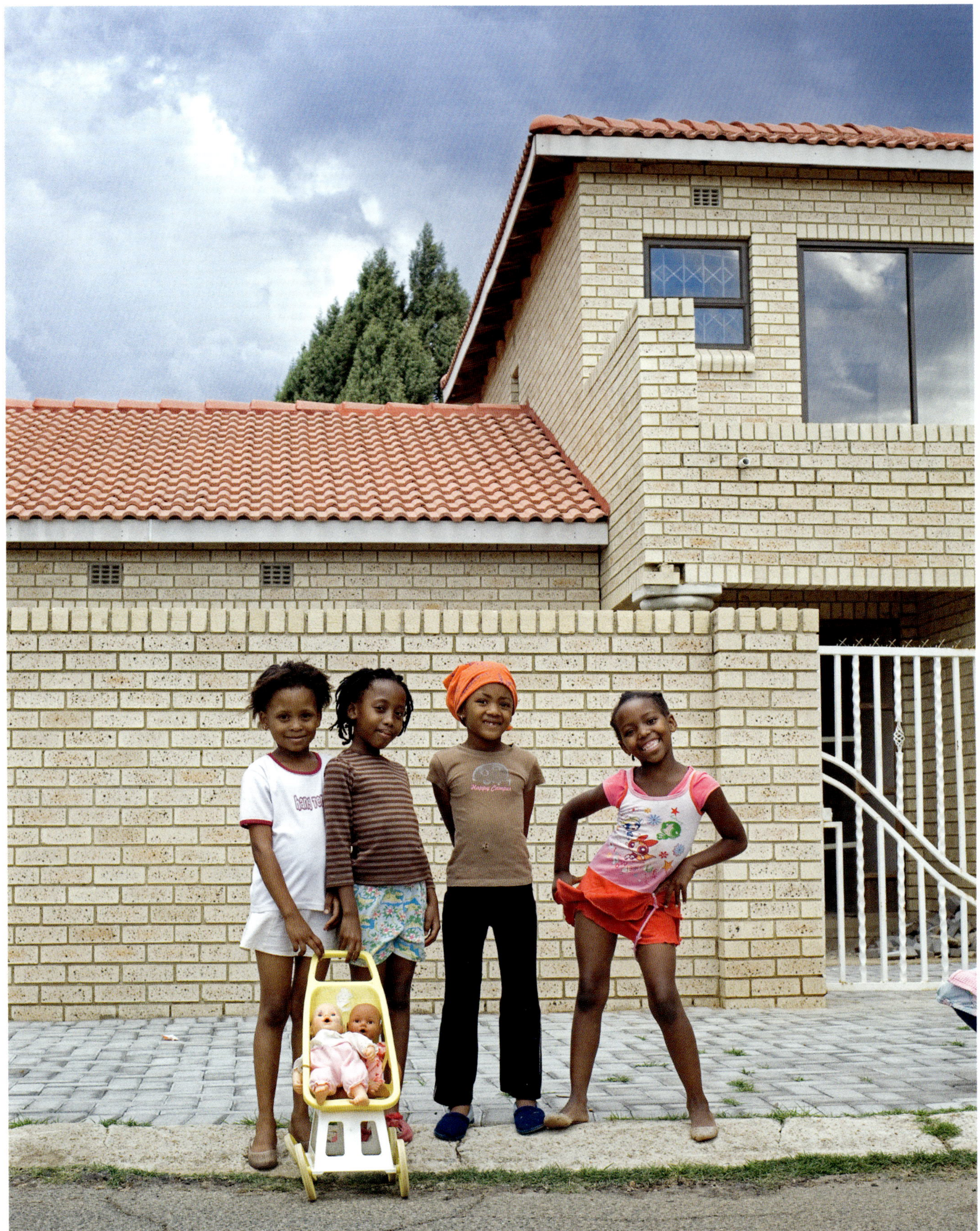

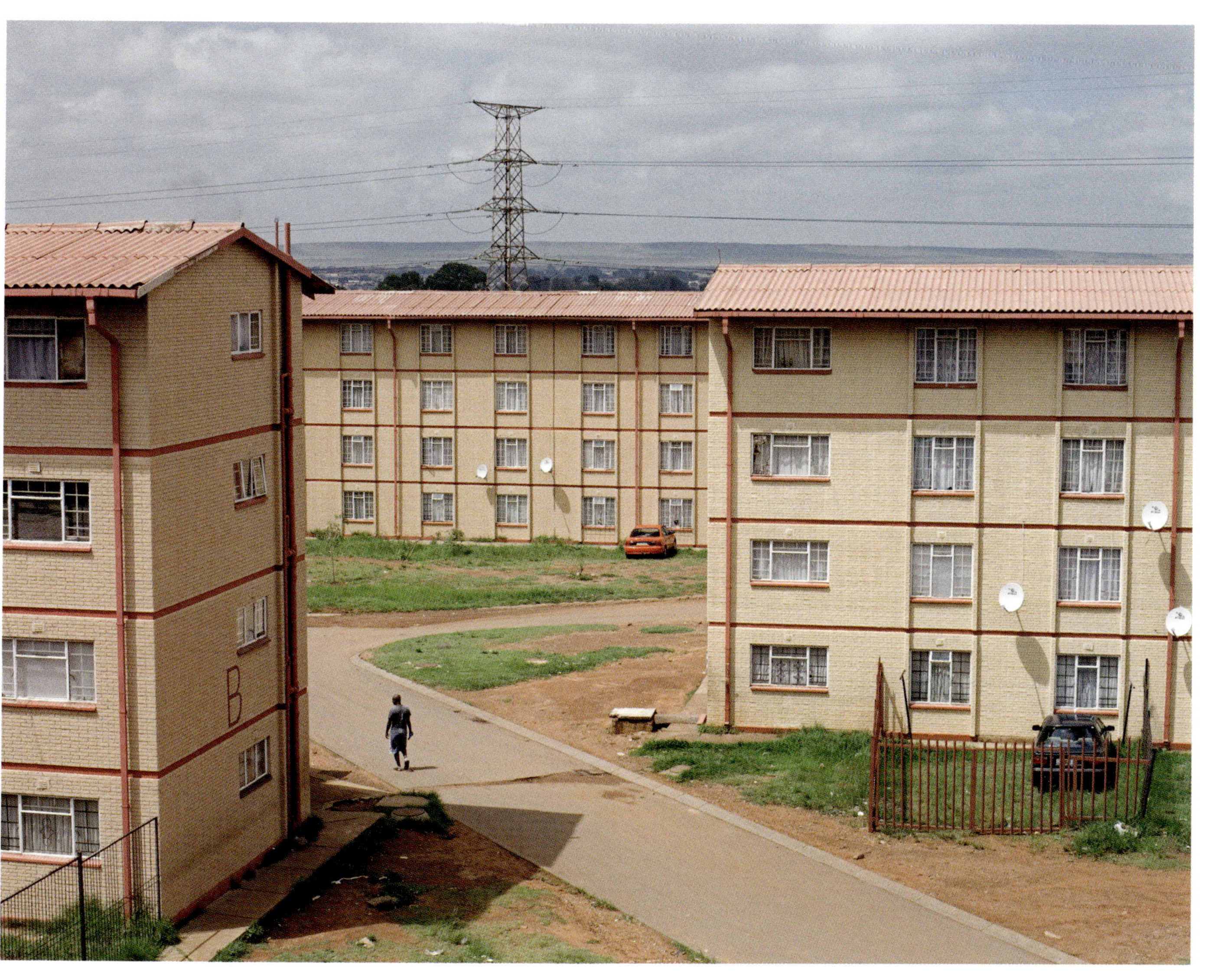

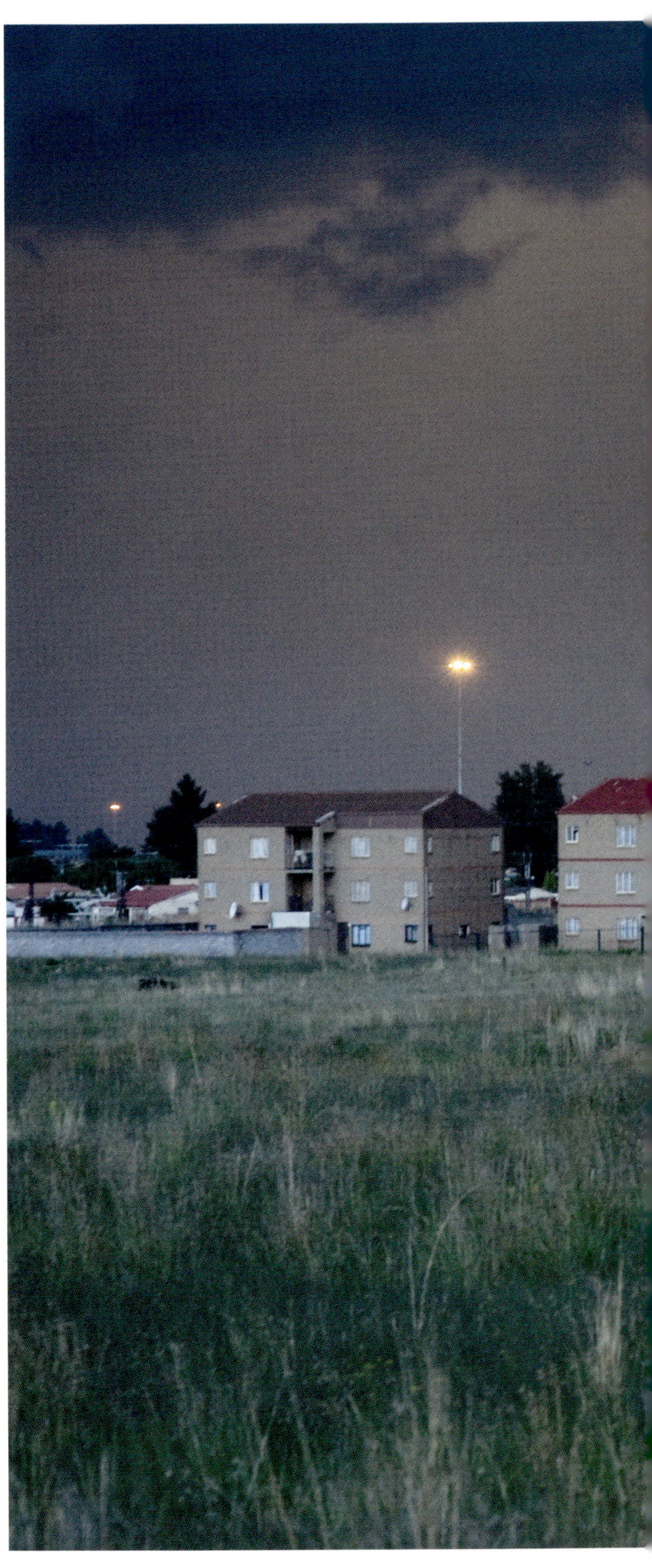

32 | Jabulani Flats, Jabulani, 2009

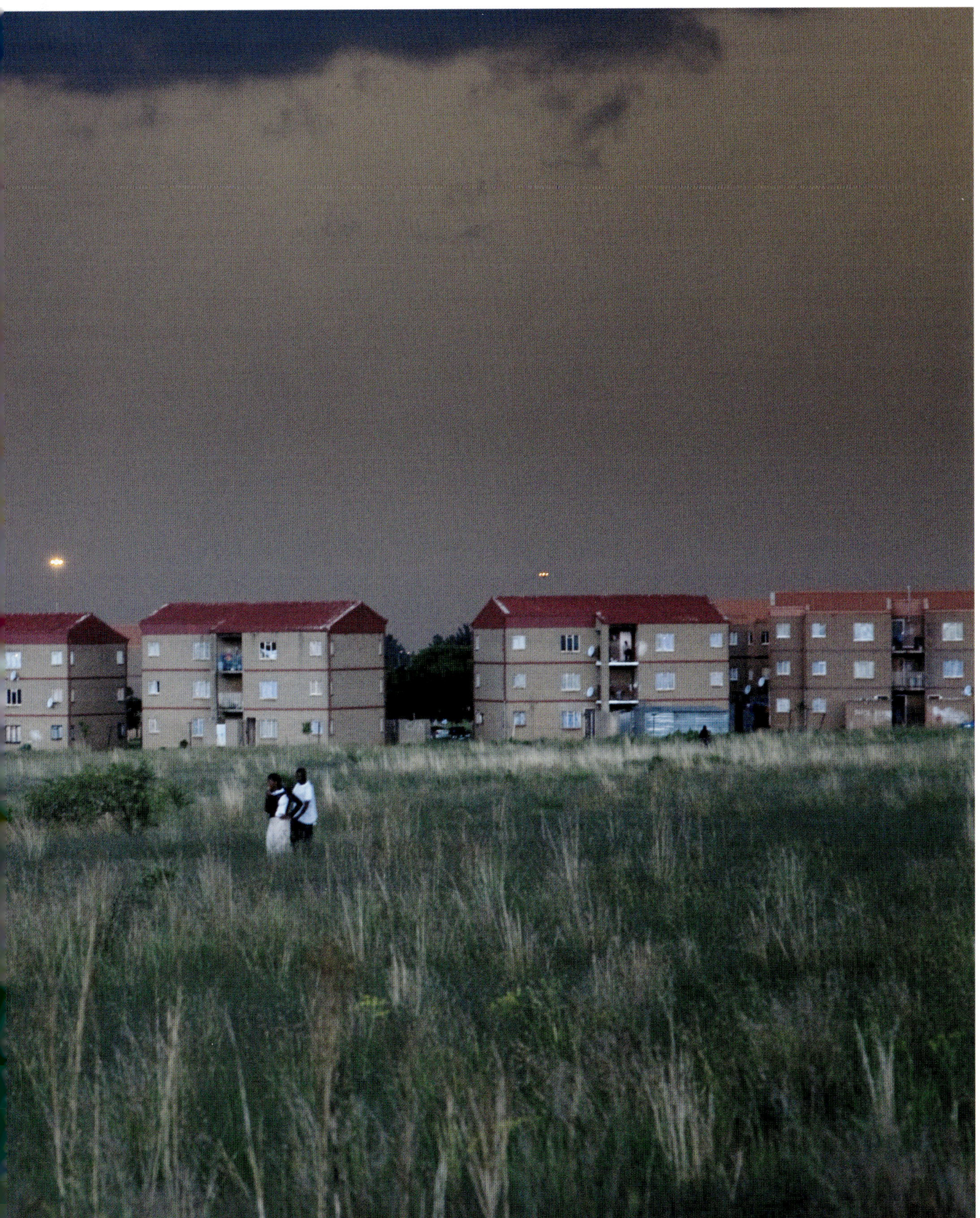

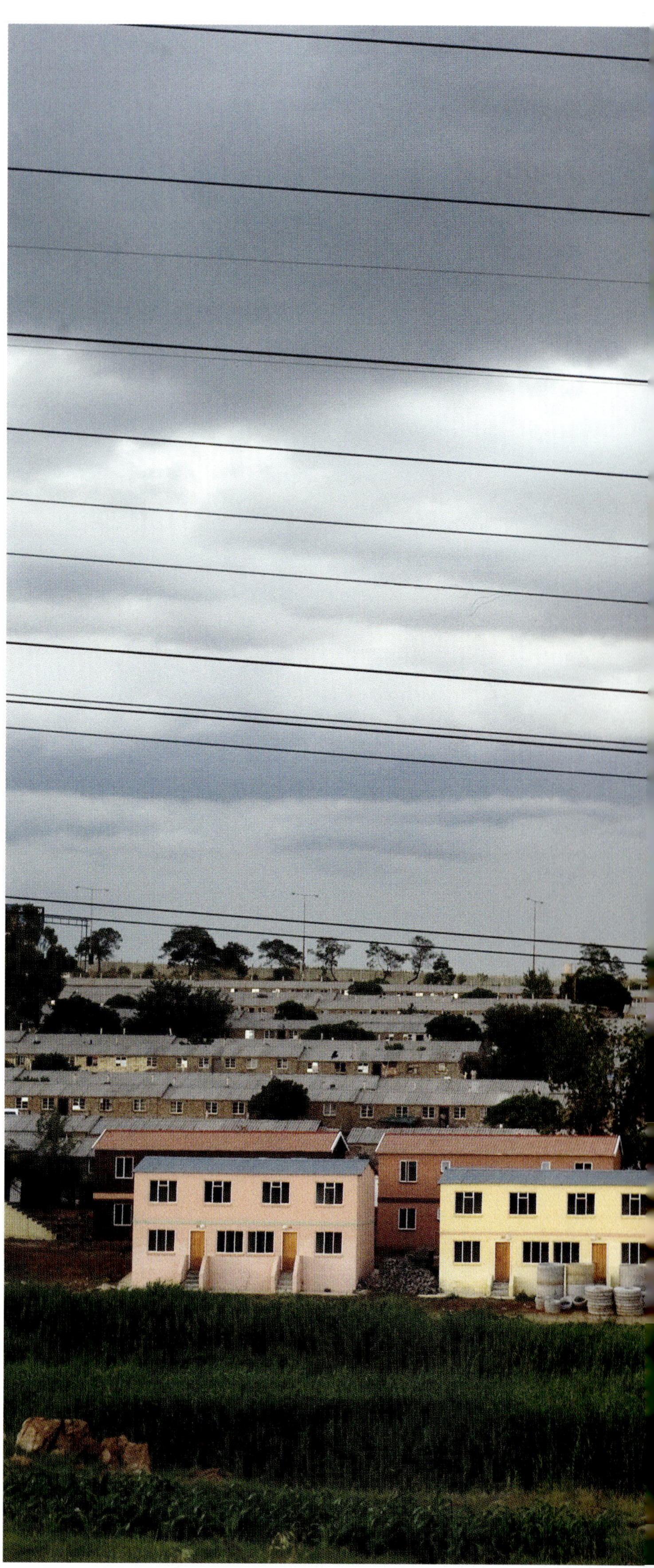

34 | Diepkloof Hostel Conversion Project,
Diepkloof, 2009

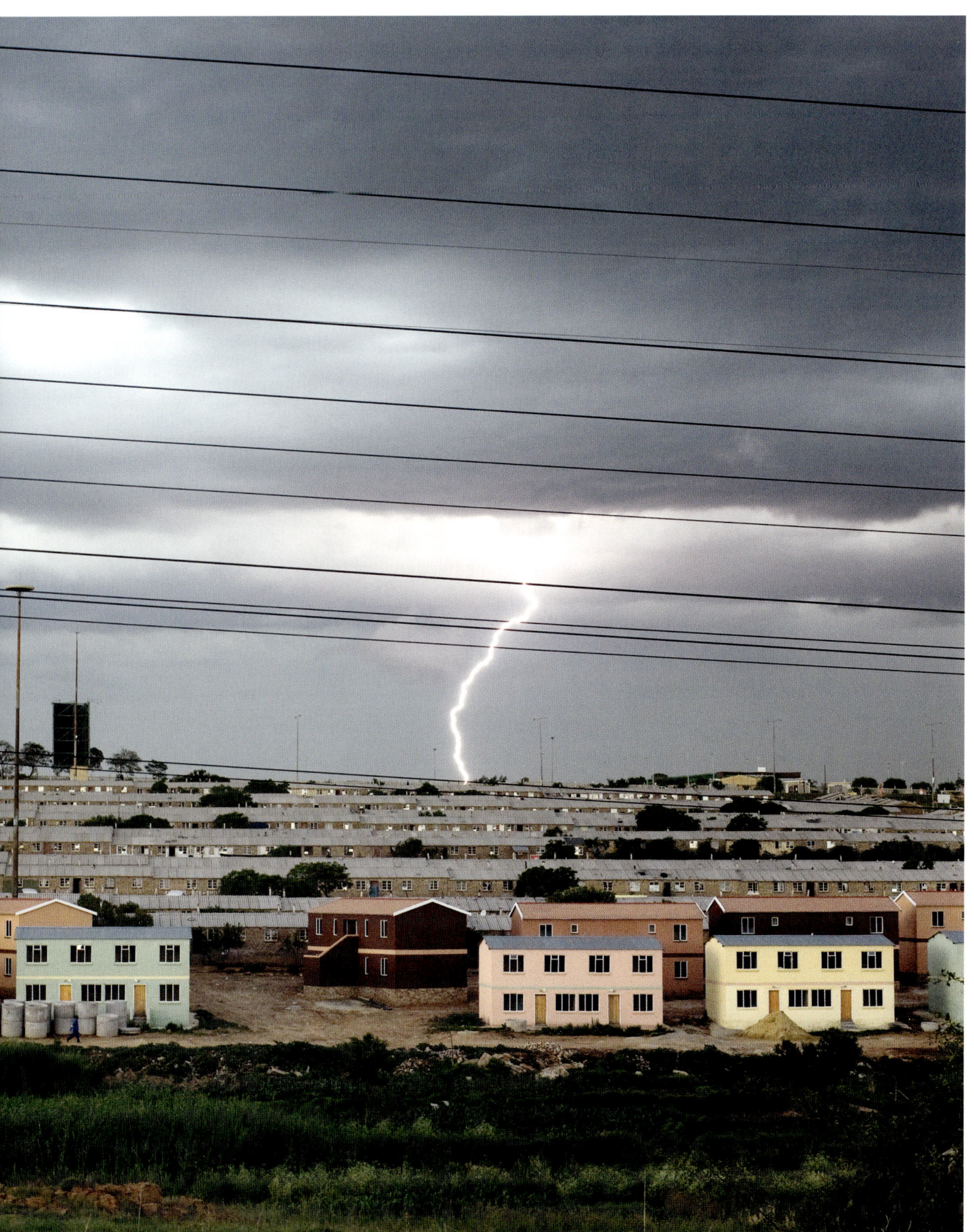

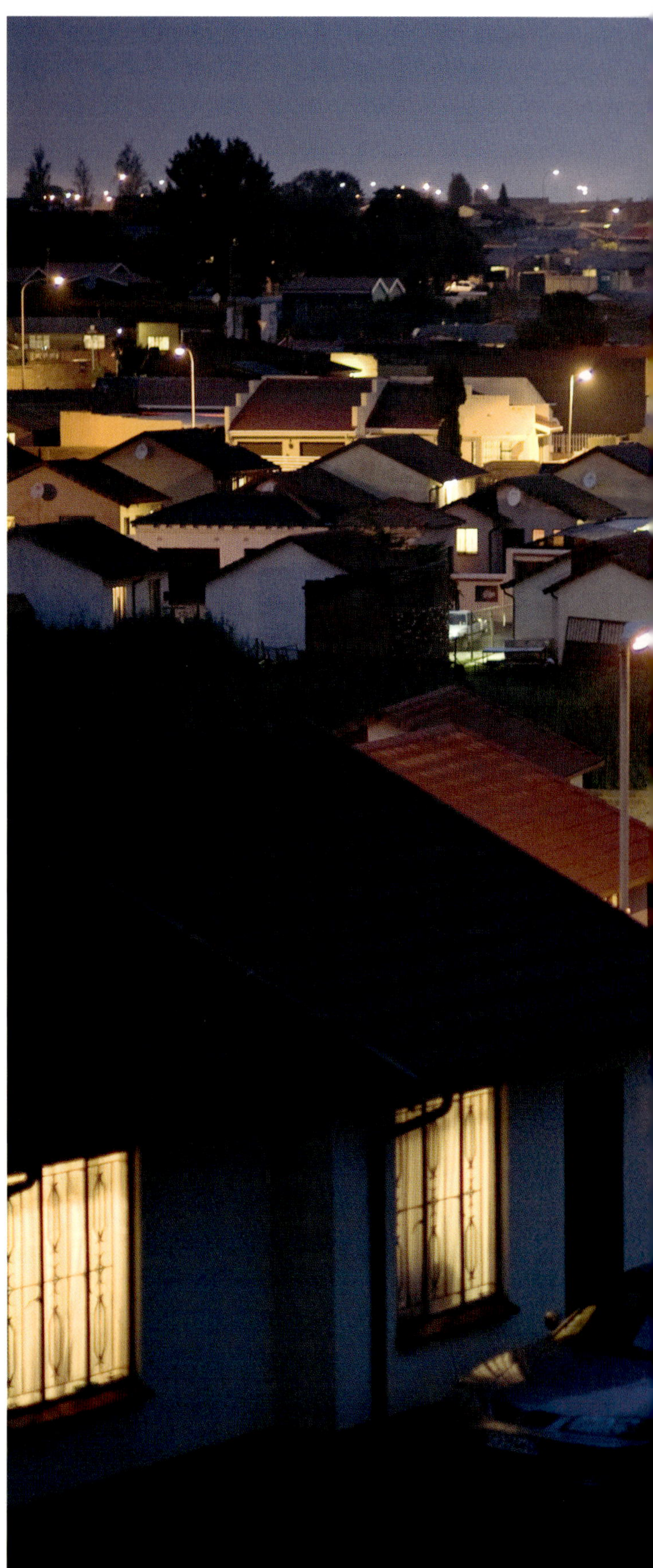

 Diepkloof as seen from the Soweto Highway,
Diepkloof, 2010

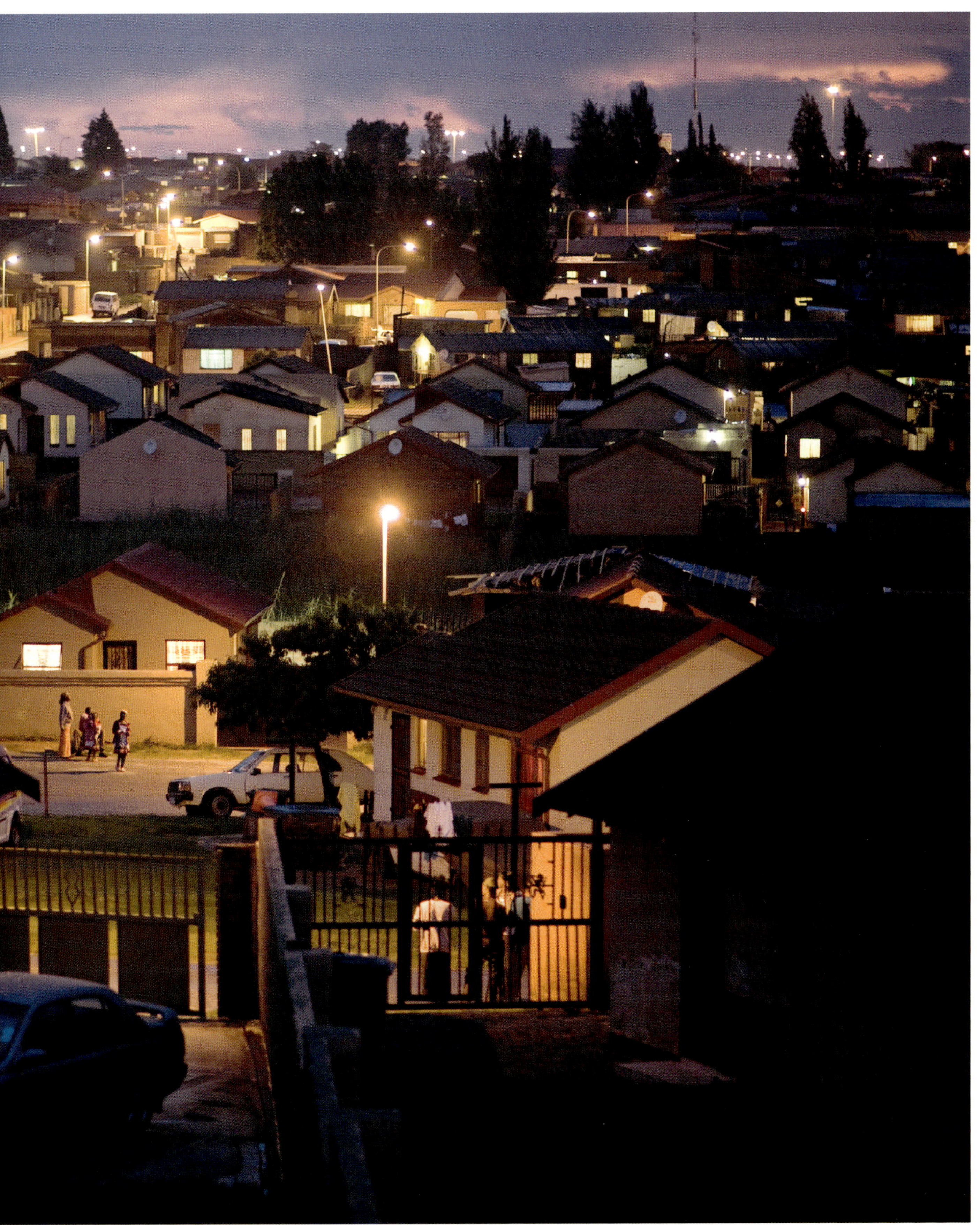

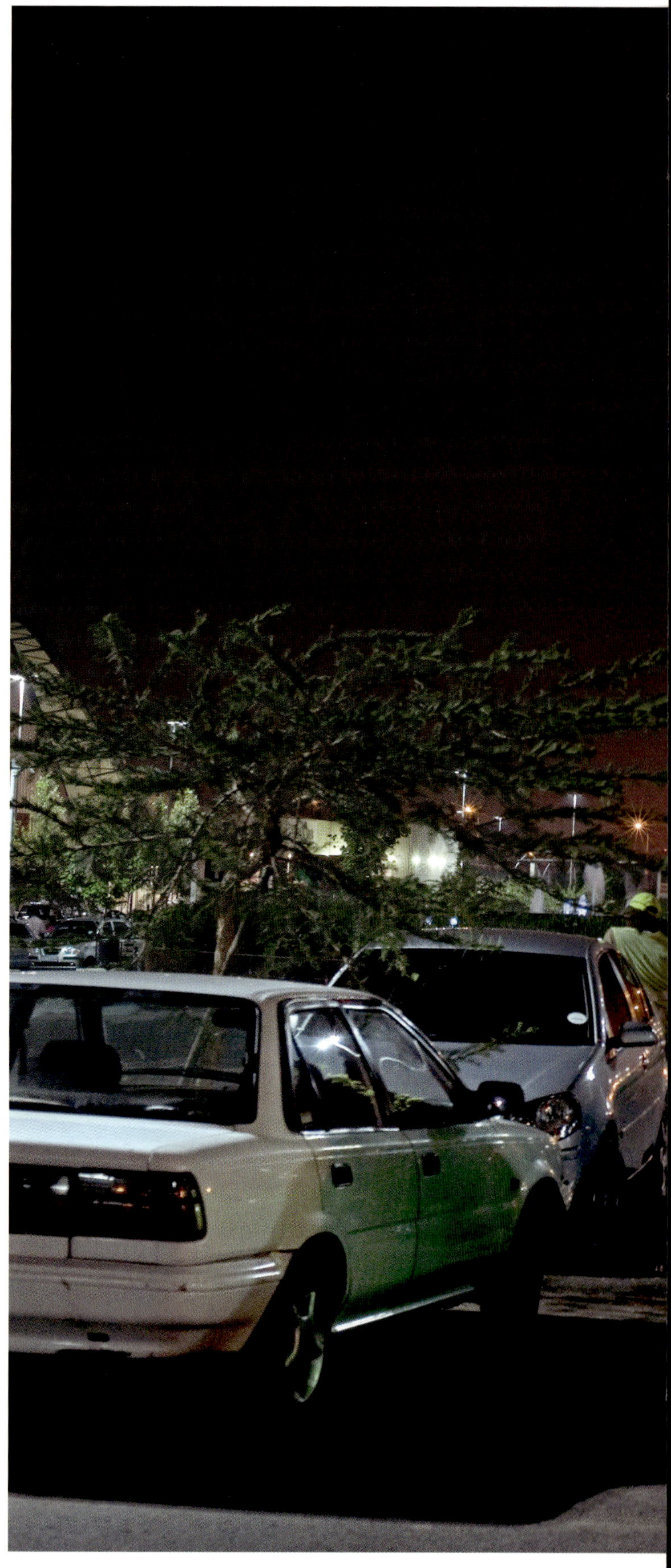

38 | Maponya Mall, Old Potchestroom Road,
Kliptown, 2010

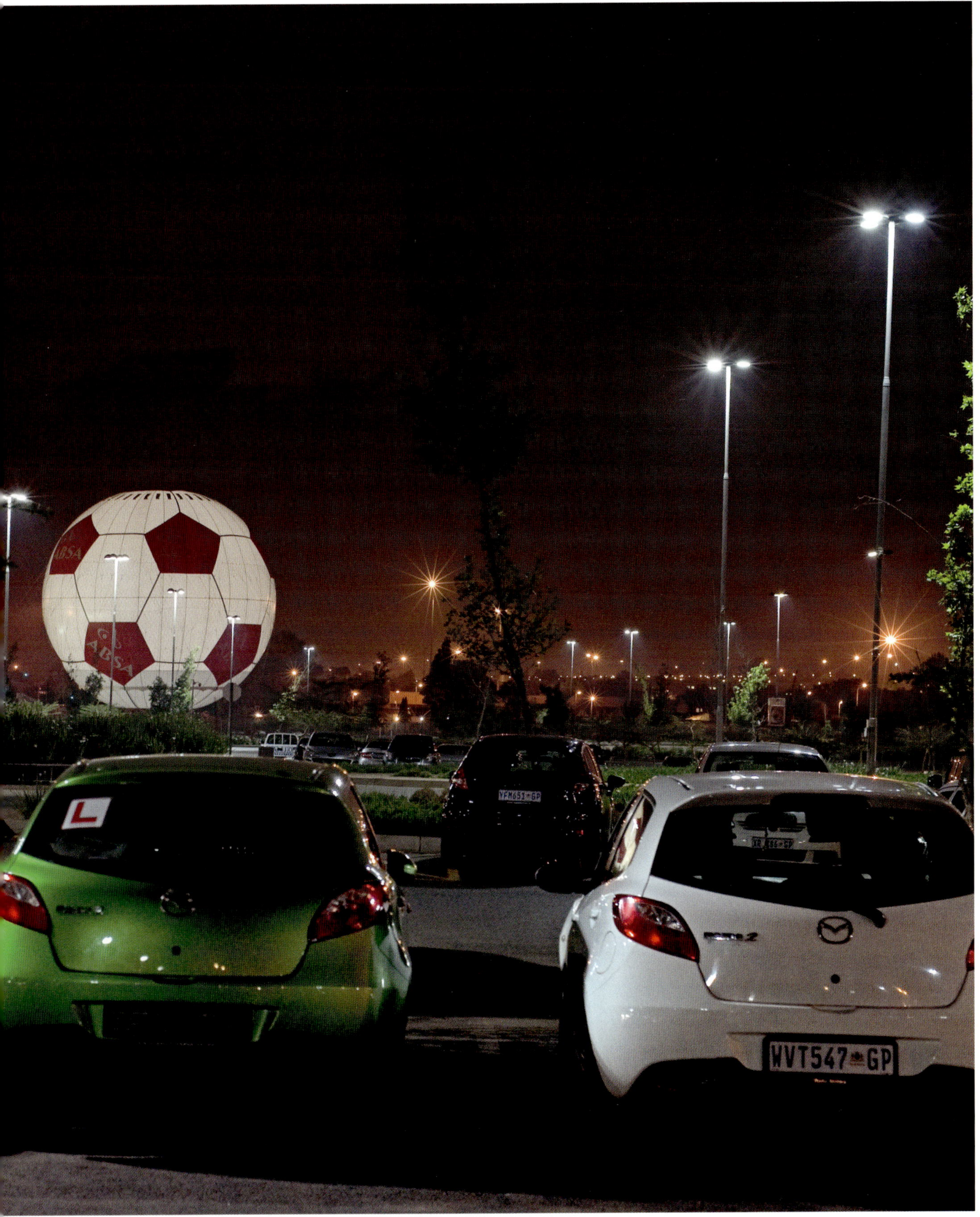

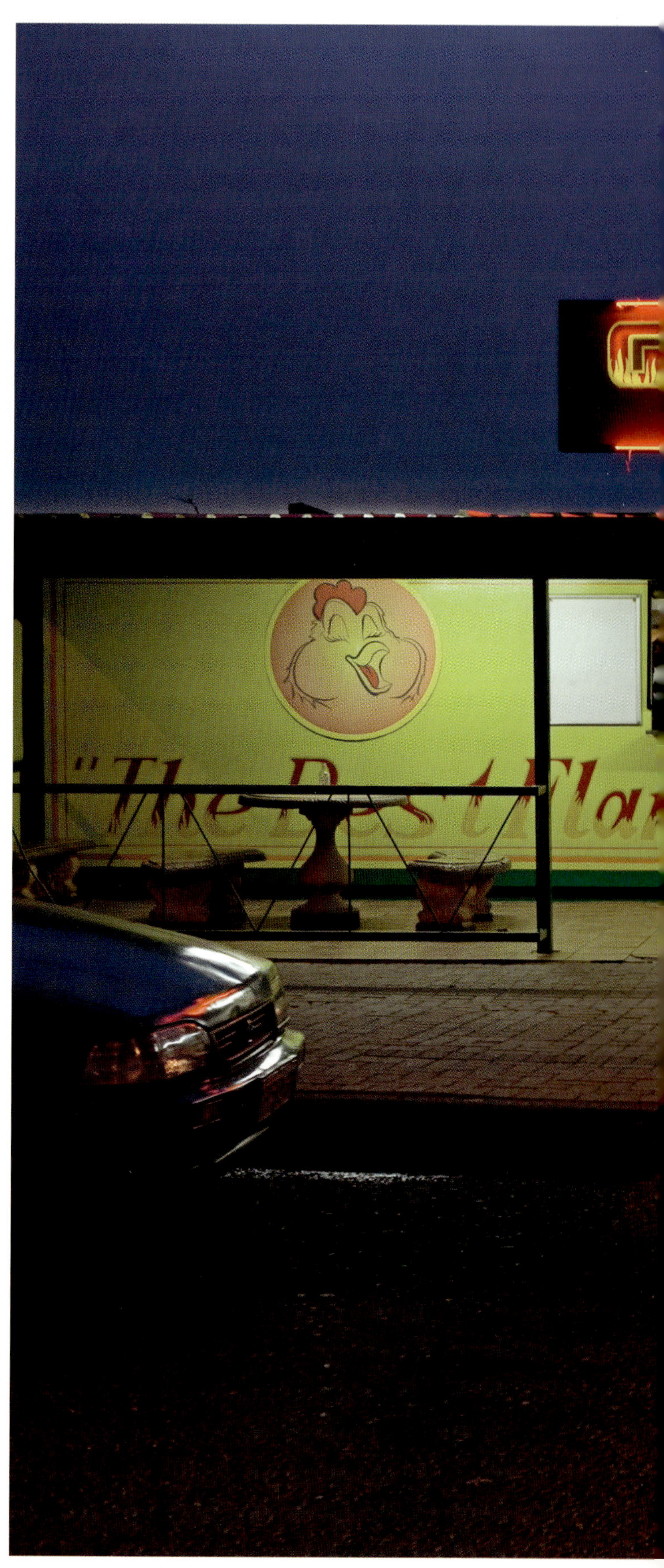

40 | Giramundo Flame Grilled Chicken, Diepkloof, 2010

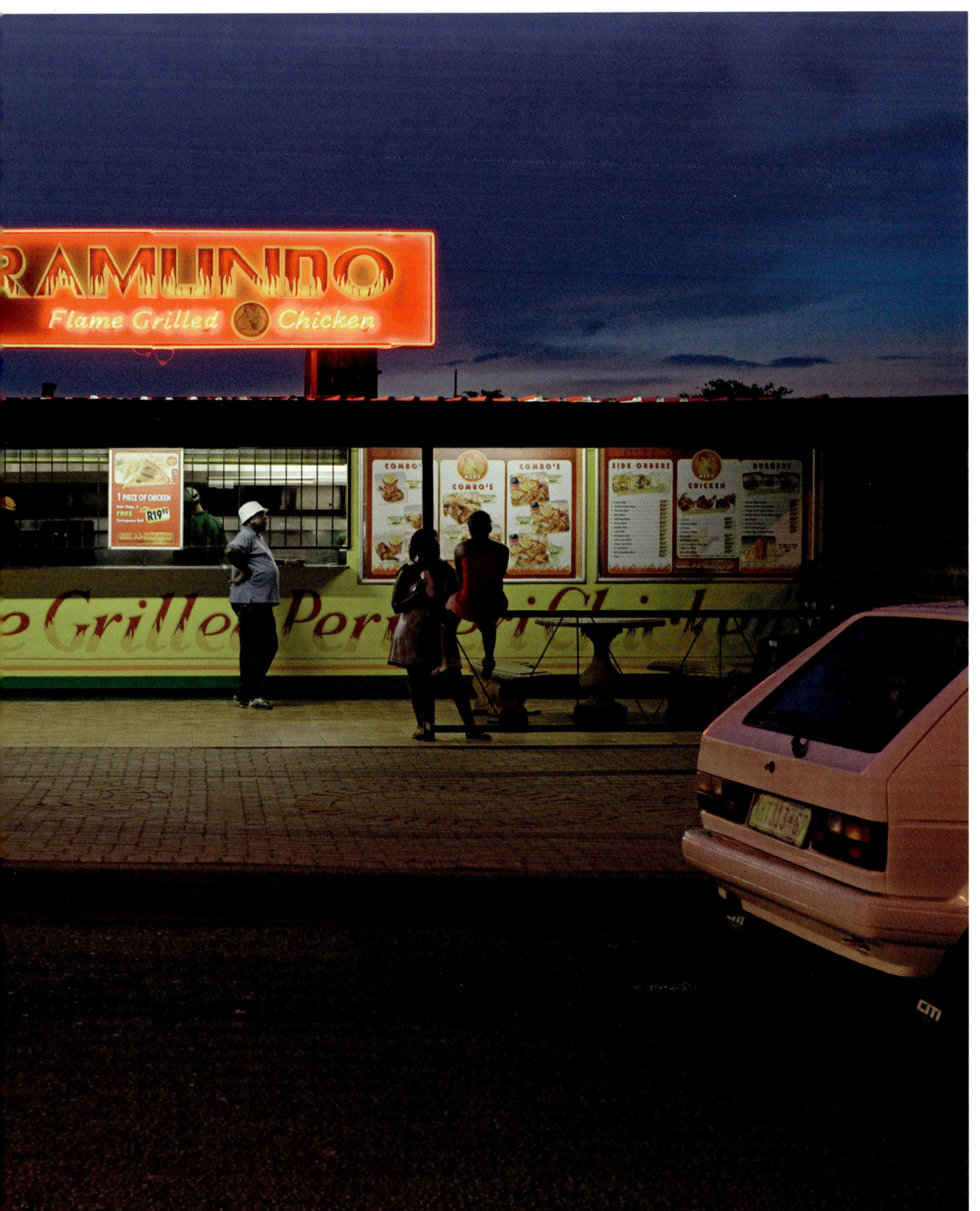
RAMUNDO
Flame Grilled Chicken
1 PIECE OF CHICKEN
FREE
R19.90
COMBO'S
COMBO'S
COMBO'S
SIDE ORDERS
CHICKEN
BURGERS
Grilled Peri Peri Chicken

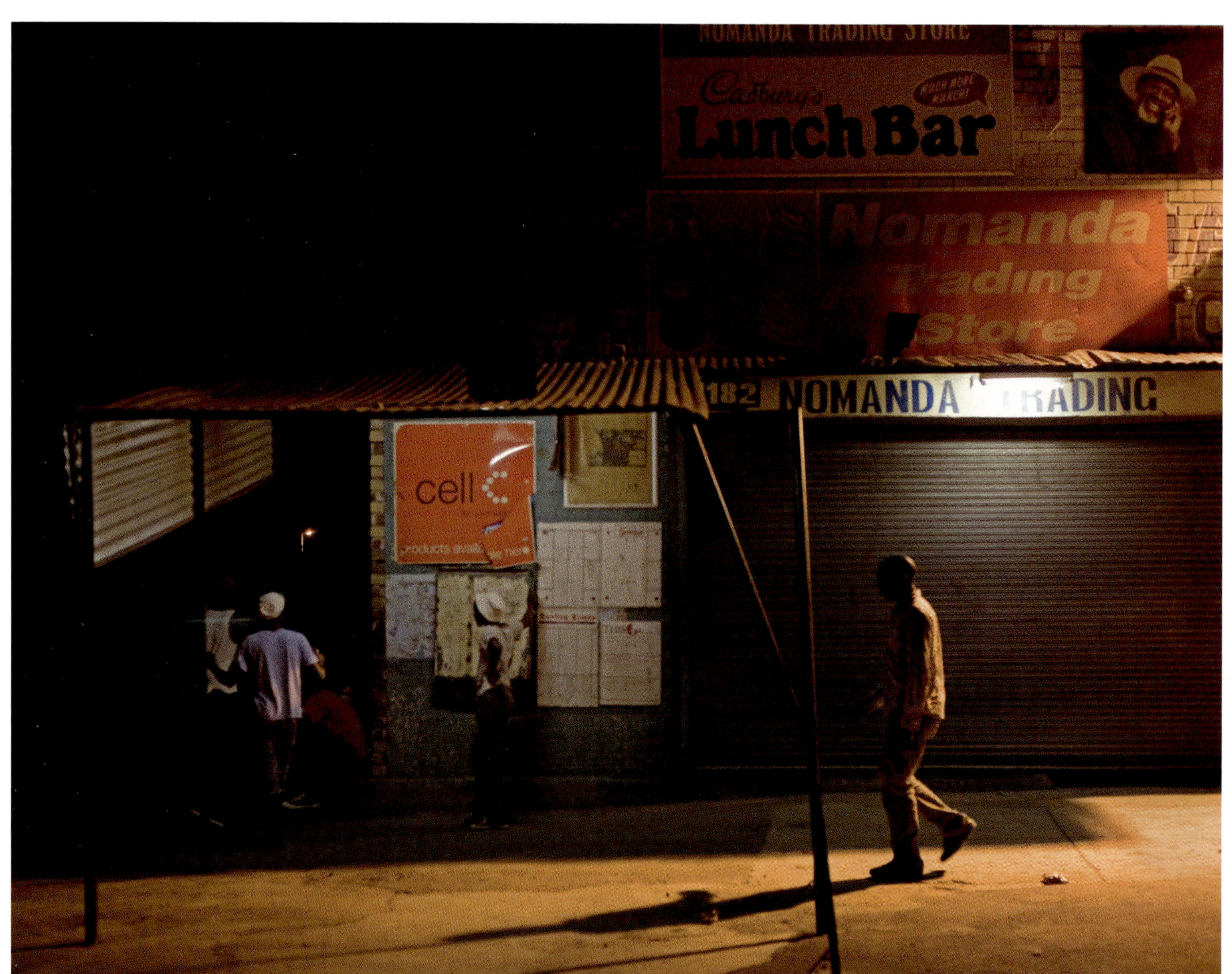

NOMANDA TRADING STORE
Cadbury's
Lunch Bar
MUCH MORE MUNCHI
Nomanda Trading Store
182 NOMANDA TRADING
cell
products available here

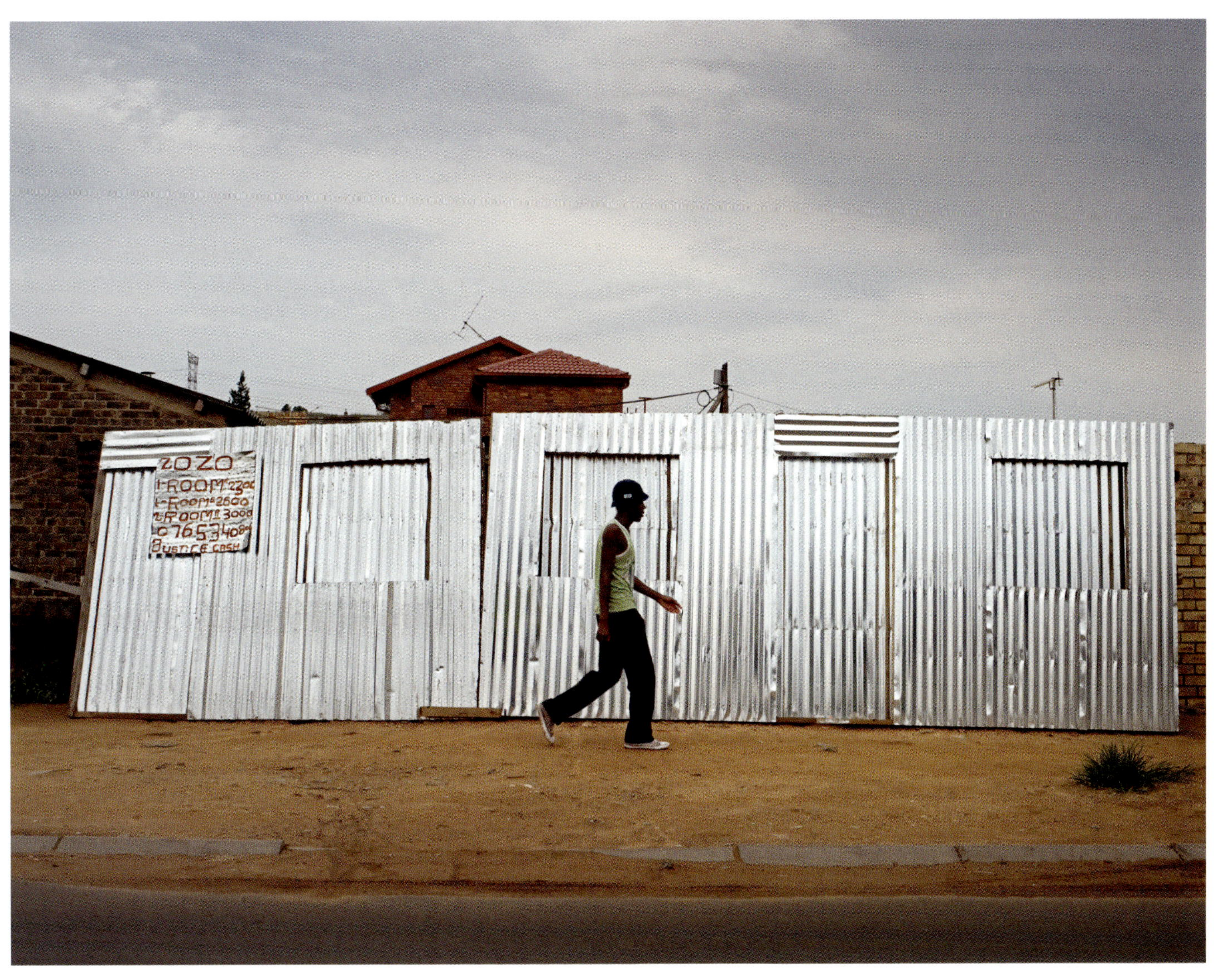

Zozo huts for sale, Dube, 2010 | 43

 Dube Young Blood Shotokan Karate Club, Dube Community Hall, Dube, 2009

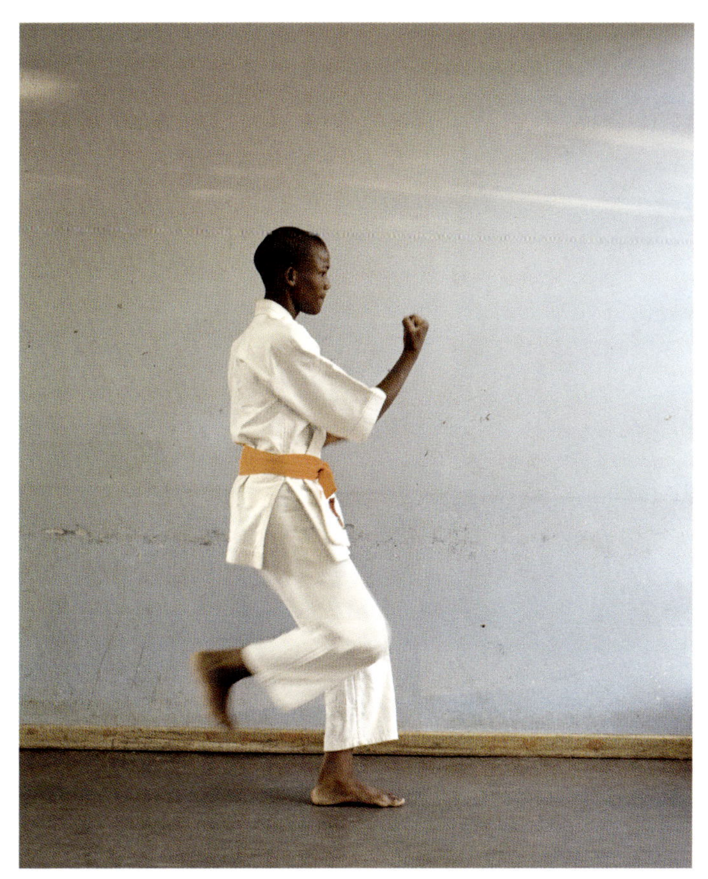

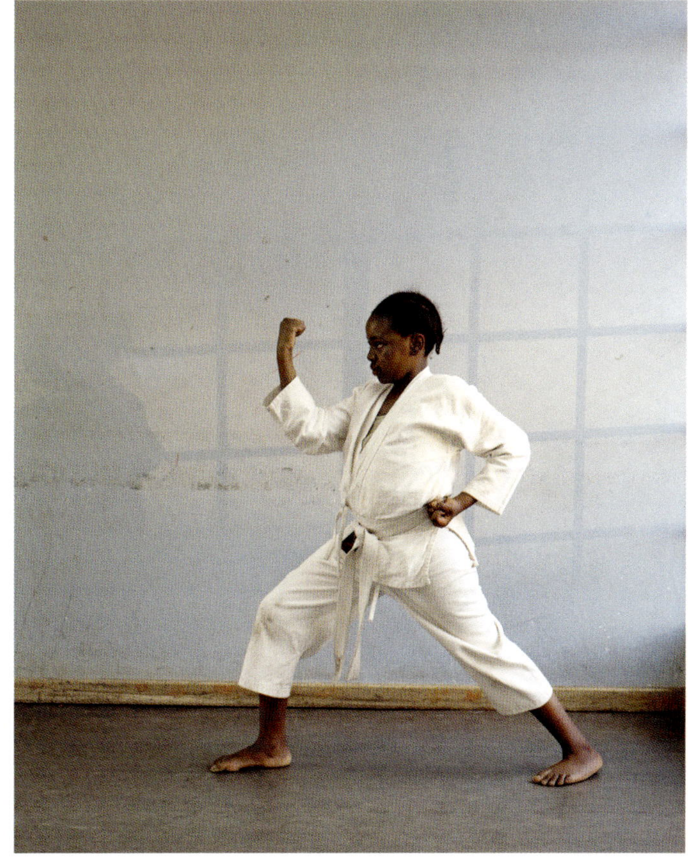

 Dube Young Blood Shotokan Karate Club, Dube Community Hall, Dube, 2009

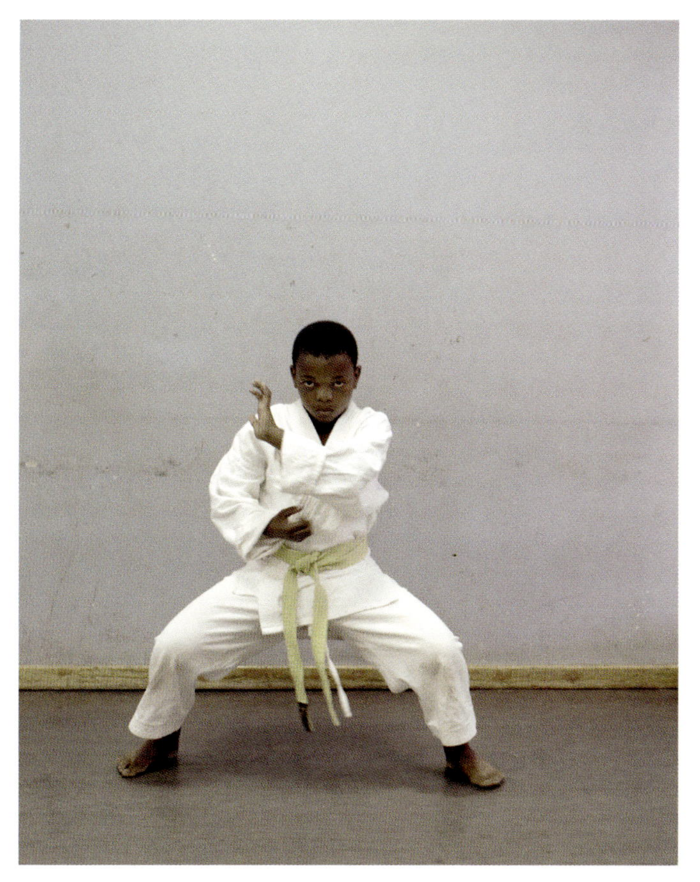
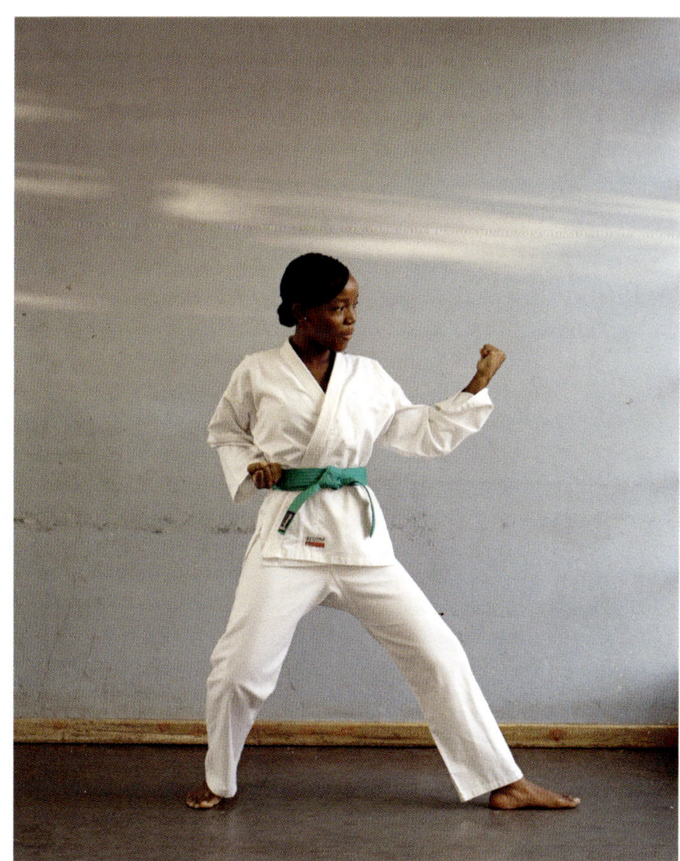
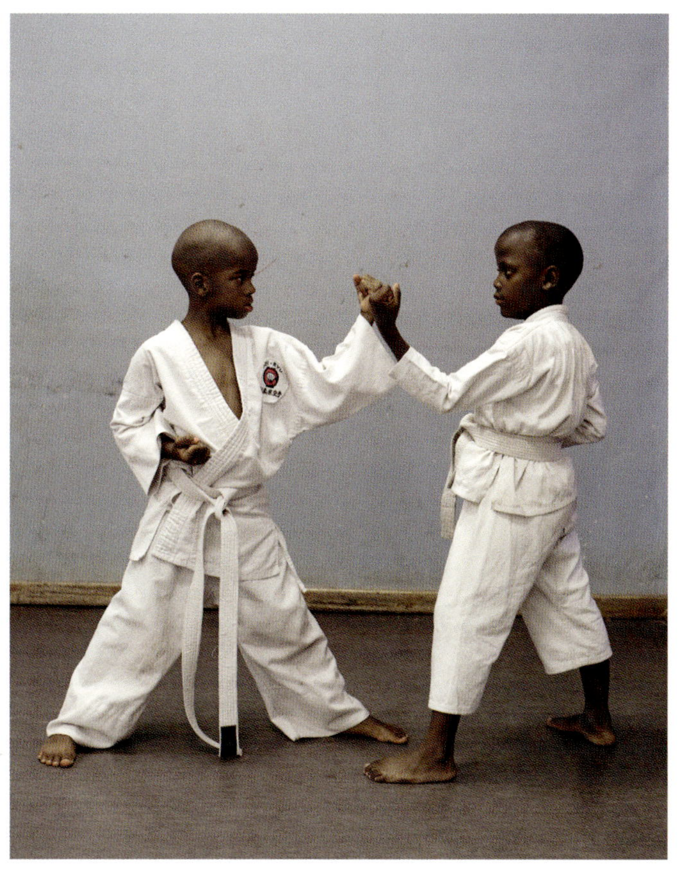
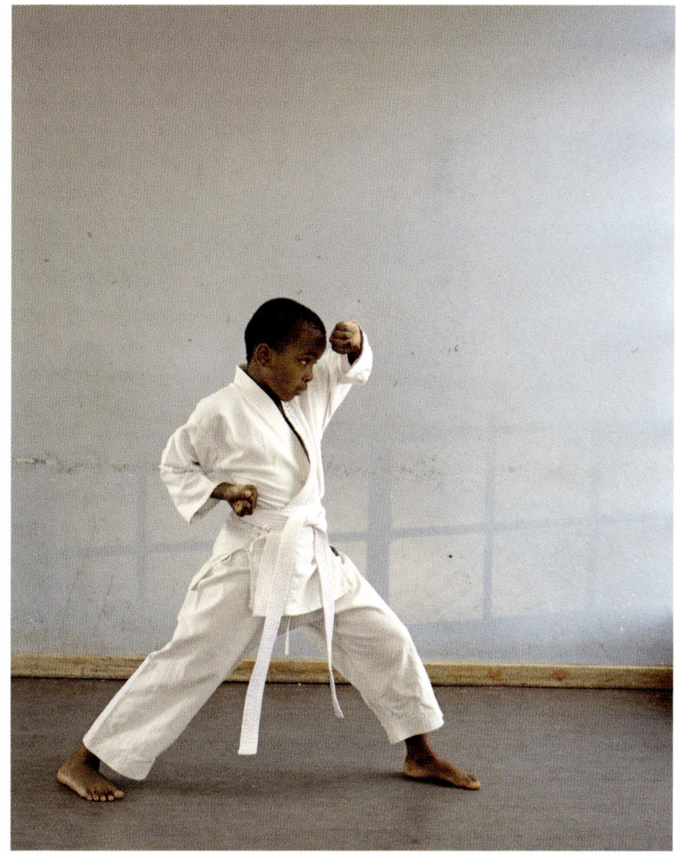

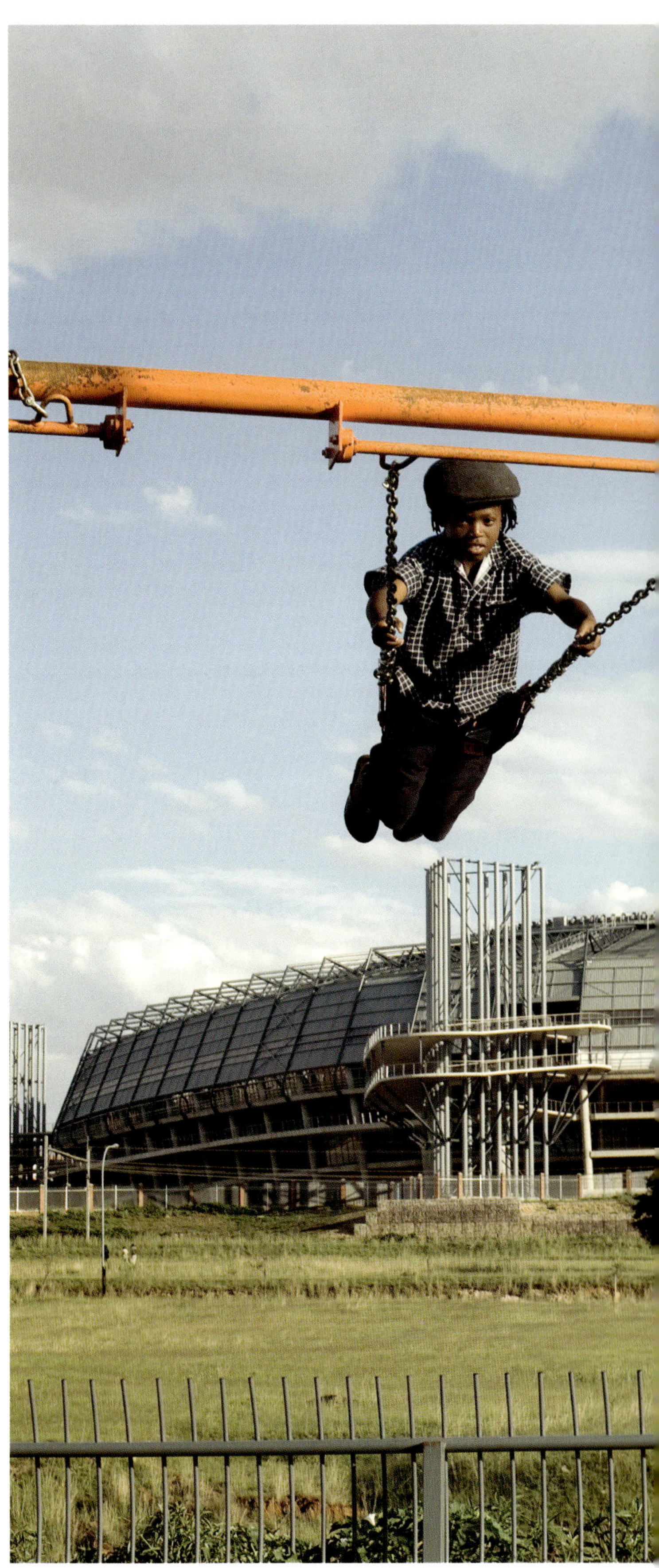

48 | Orlando West Regional Park, Orlando West, 2009

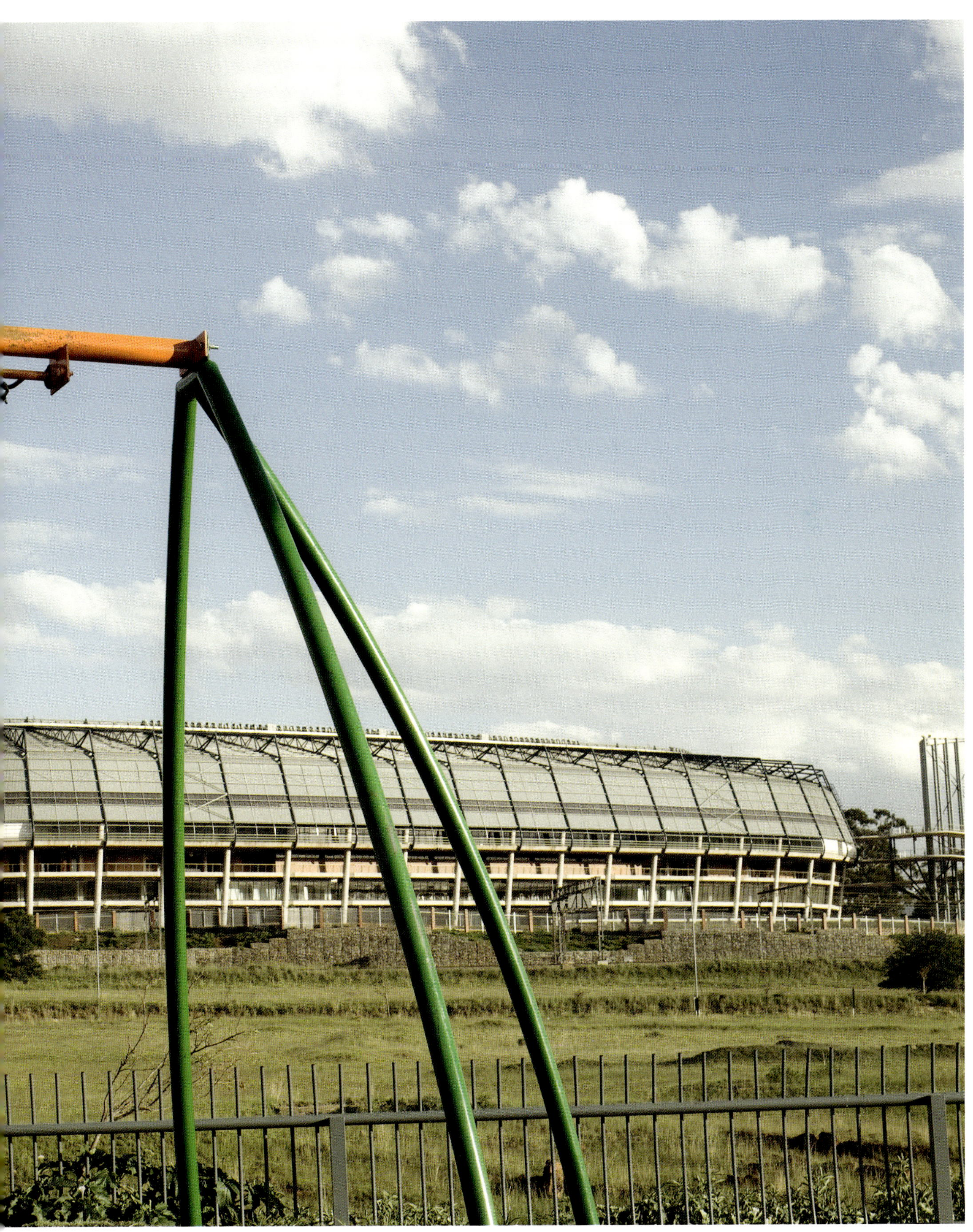

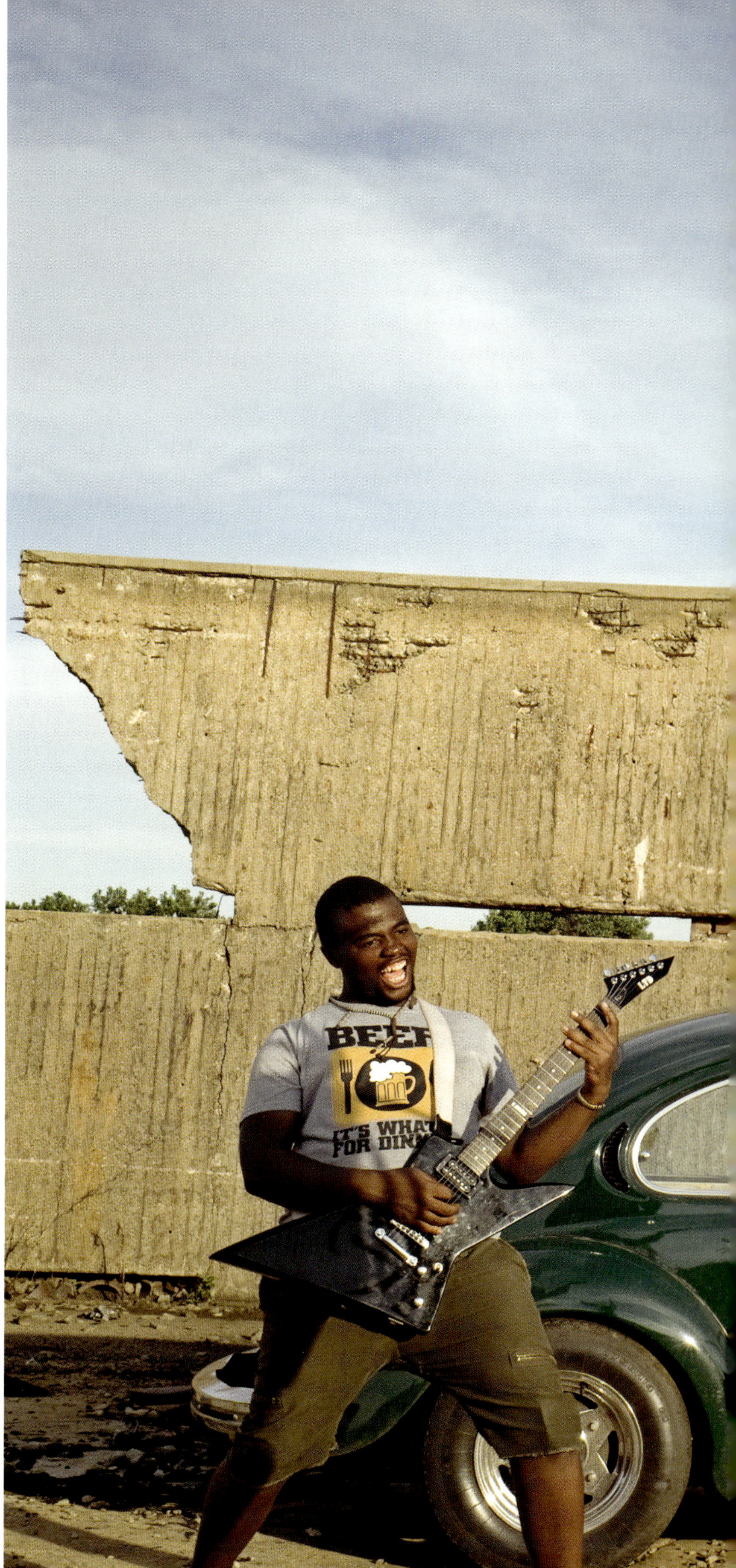

50 | Alternative rock band Ree-Buurth,
Pimville, 2009

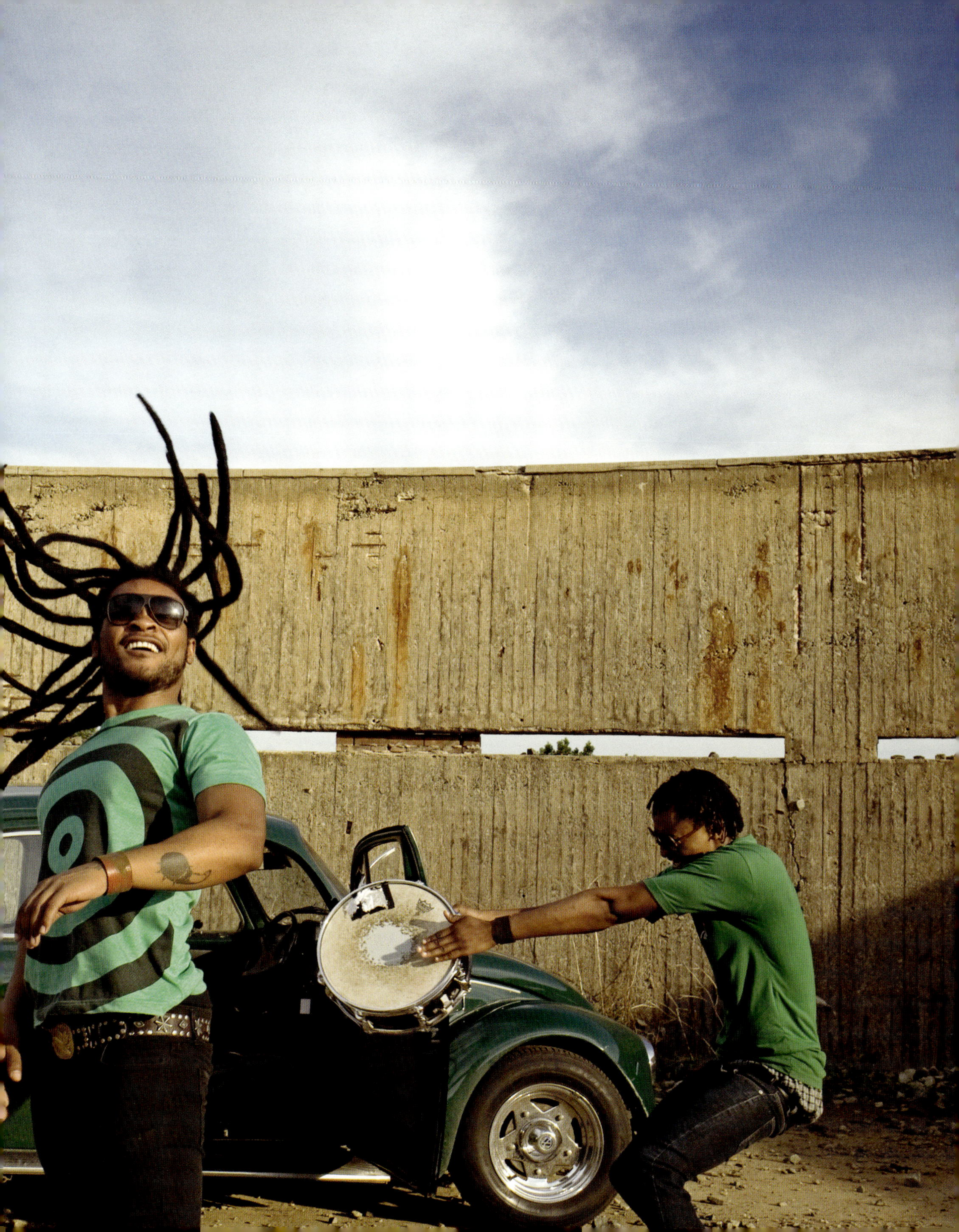

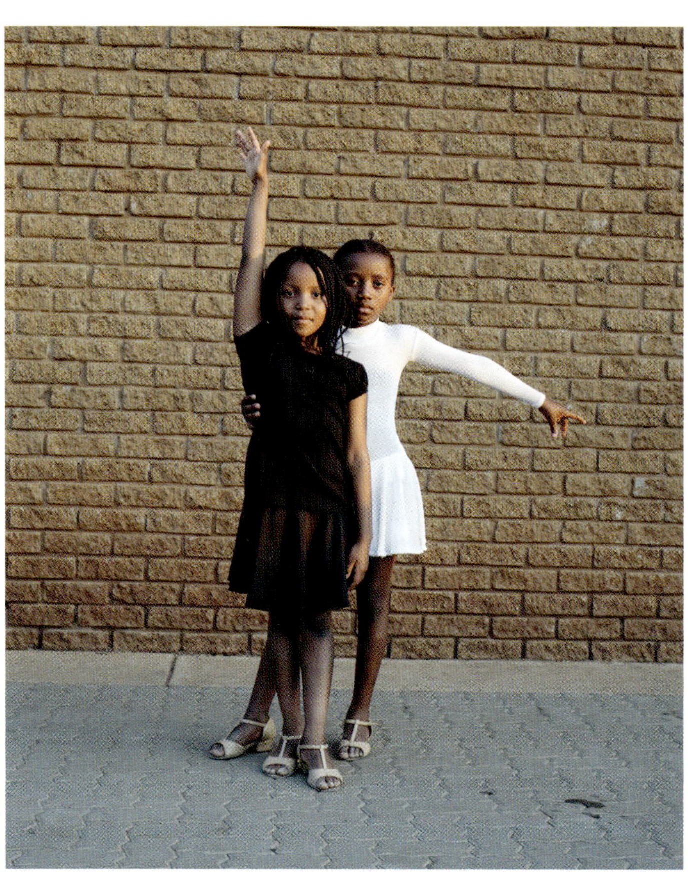

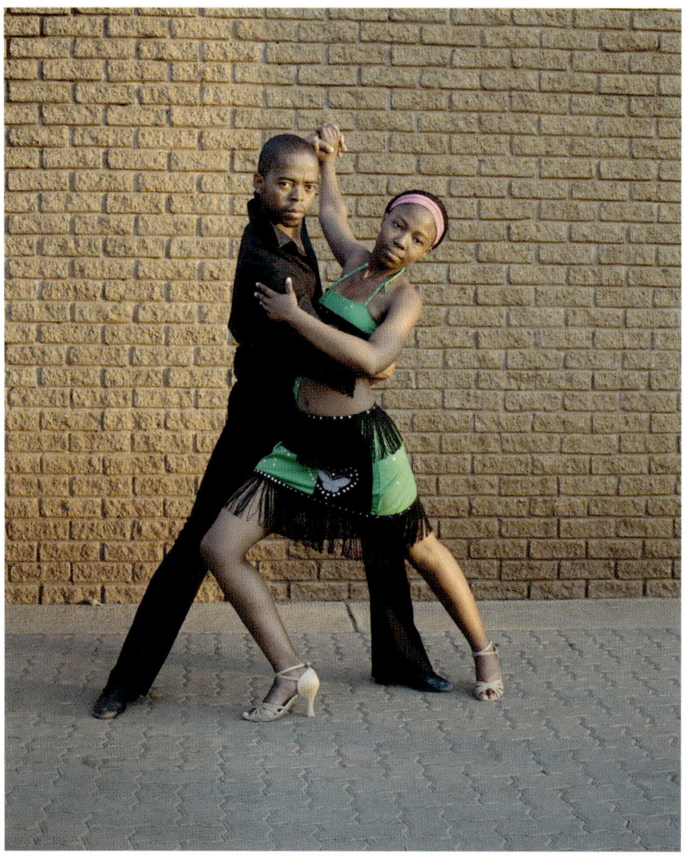

52 | Magic Feet Dance School, Chiawelo
Community Centre, Chiawelo, 2009

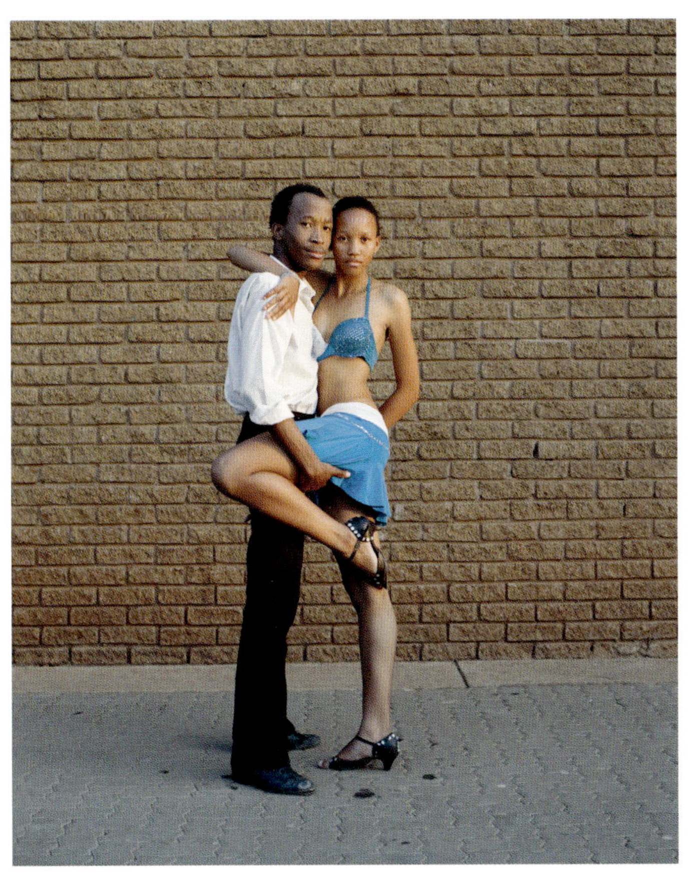
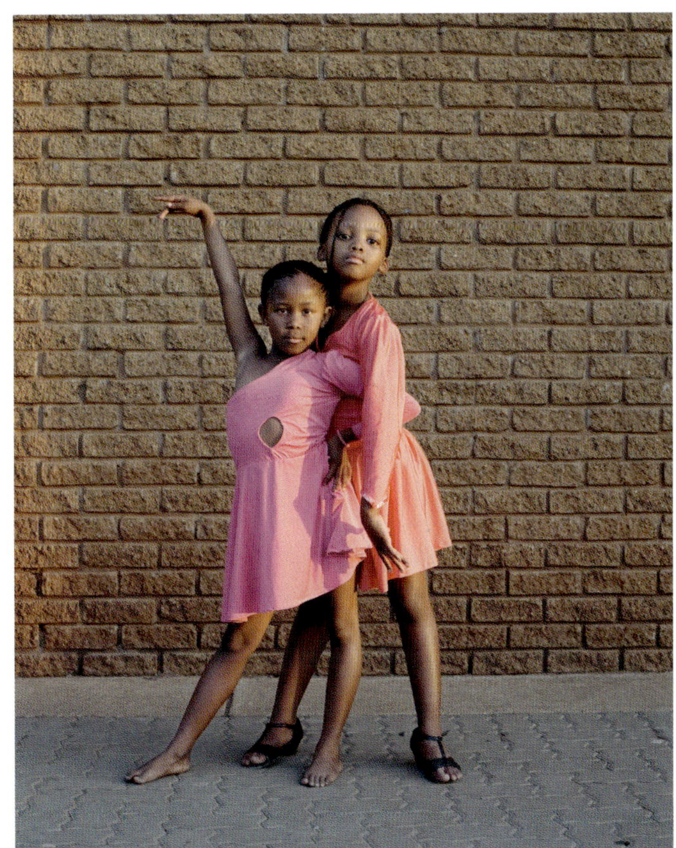
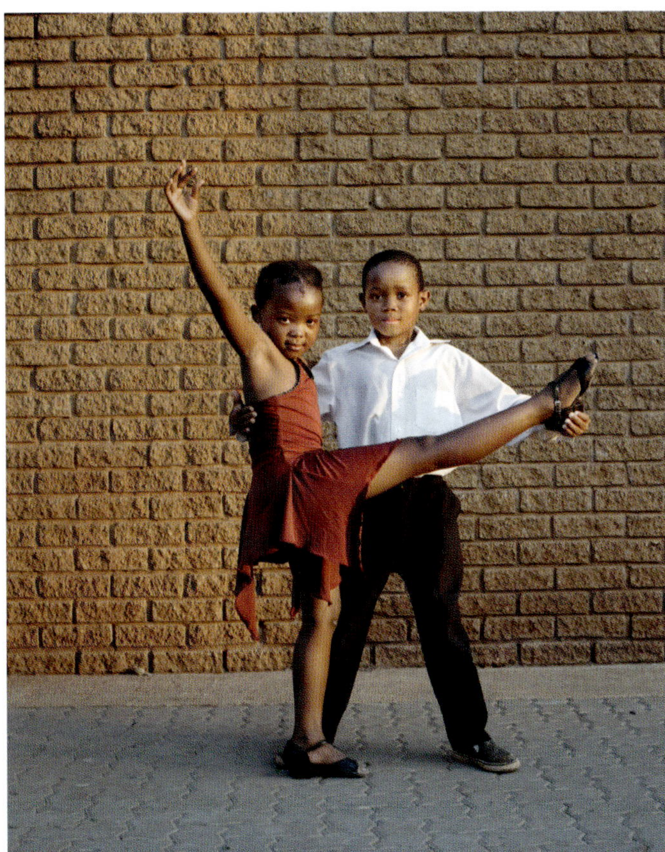
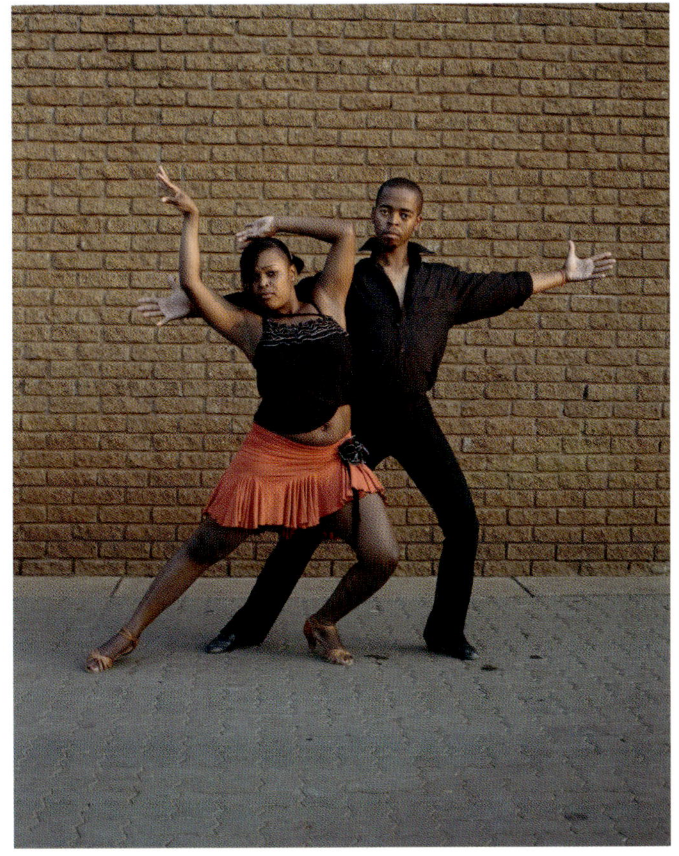

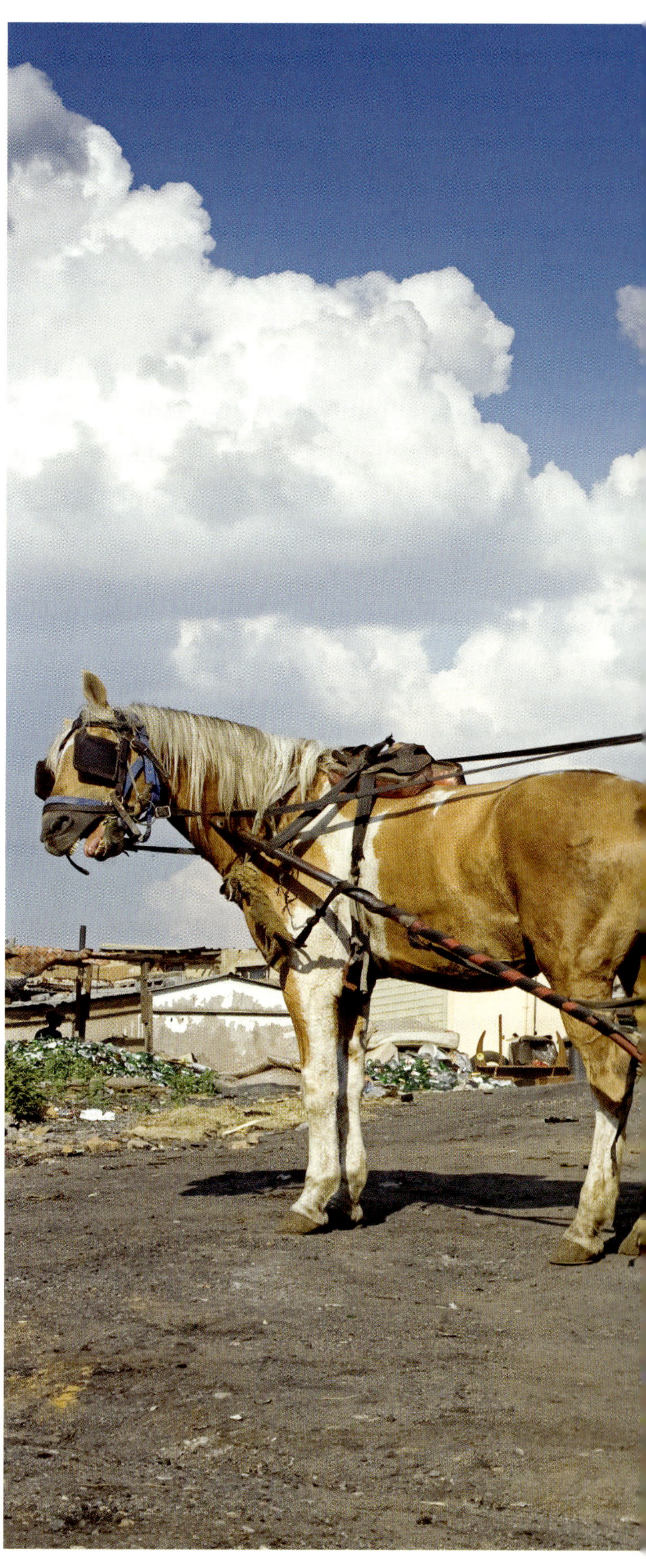

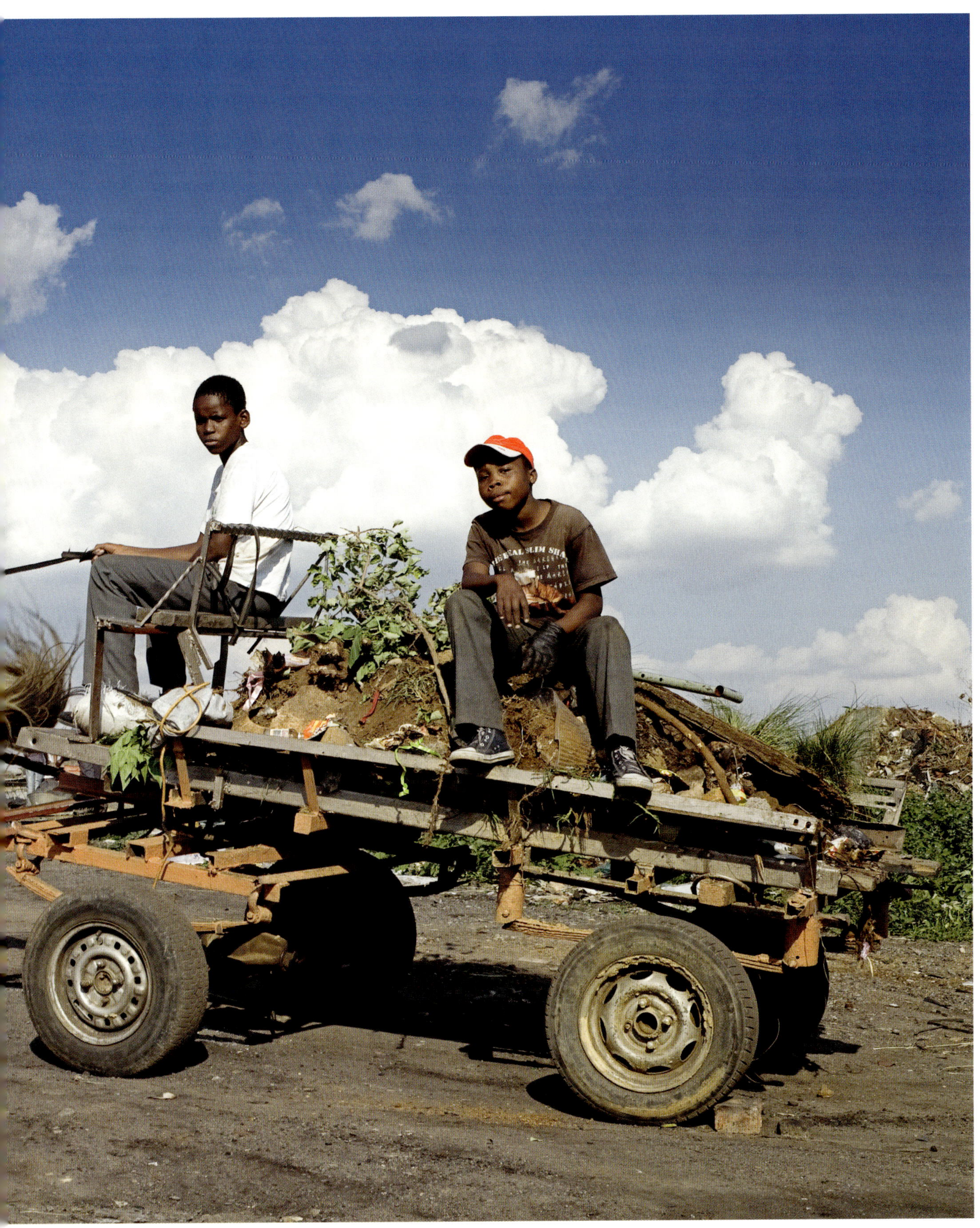

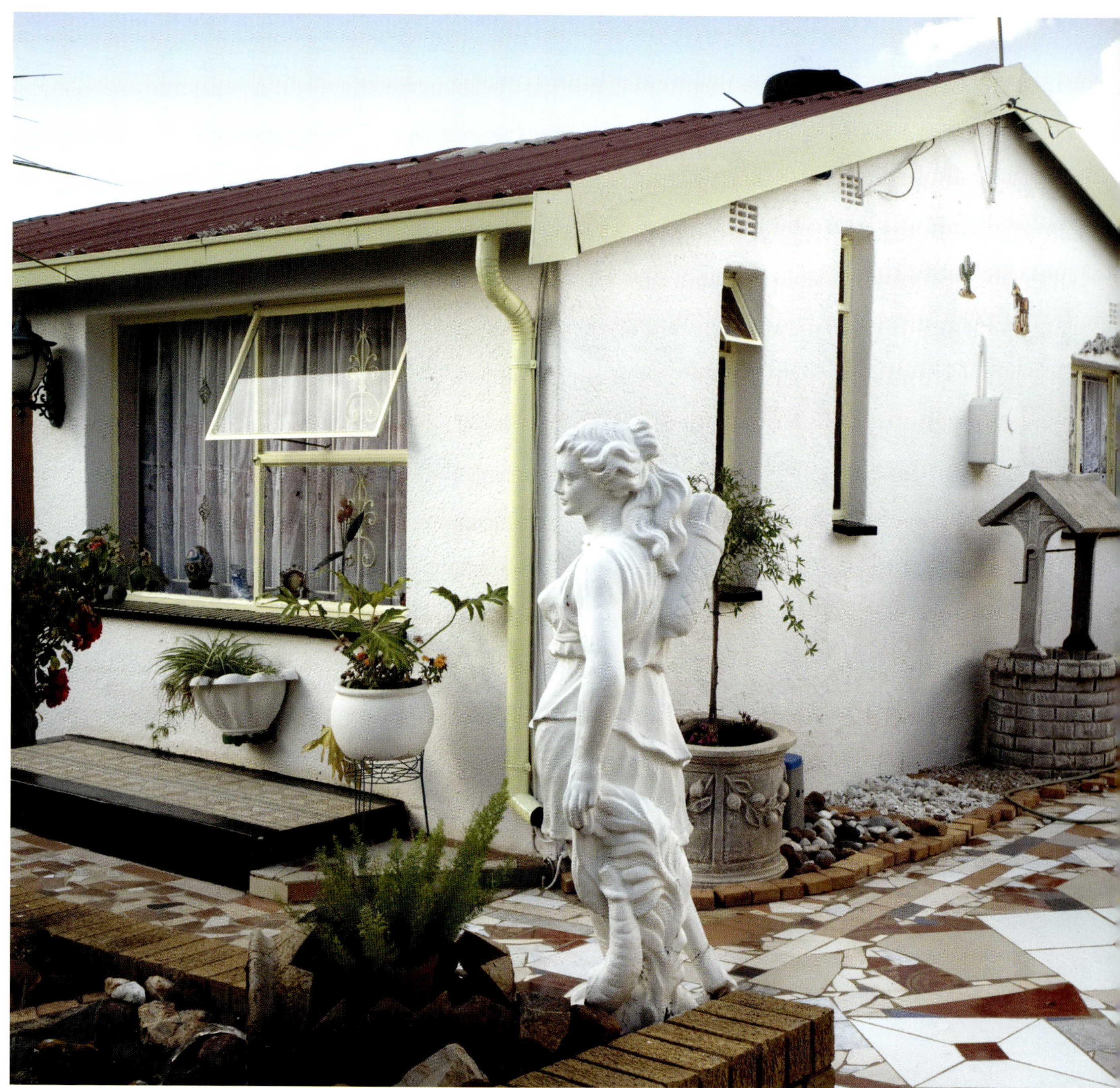

 Tryphina Nhlapo's house, Phiri, 2009

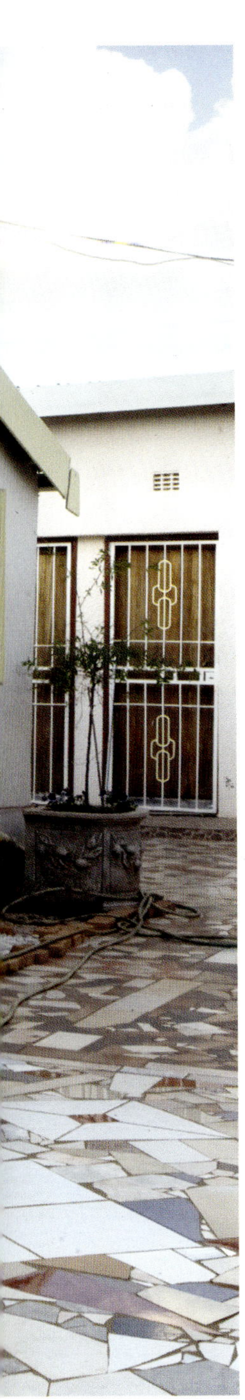

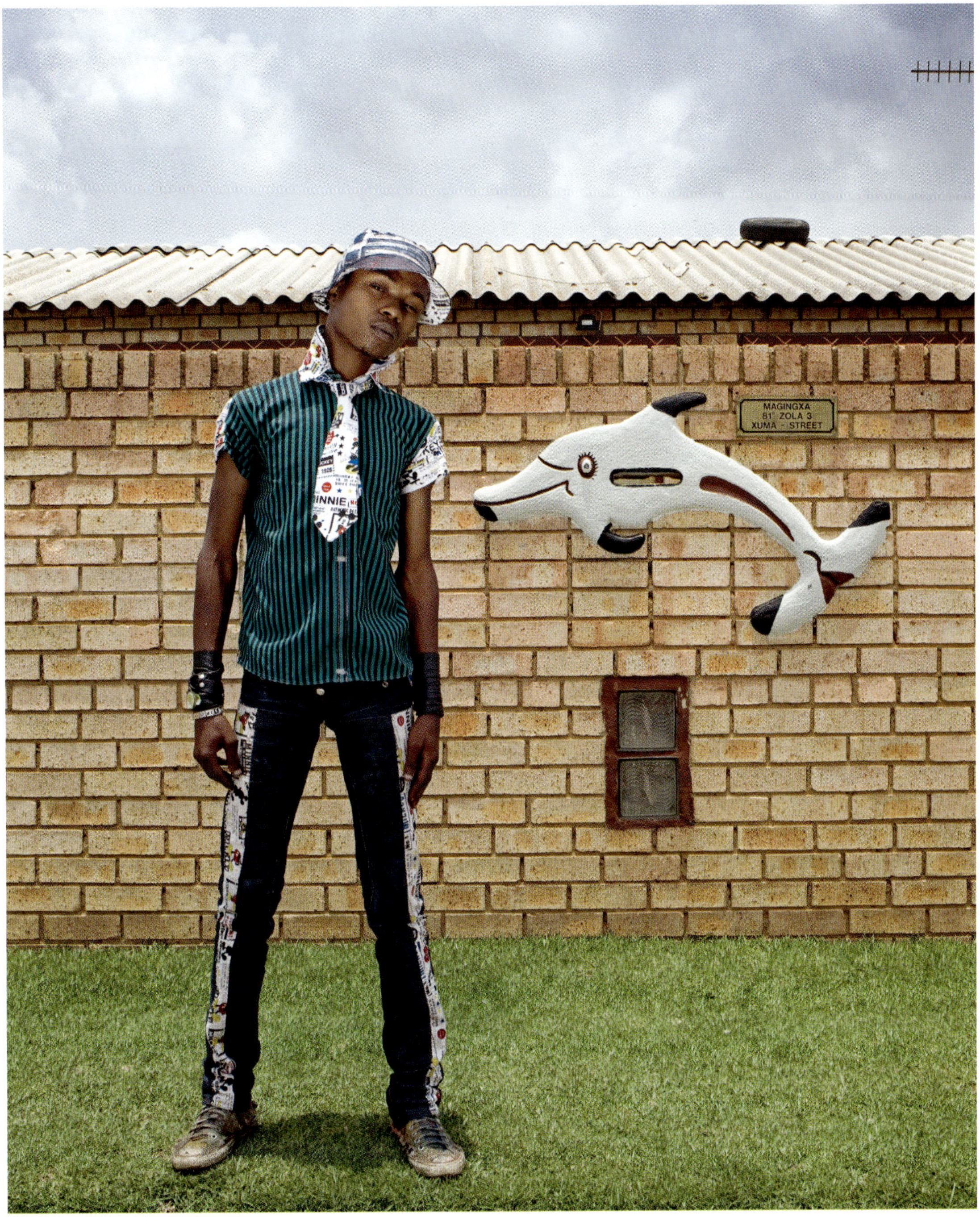

Bongani Sithole – Semen Seed Clothing, Zola 3, 2009 | 57

58 | Noria Chauke, Chiawelo, 2009

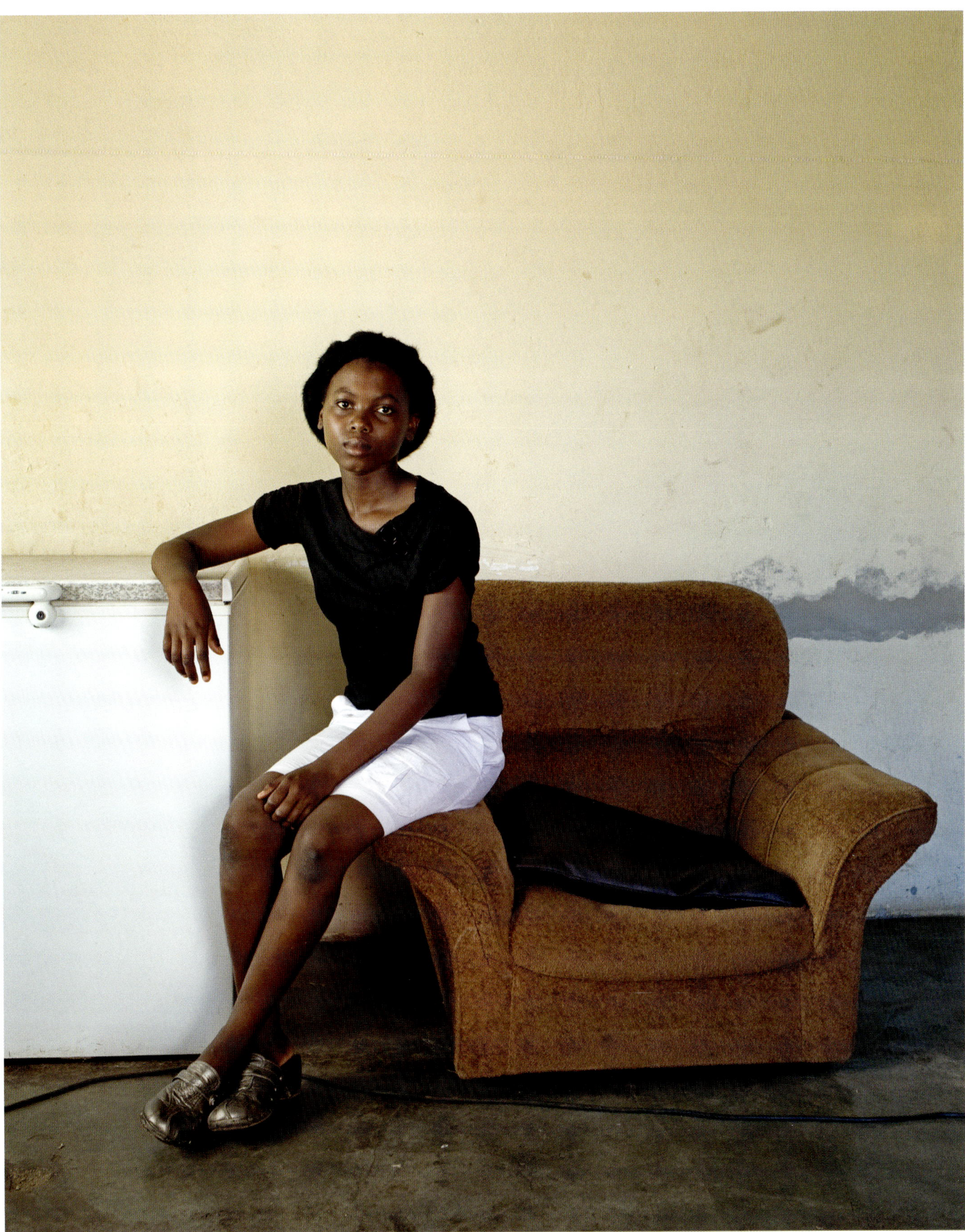

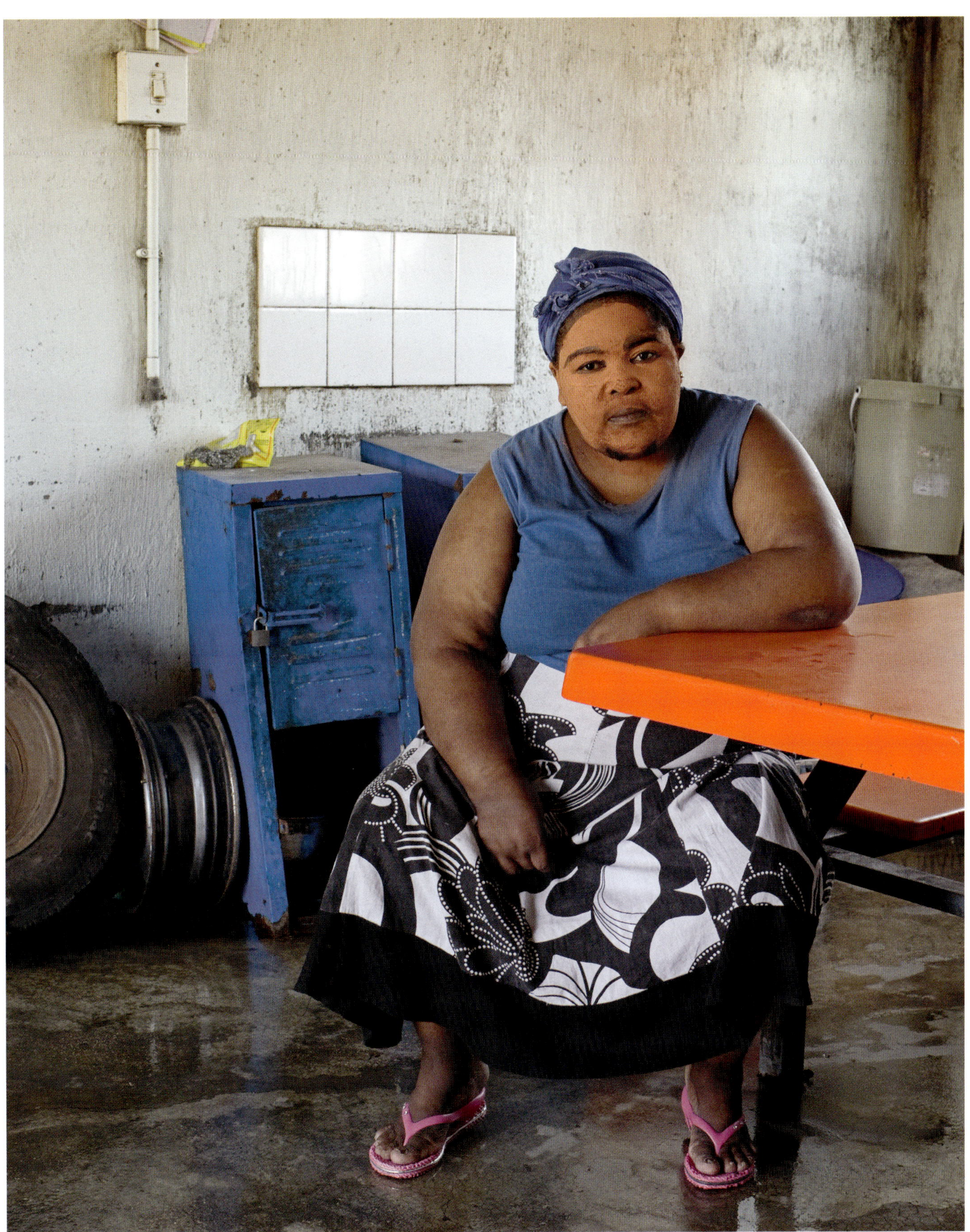

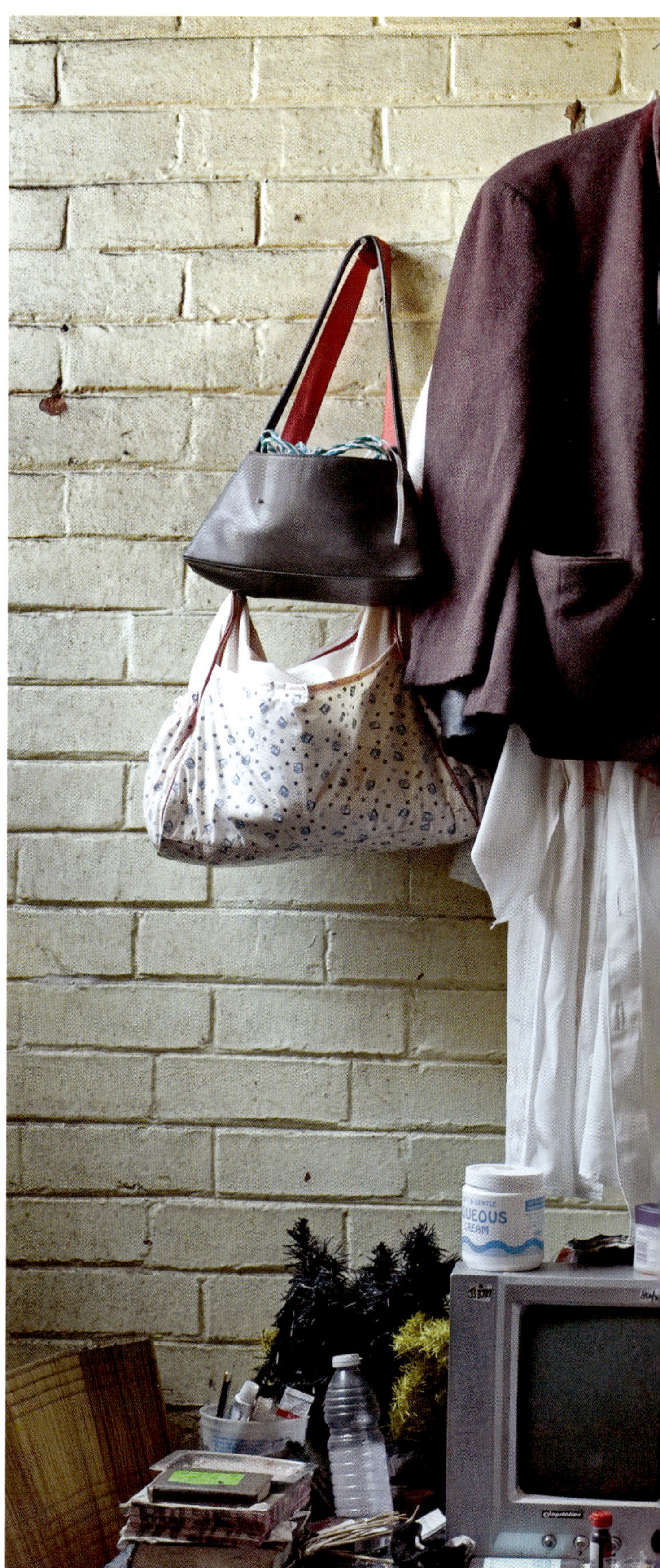

62 | Tholakele Mdluli, Nancefield Hostel,
Klipspruit, 2009

[Next page left] "A good wife respects her
husband", Songiseni and Princess Zungu's
home, Mzimhlophe Hostel, Mzimhlope,
Zone 11, 2009
[Next page right] Princess Zungu and
her son, Nolunge, Mzimhlophe Hostel,
Mzimhlophe, Zone 11, 2009

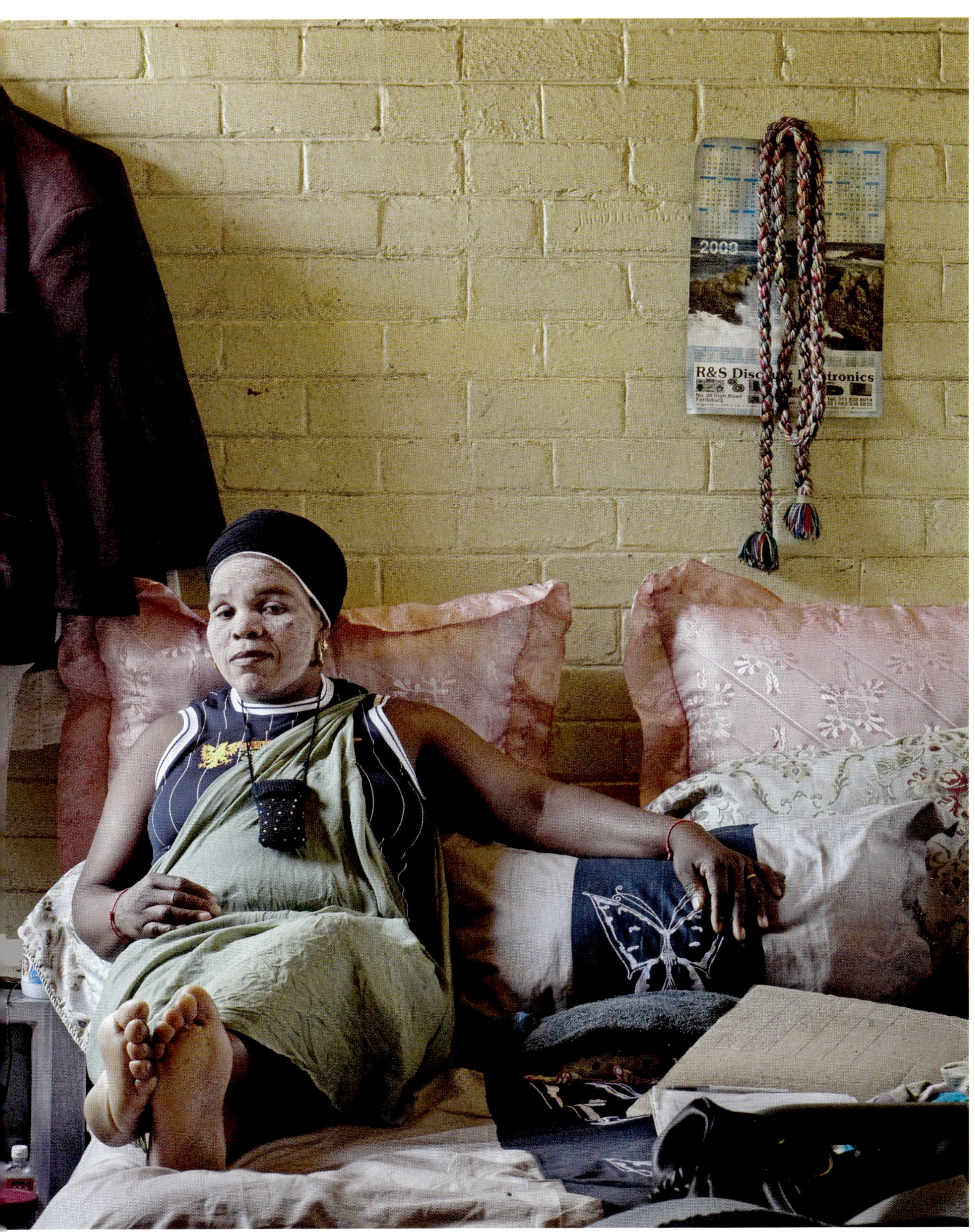

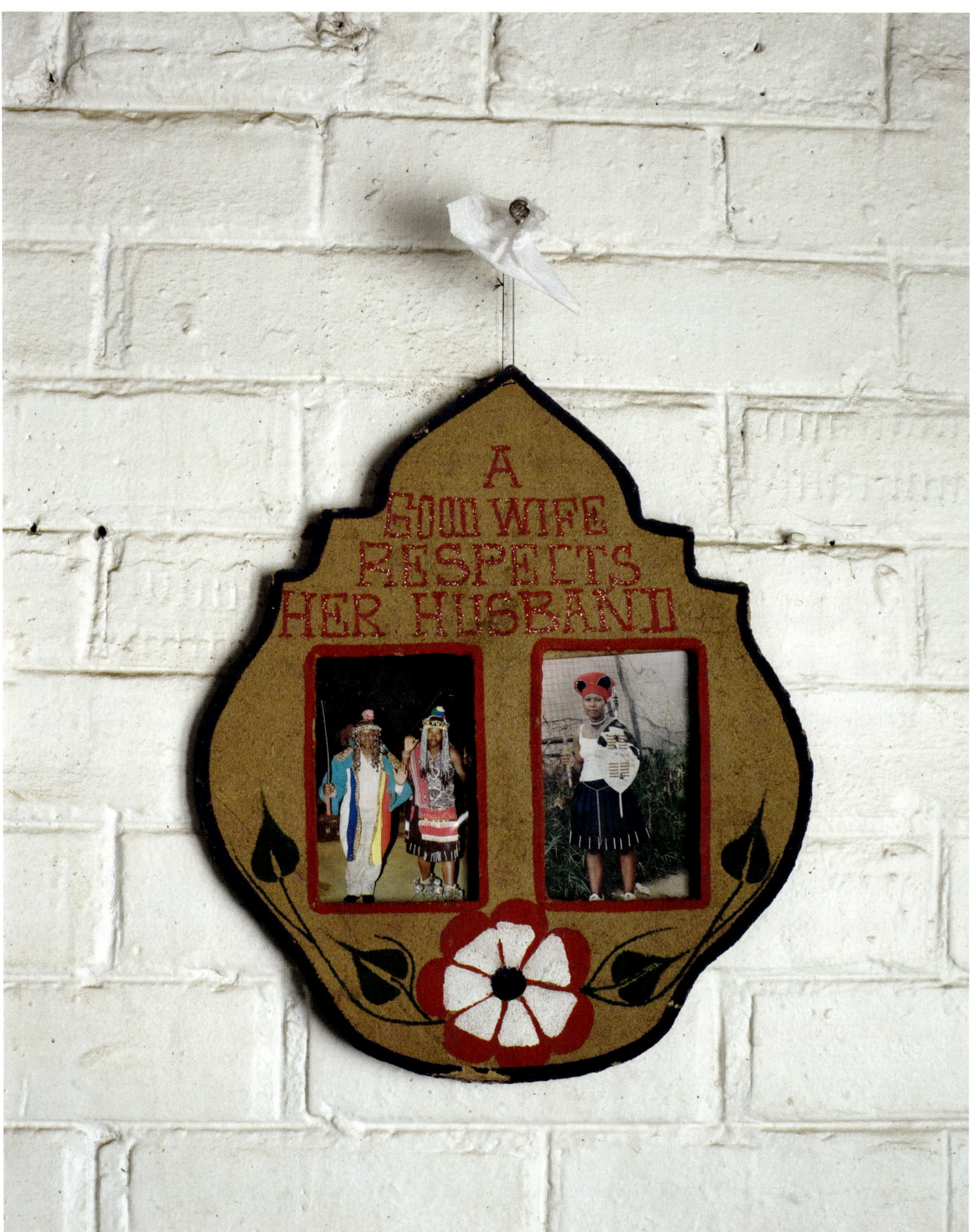
A
GOOD WIFE
RESPECTS
HER HUSBAND

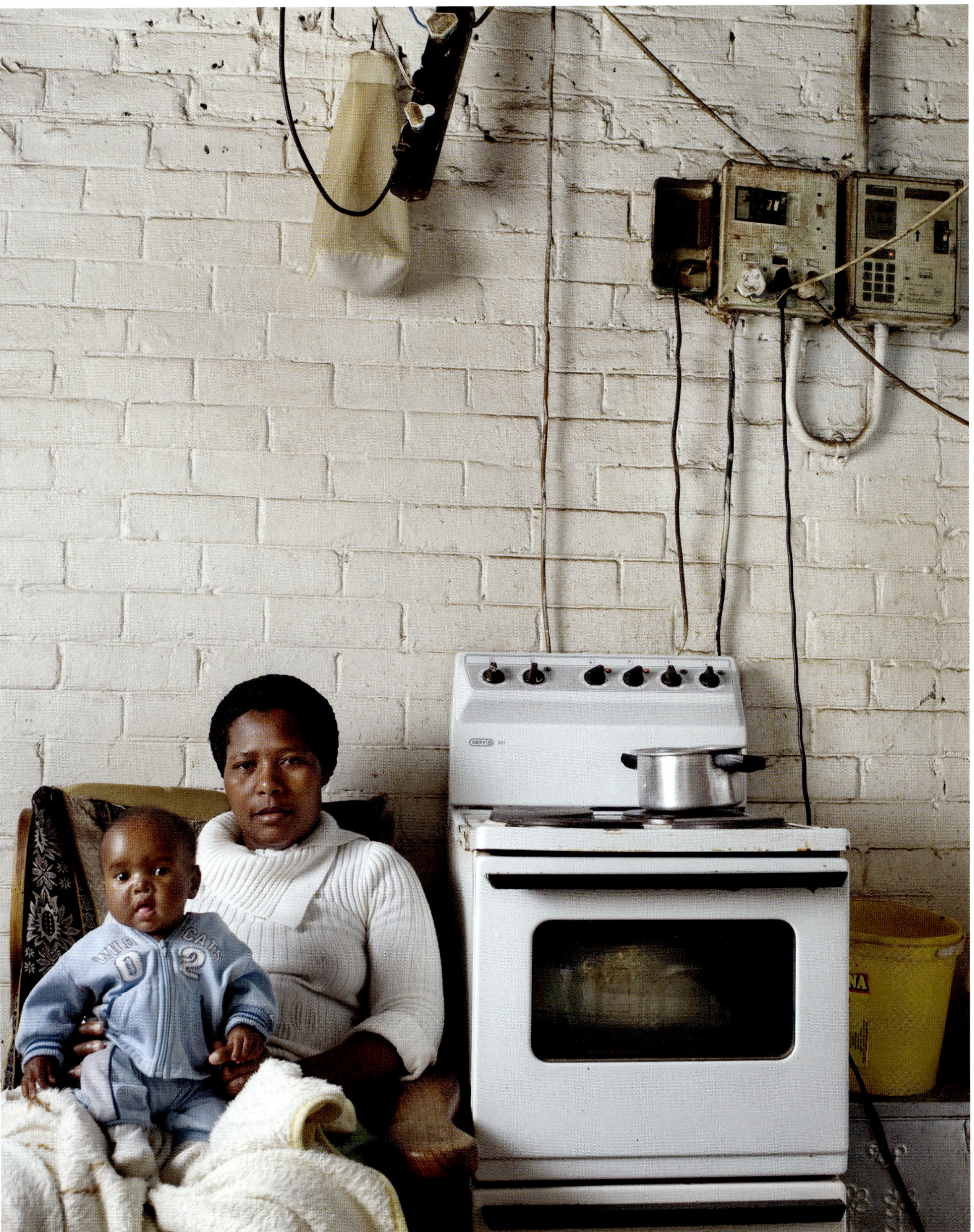

 Themba and Josephine Kunene, Meadowlands, Zone 6, 2009

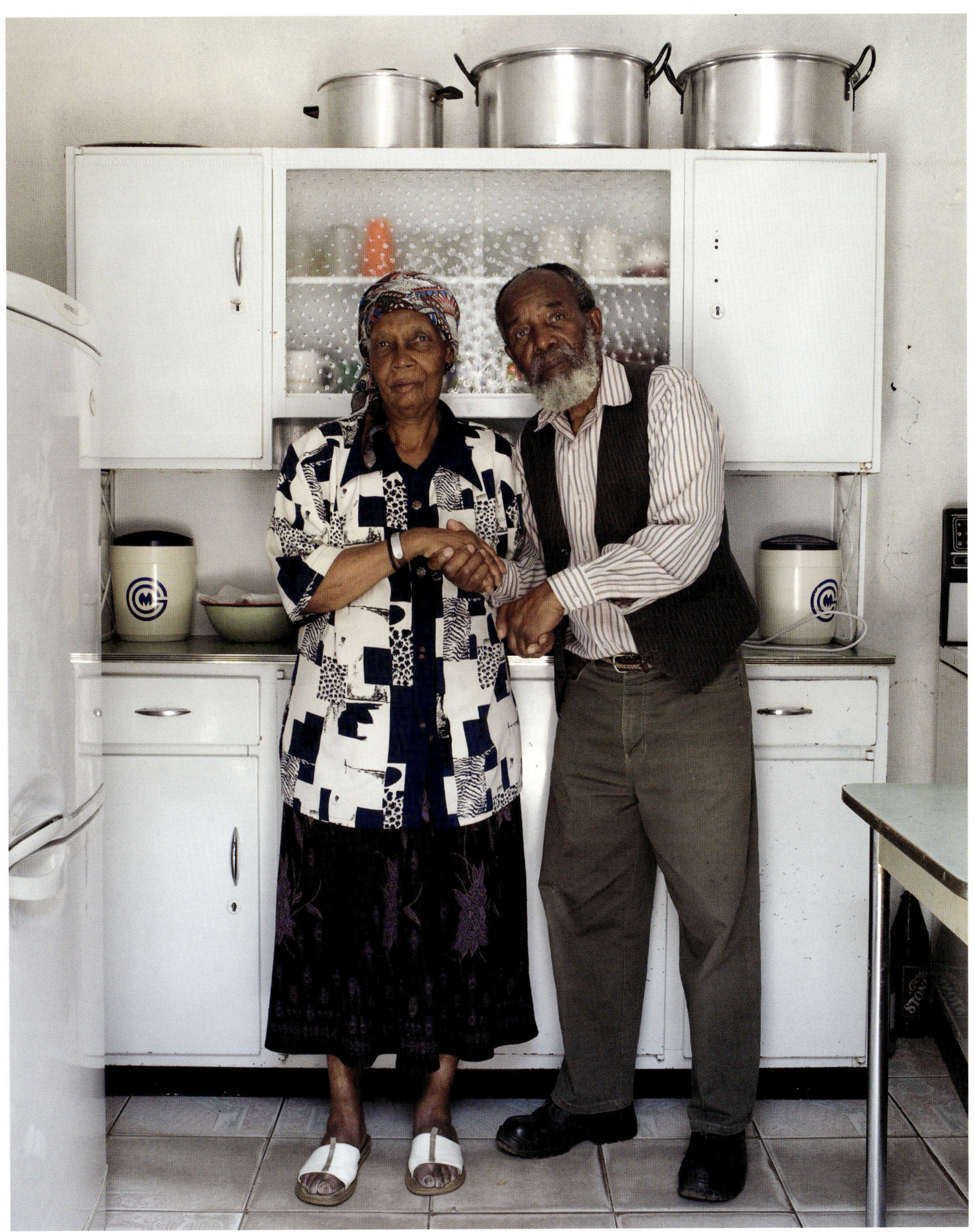

68 | Francina and Shadrak Mahlangu, Zola 3, 2009

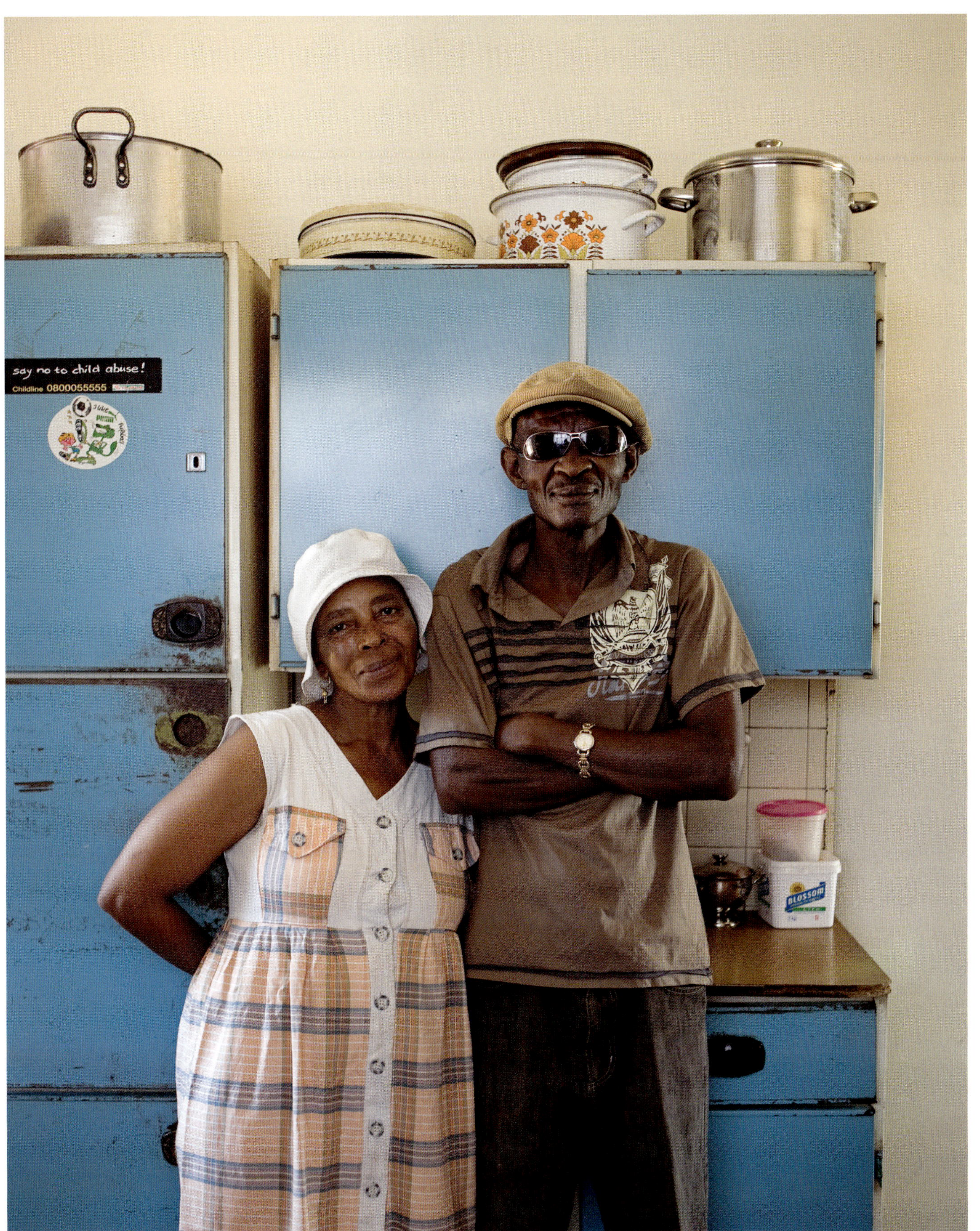

say no to child abuse!
Childline 0800055555

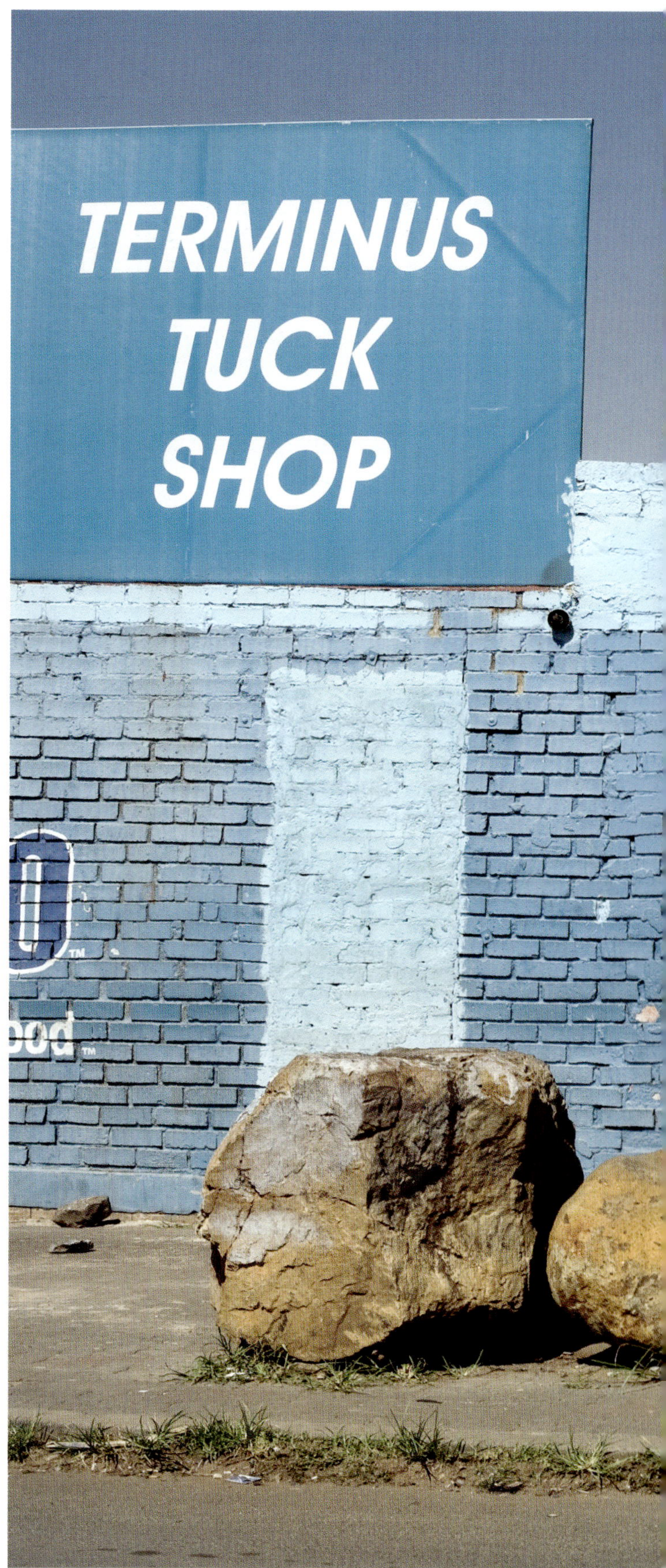

TERMINUS
TUCK
SHOP

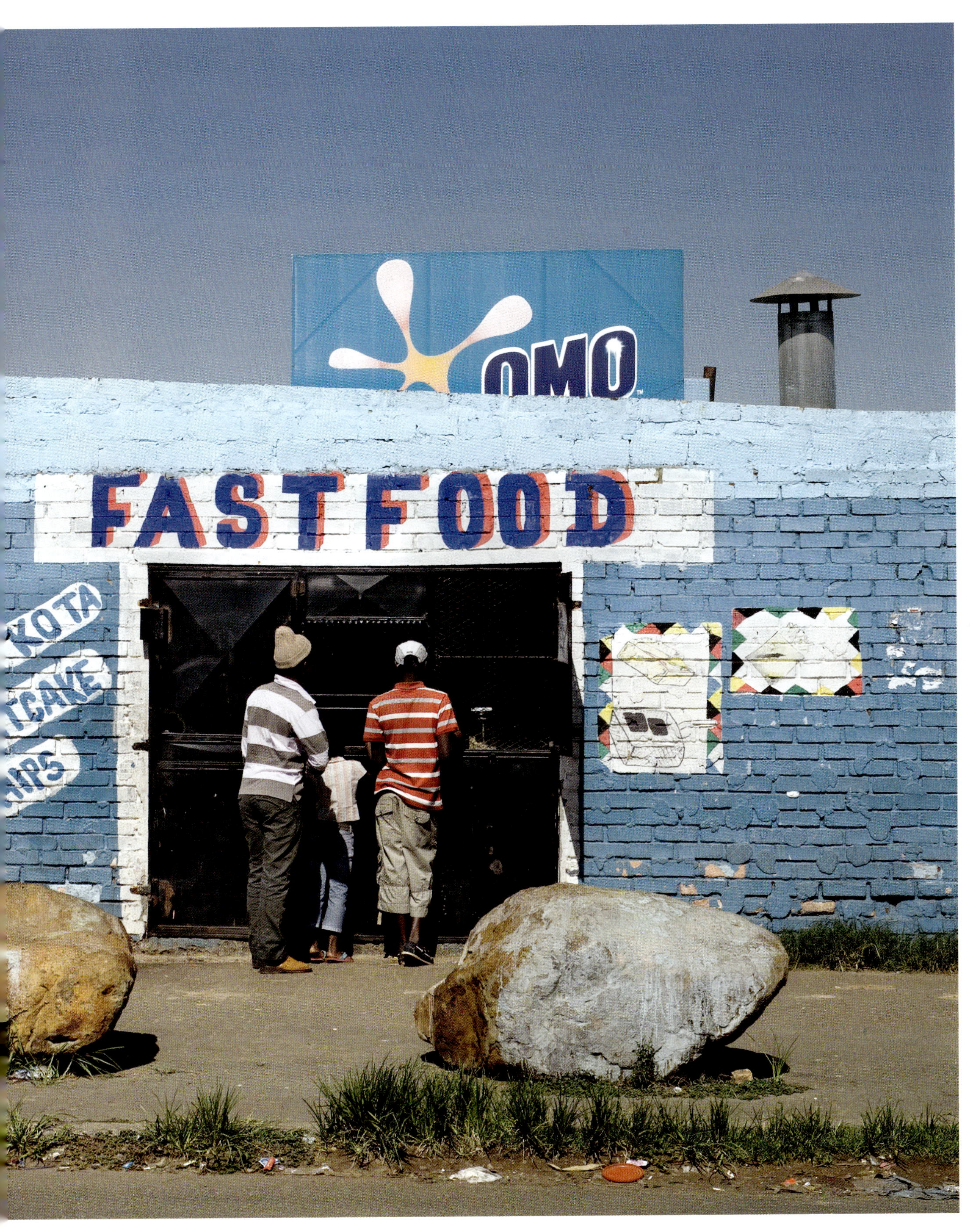

OMO
FAST FOOD
KOTA
CAKE
PS

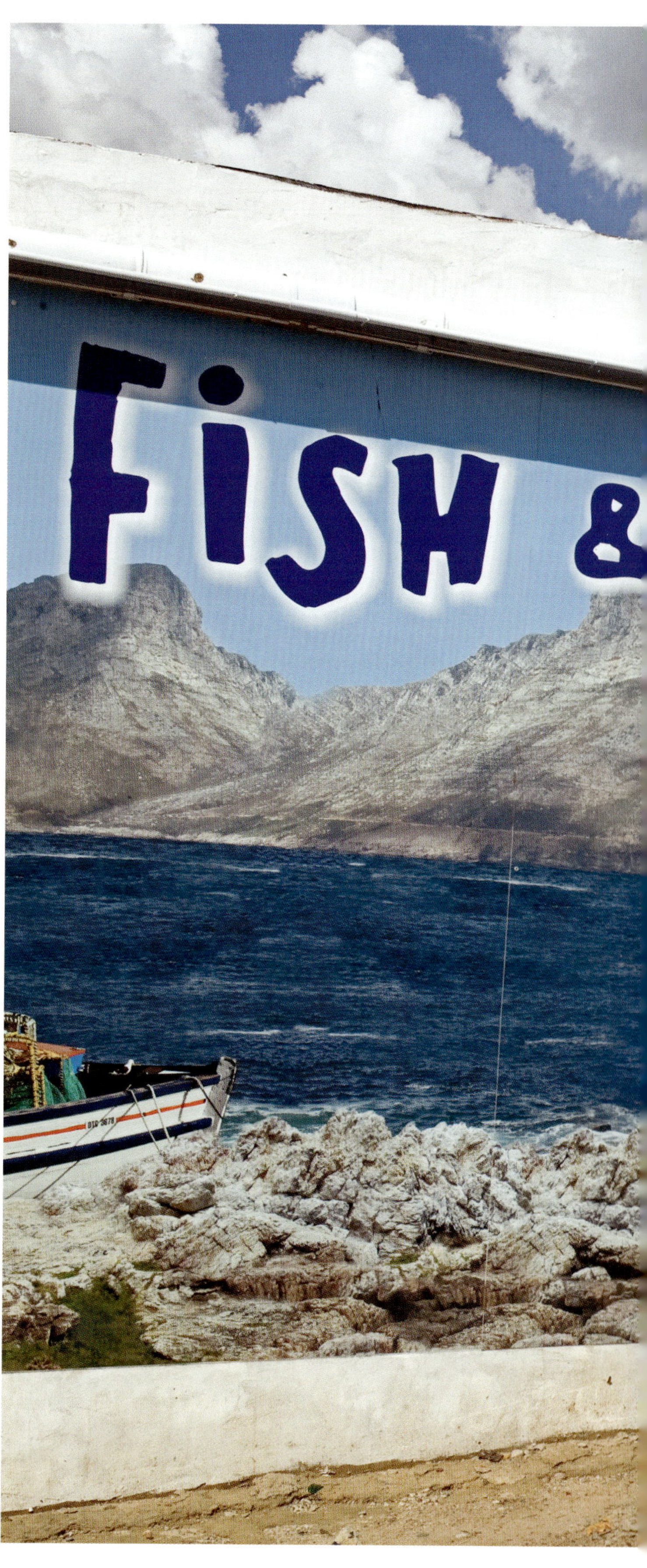

72 | Fish and Chips, Chiawelo, 2009

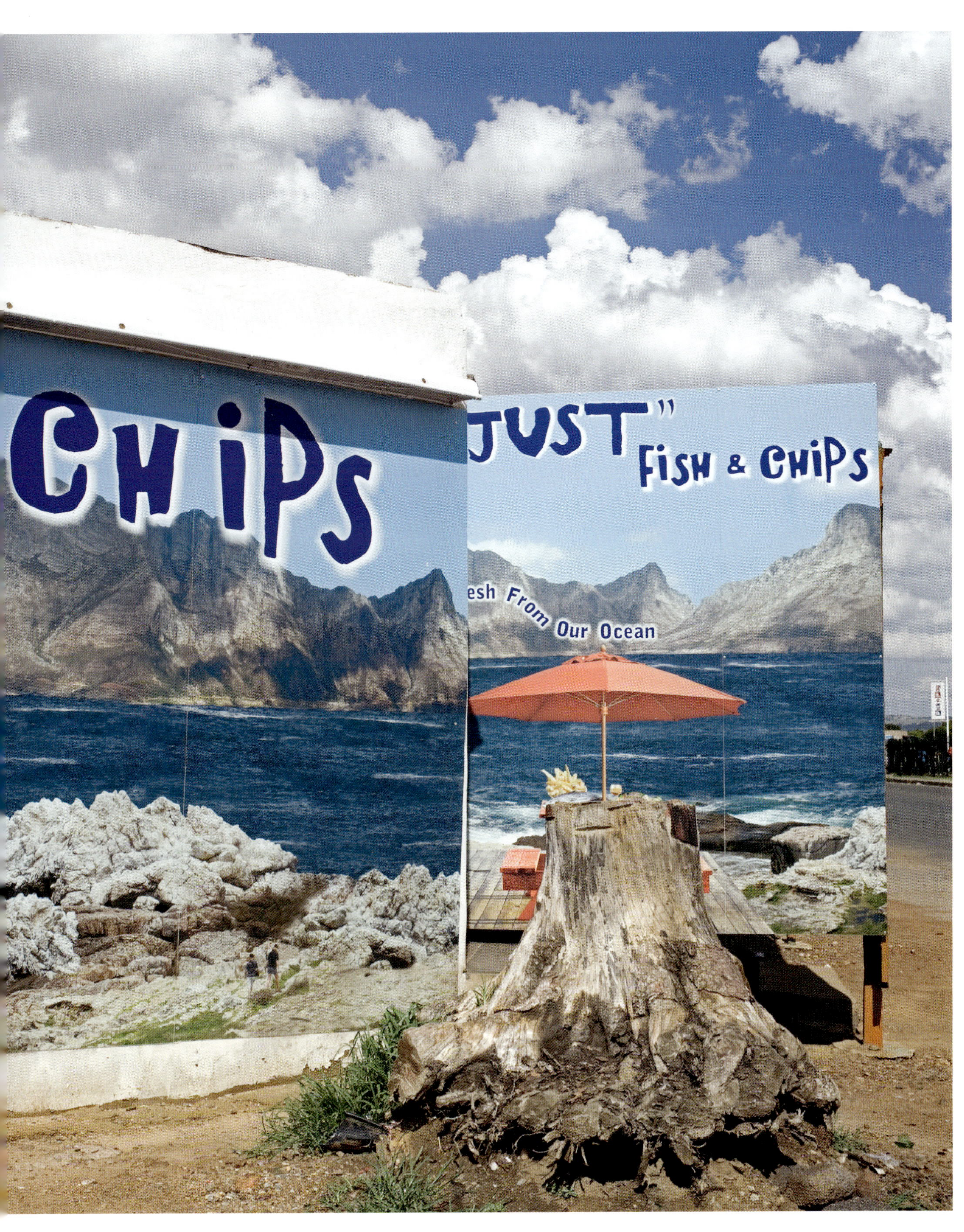

CH iPS
"JUST" FiSH & CHiPS
...esh From Our Ocean

 Orlando West Swimming Pool, Orlando West, 2009

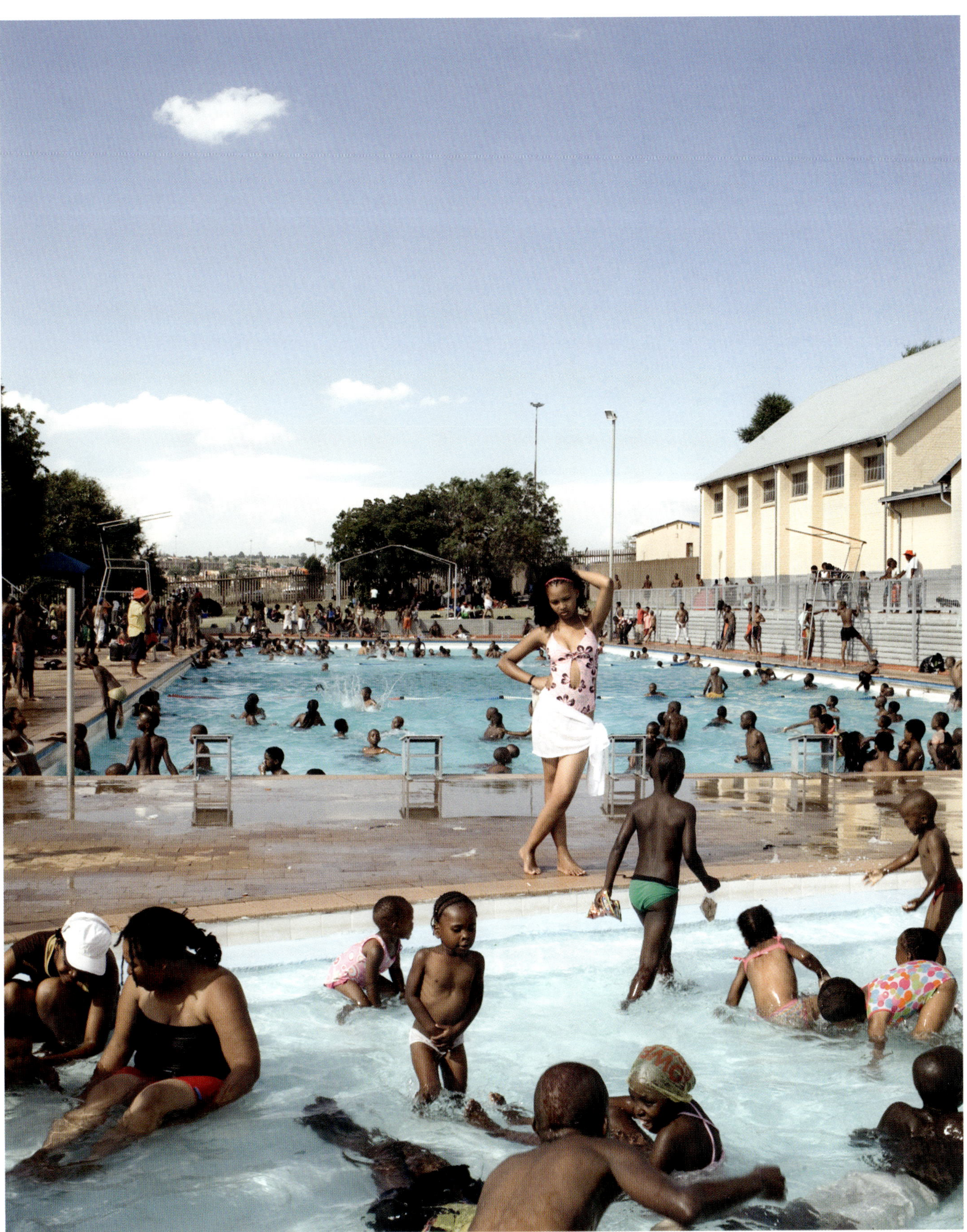

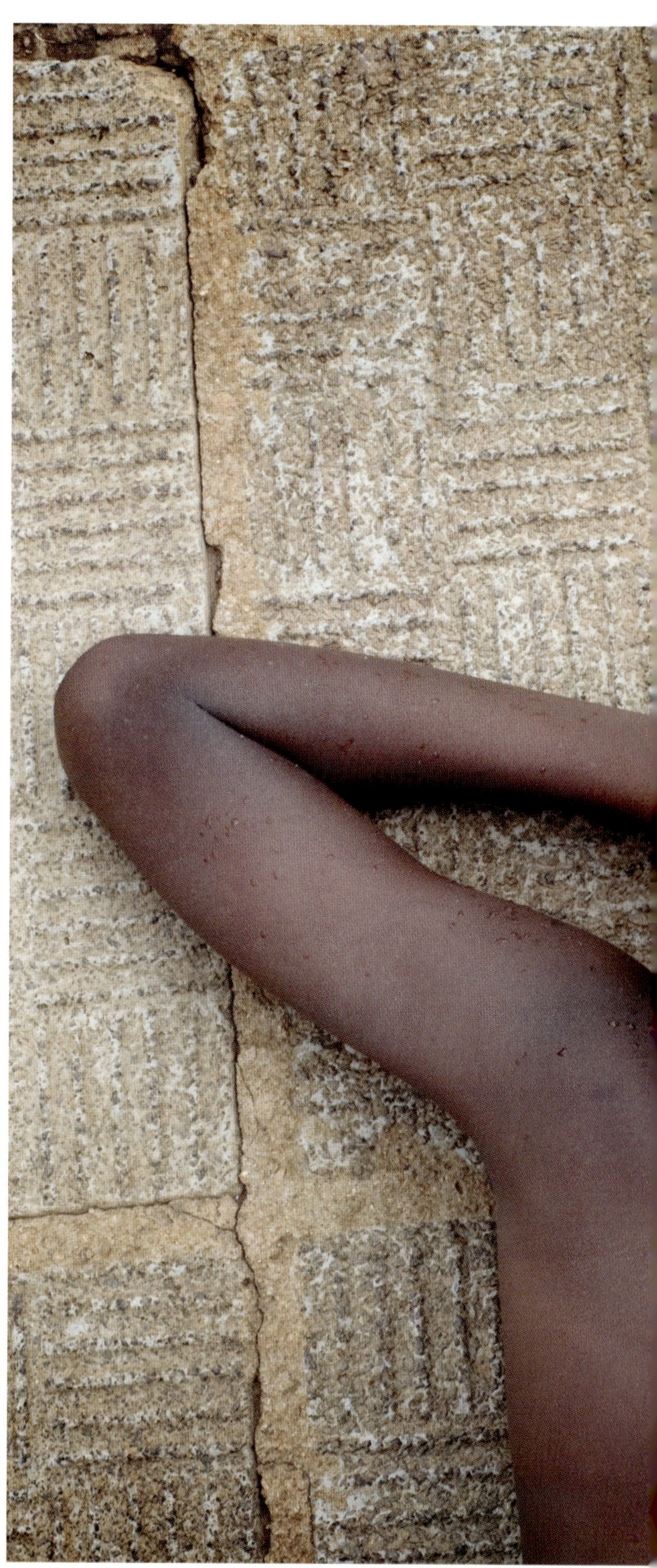

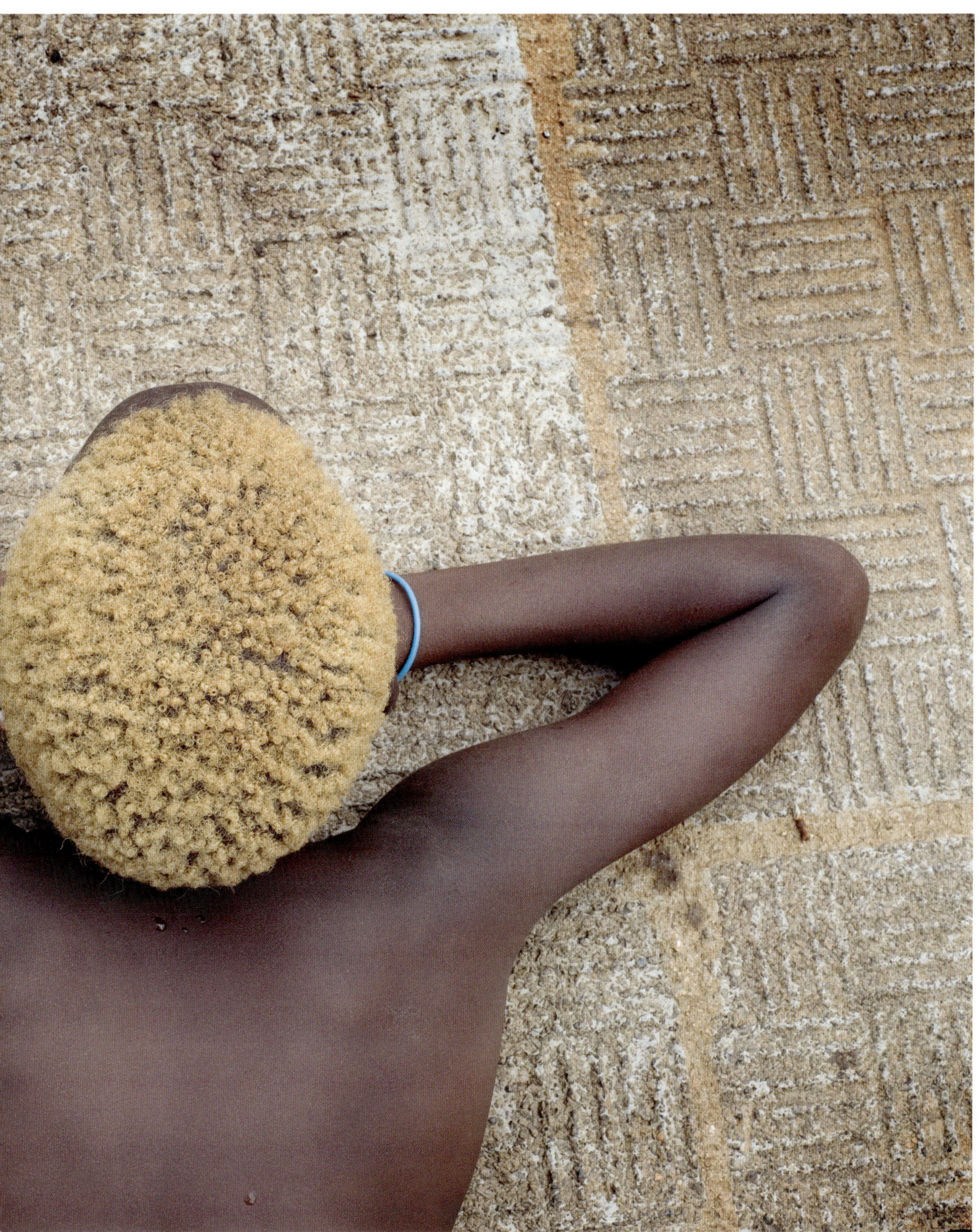

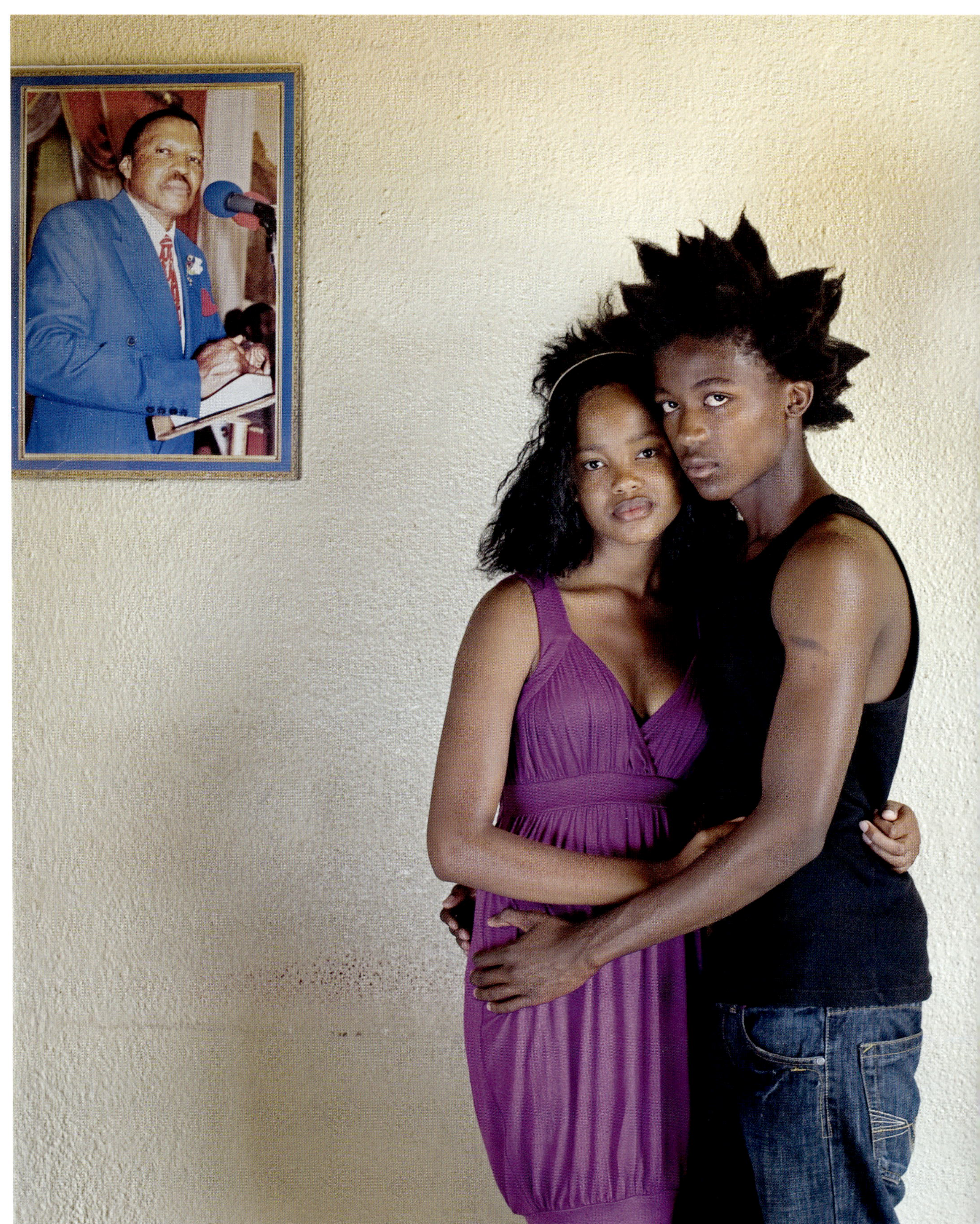

Tumi Tlou and Ali Mbalati, with a portrait of Pastor Modise
on the wall, Chiawelo Flats, Chiawelo, 2010 | 79

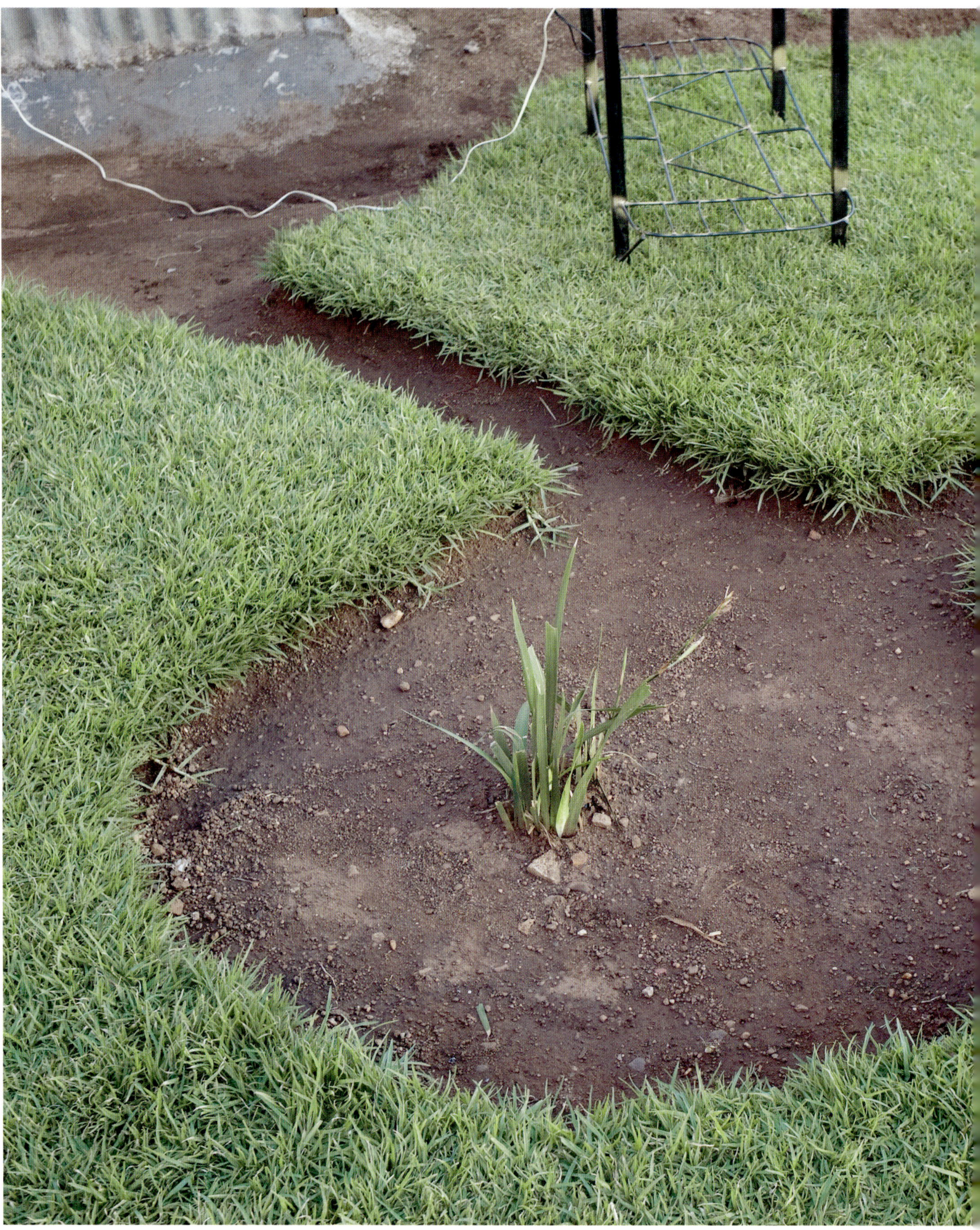

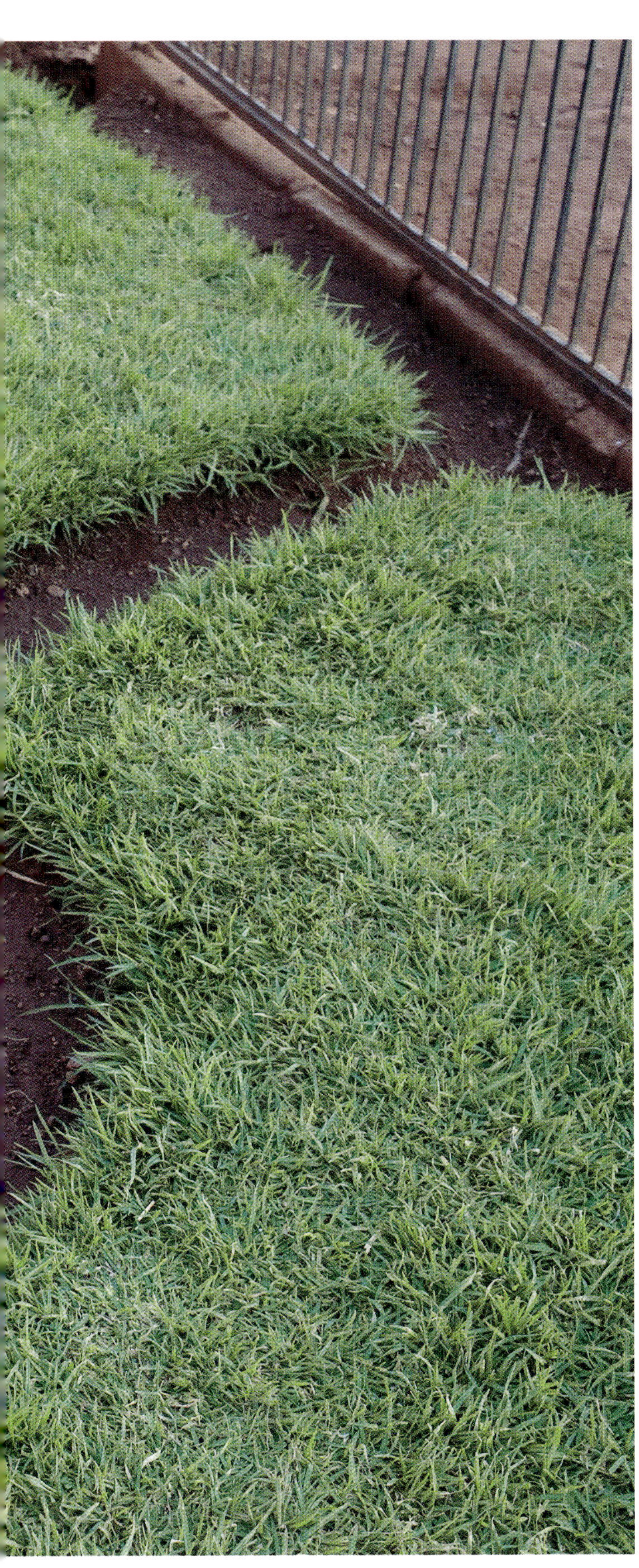

HIV/Aids ribbon in a garden being used to run an informal
telephone business, Chiawelo, 2009 | 81

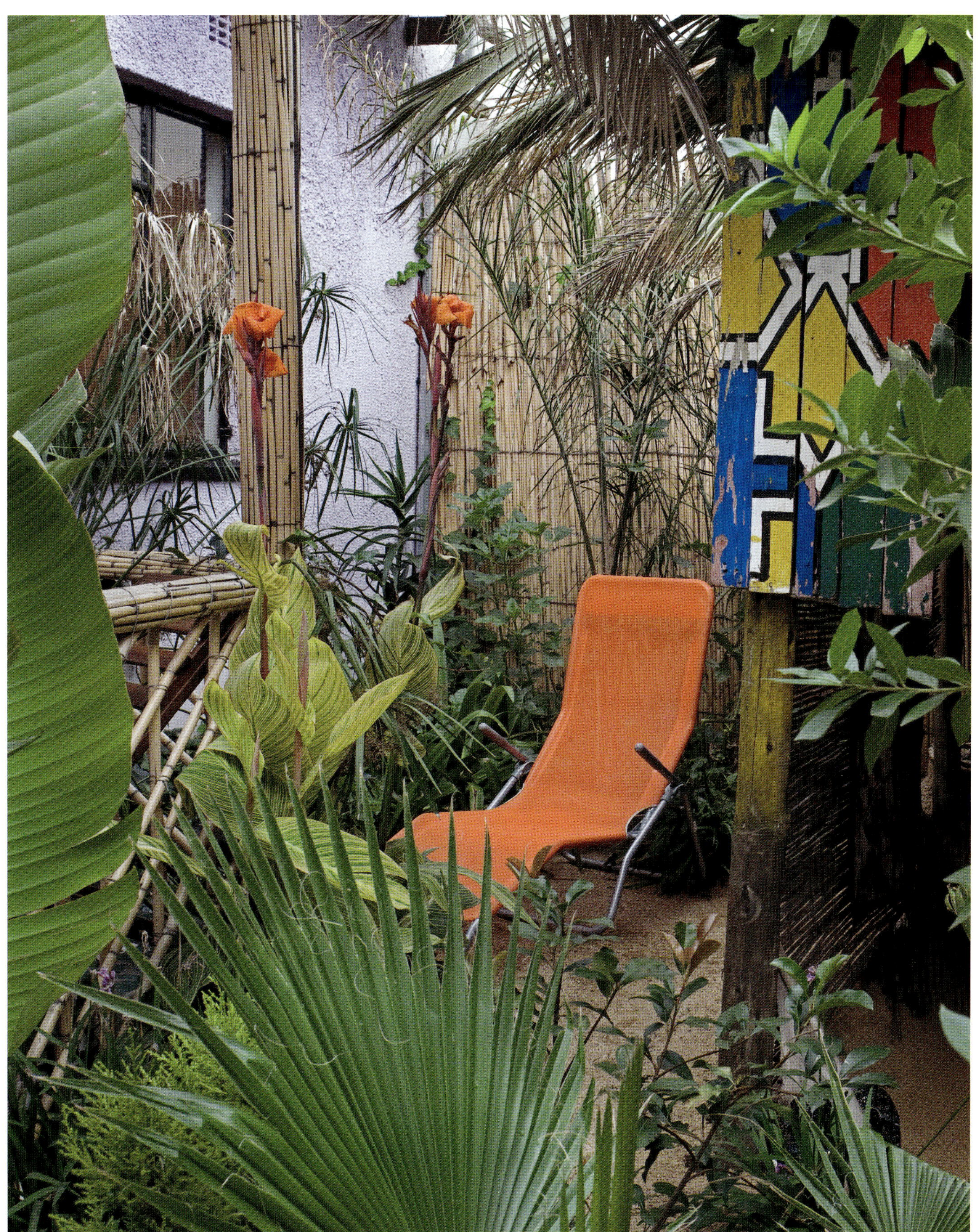

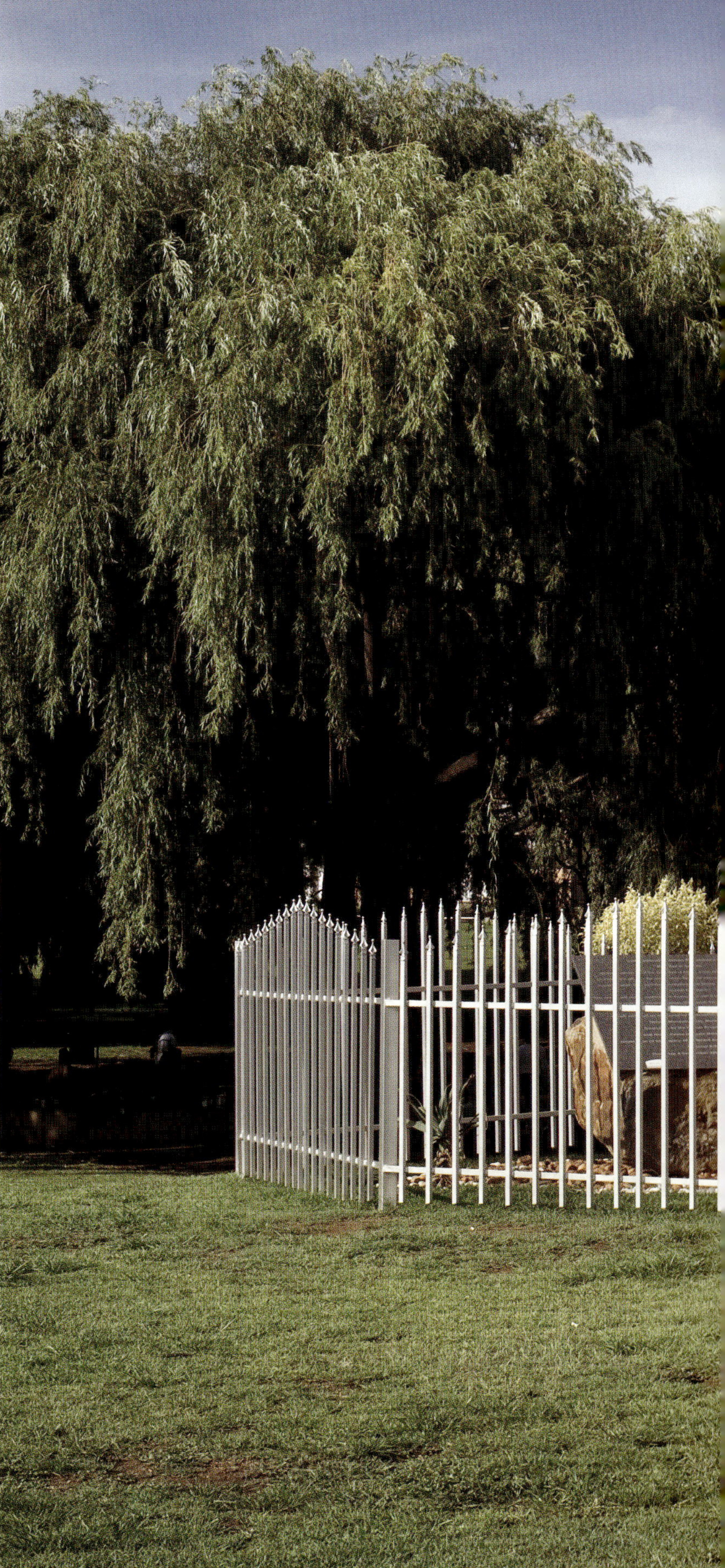

84 | Nelson Mandela, Thokoza Park, 2009

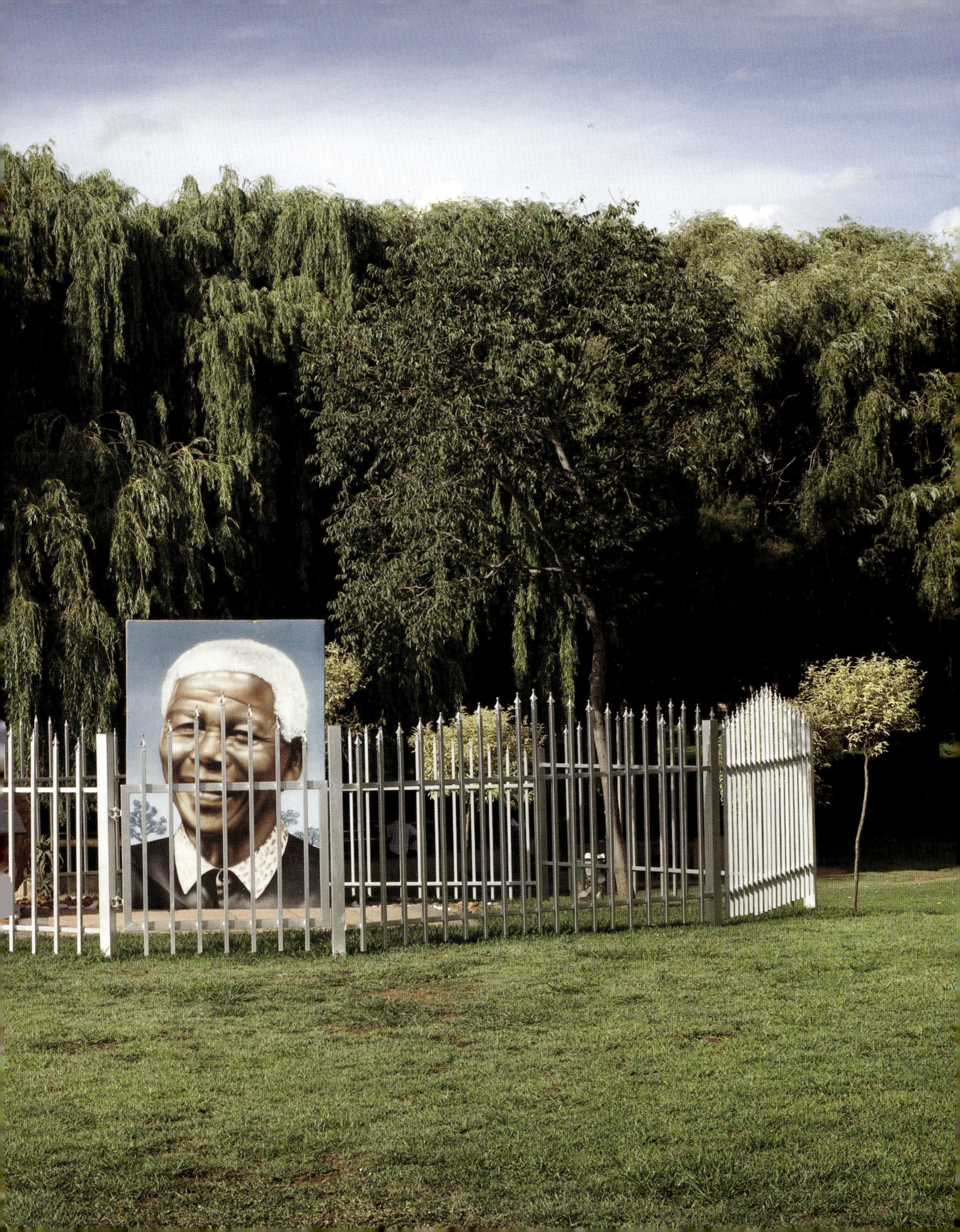

 Mural painted in memory of Hector Pieterson, Chiawelo Flats, Chiawelo, 2010

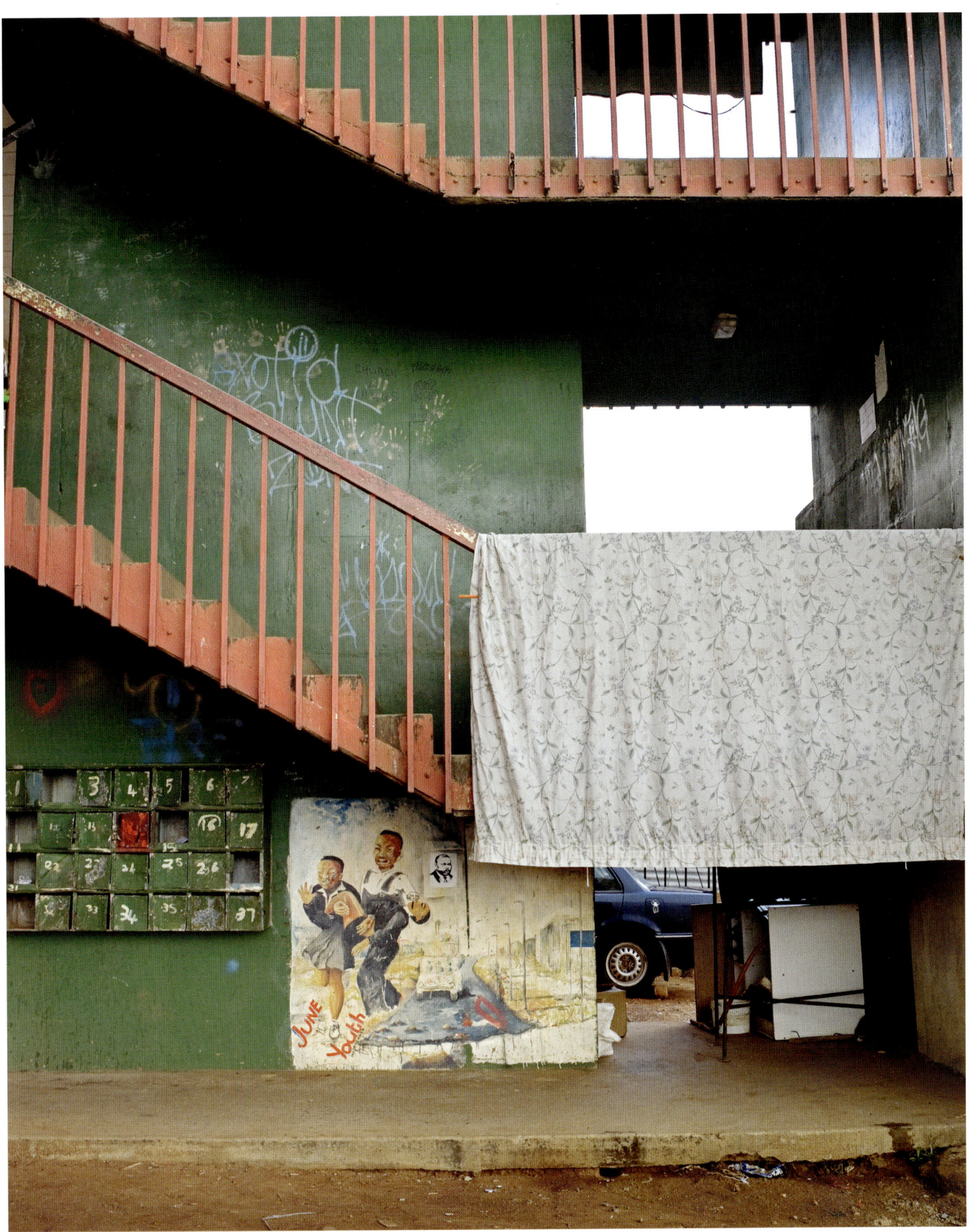
June
Youth

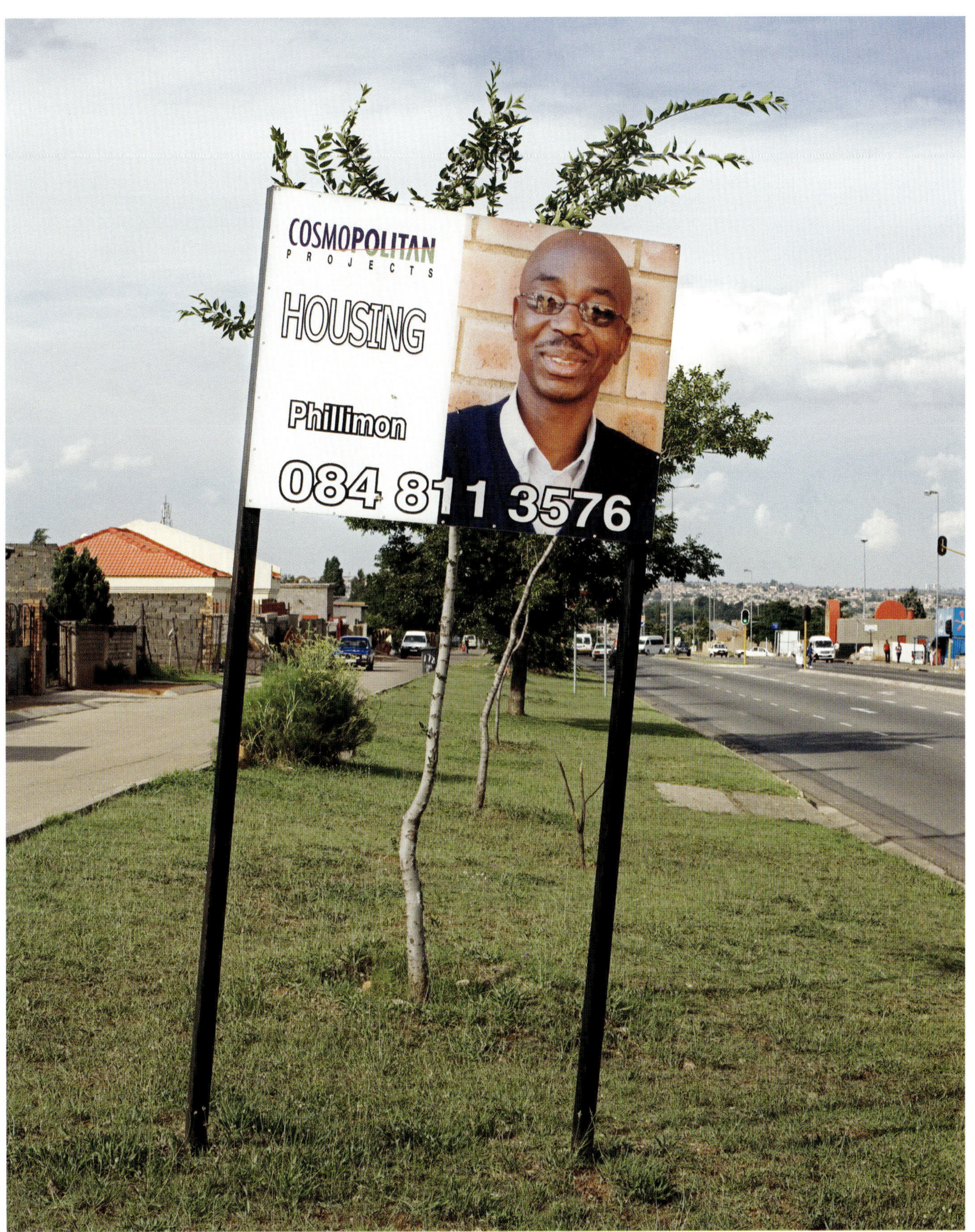

COSMOPOLITAN
PROJECTS
HOUSING
Phillimon
084 811 3576

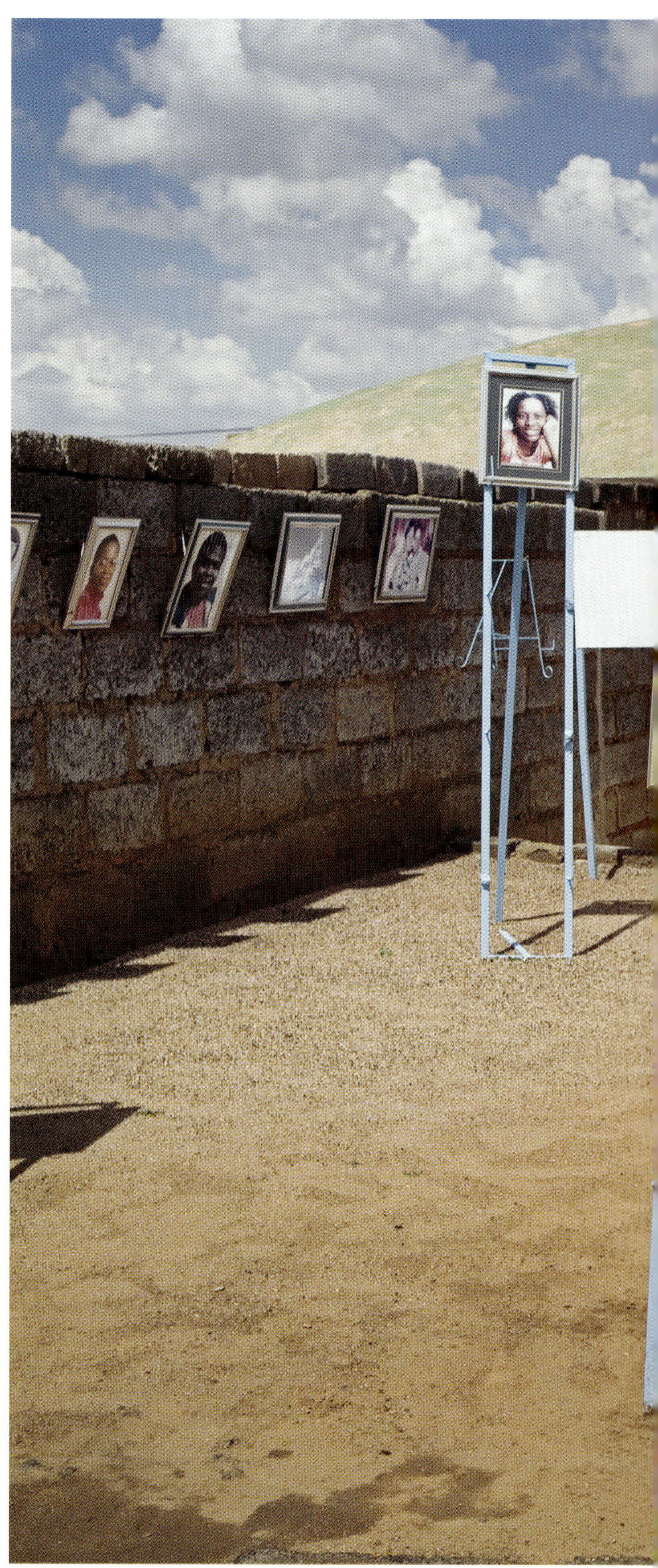

90 | Johnny Moloisane's Sunrise Photographic
Studio, White City Jabavu, 2009

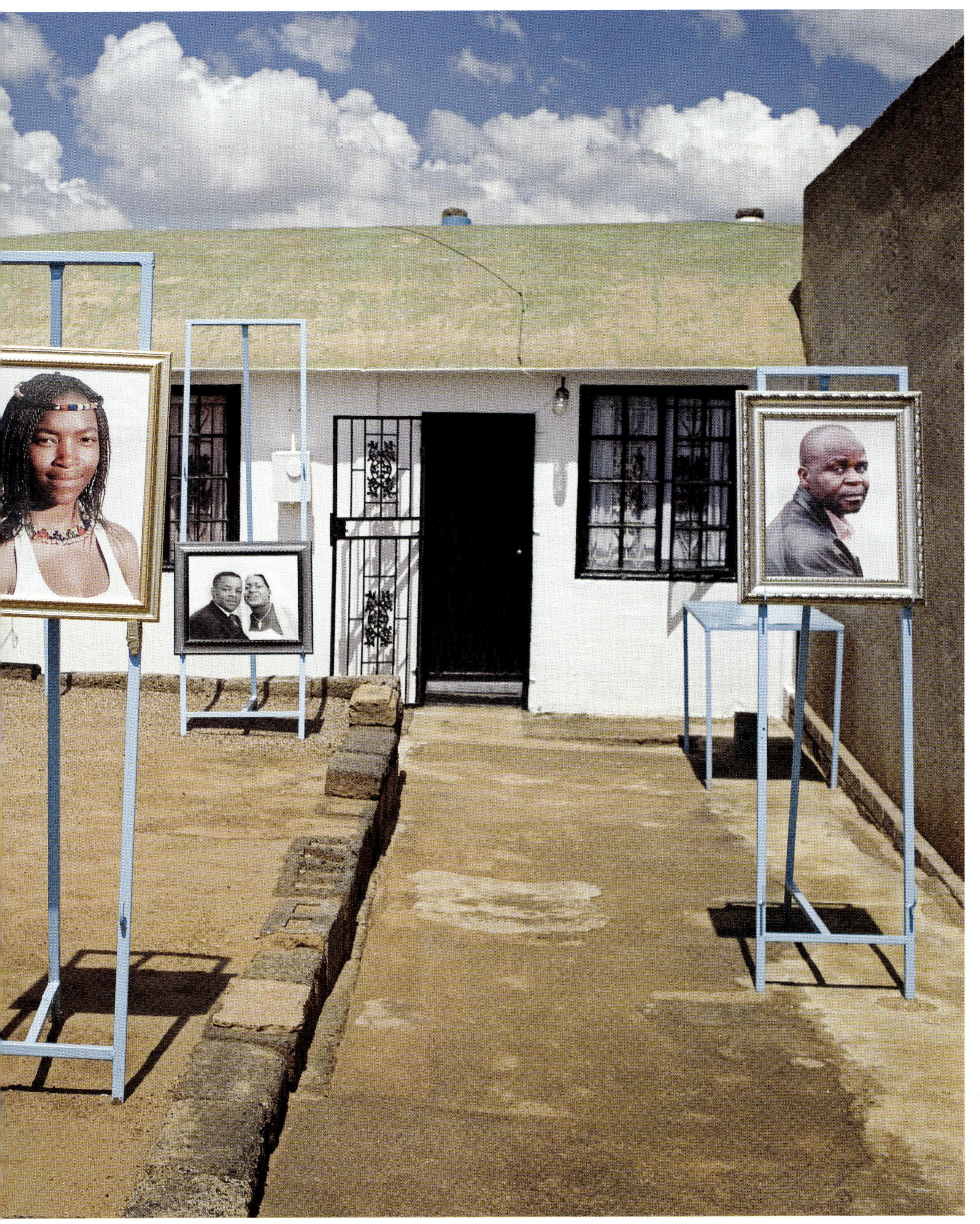

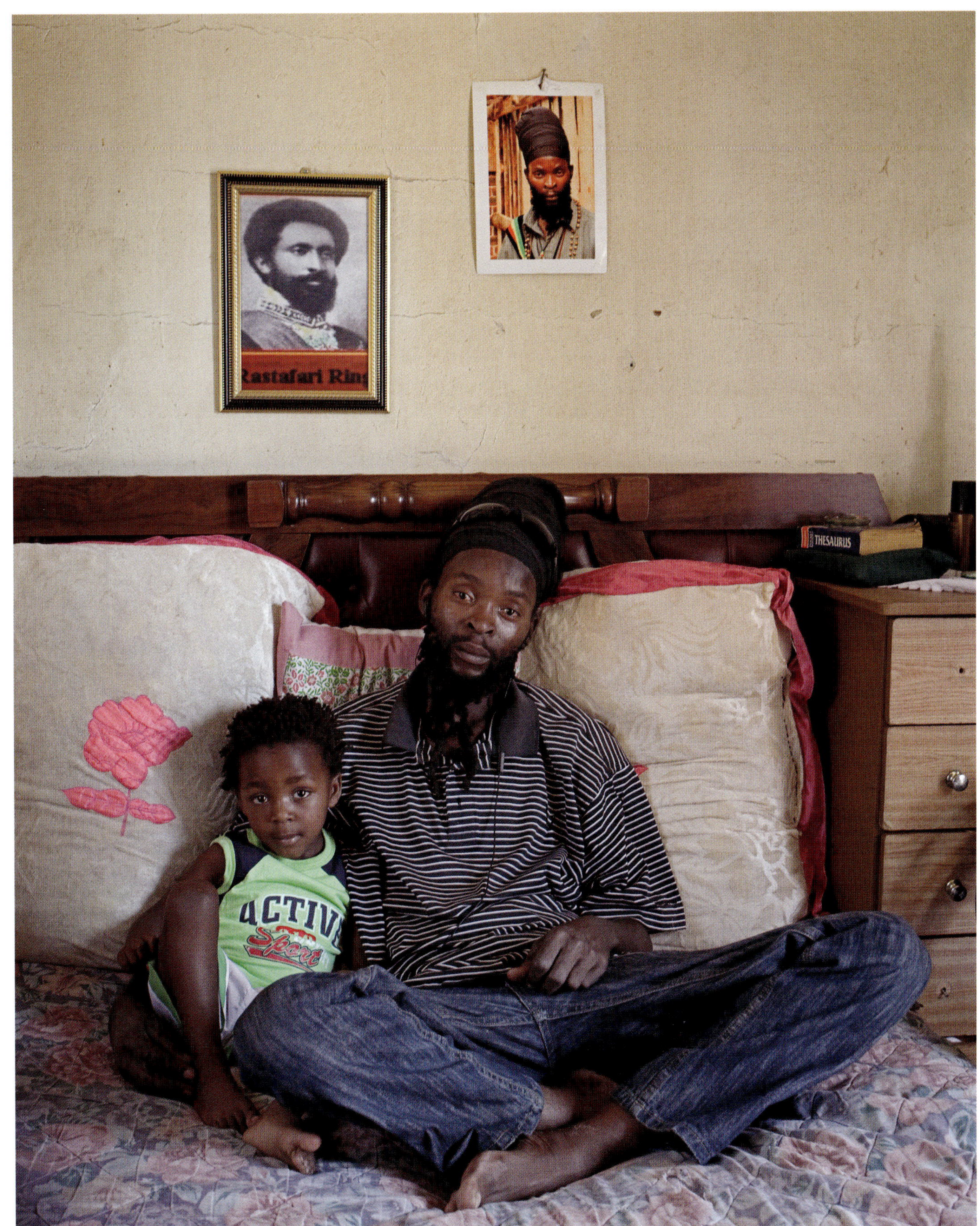

Rastafari Ring

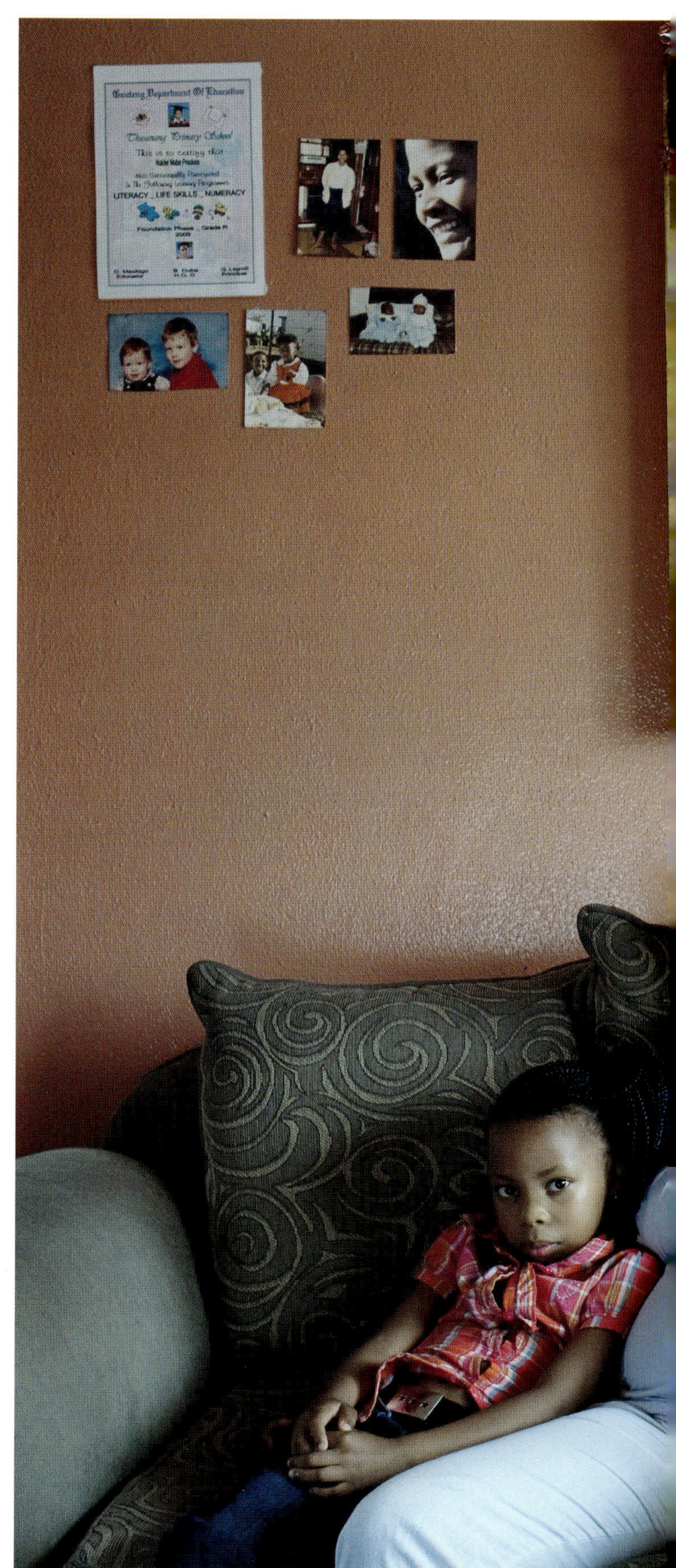

94 | Chris and Mpho Nalder and their children,
Lebohang and Ofentse, Rockville, 2010

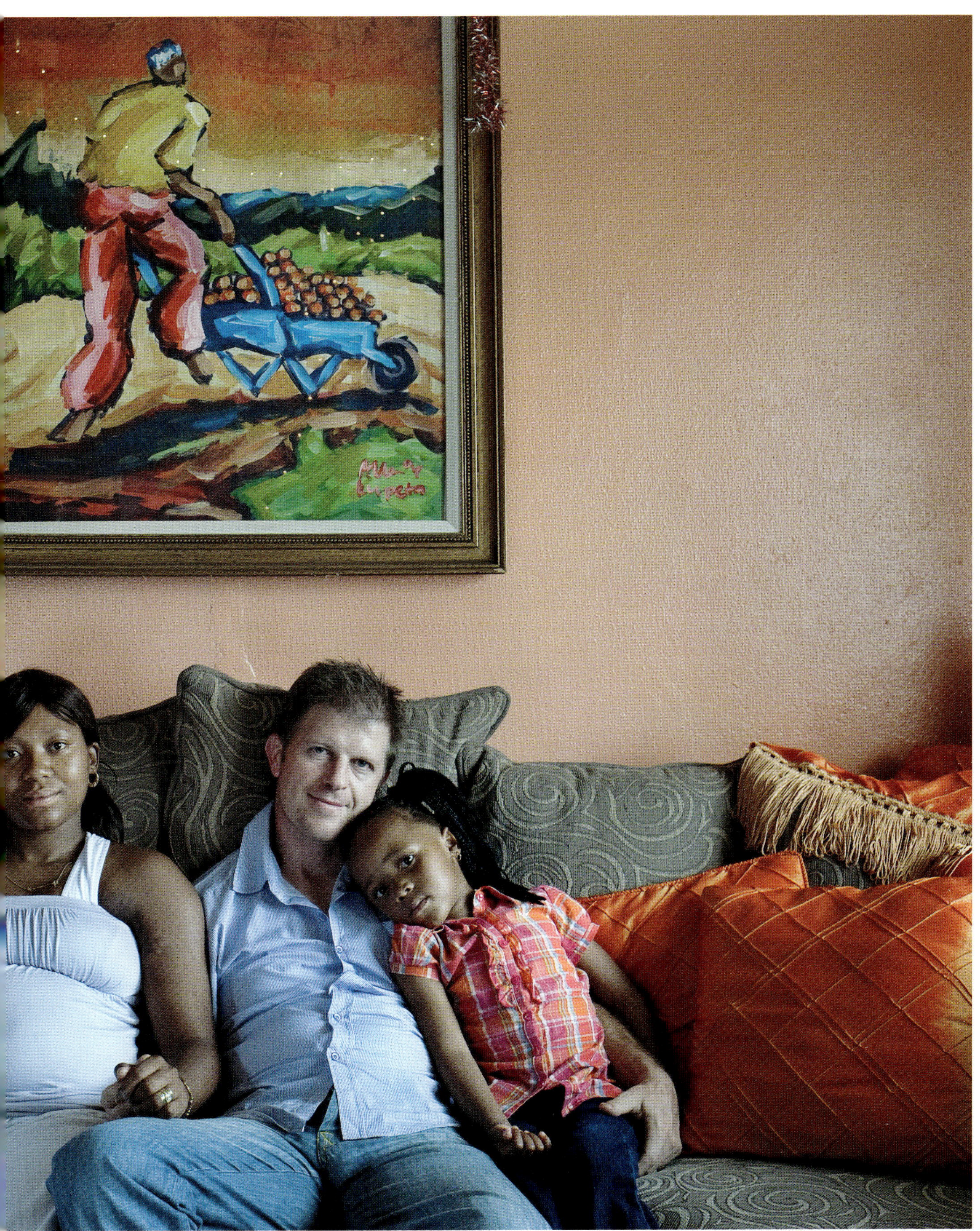

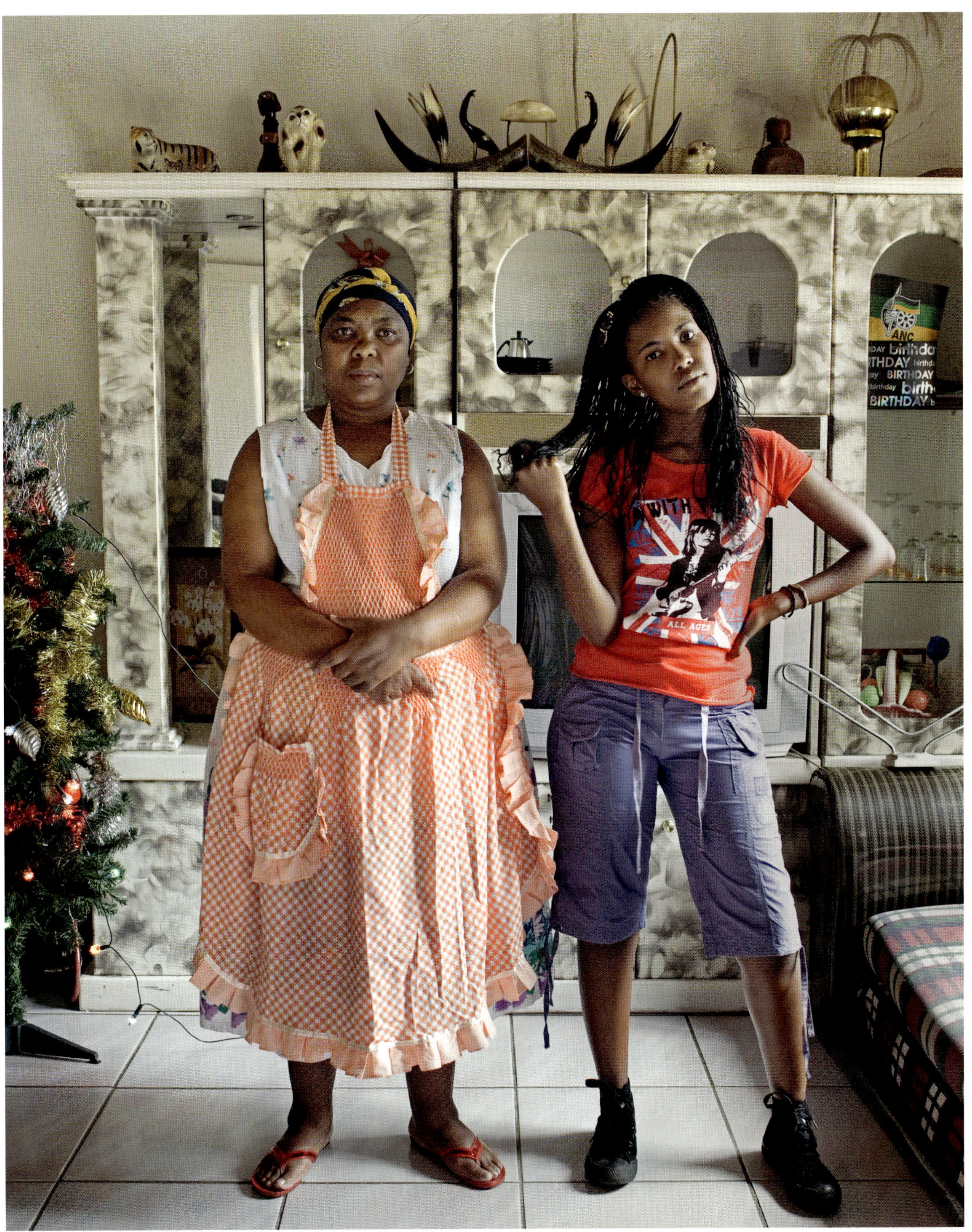

98 | Mkhulu Nyengelezi, a sangoma (traditional healer), and her assistant, Thwasa Gogo Lungi, Senoane, 2009

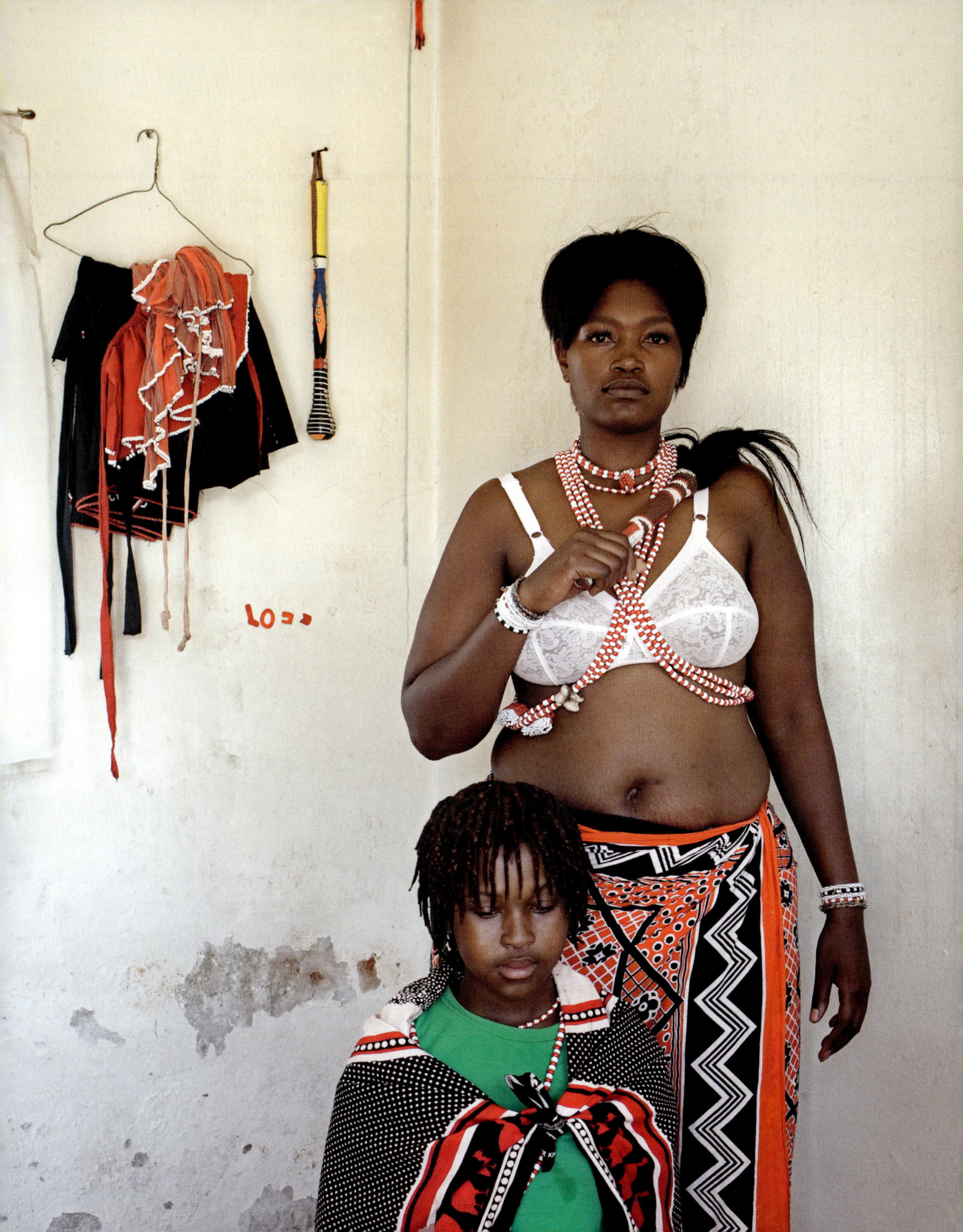

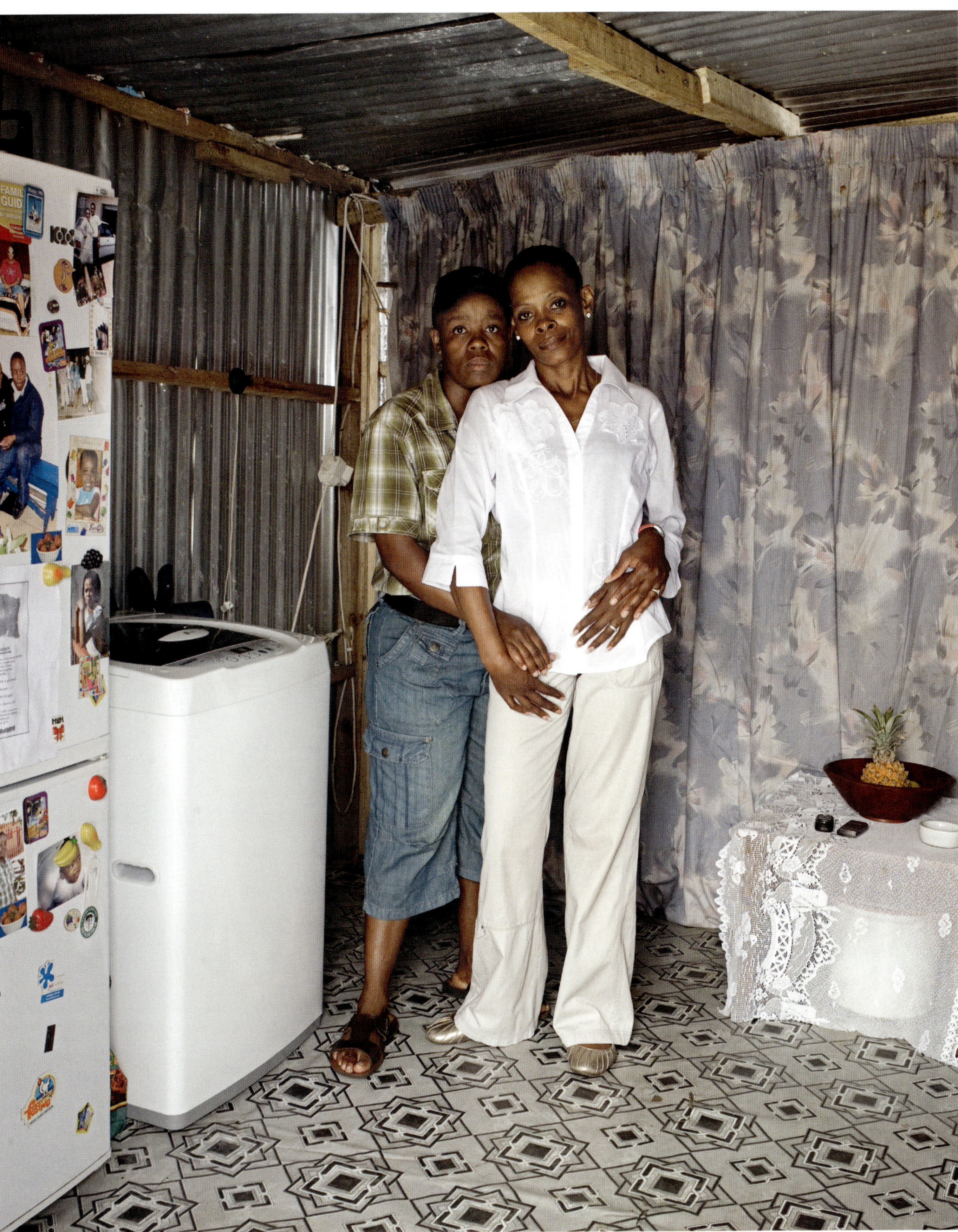

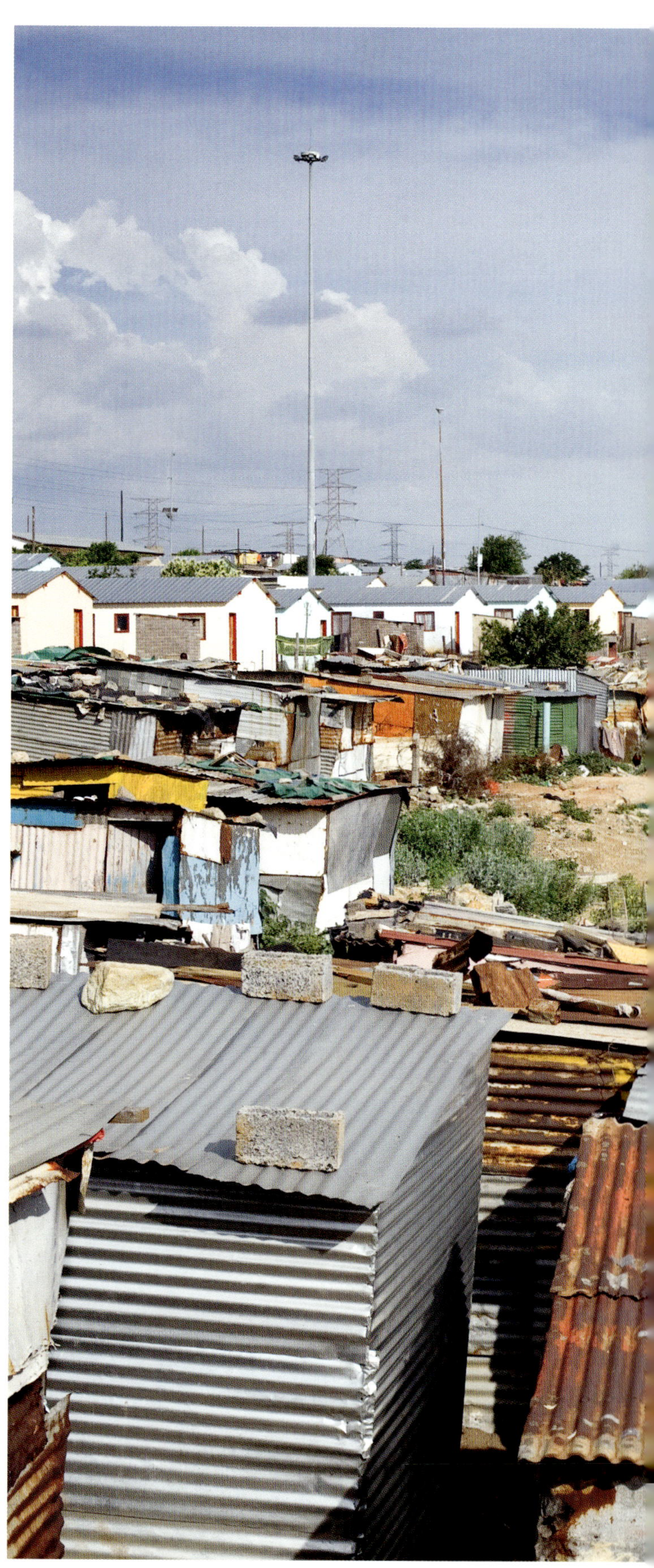

102 | Nomzamo Park Informal Settlement,
Orlando East, 2009

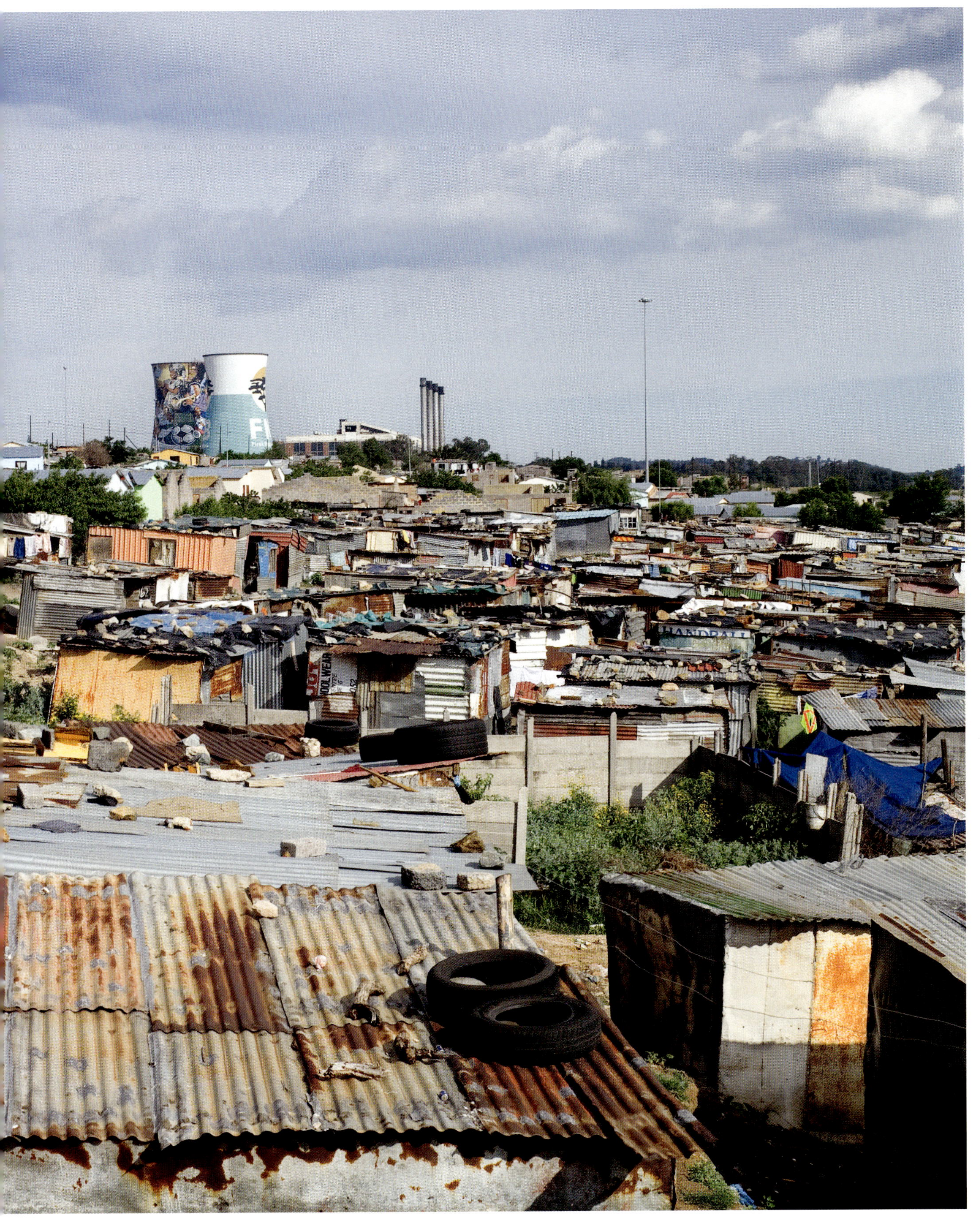

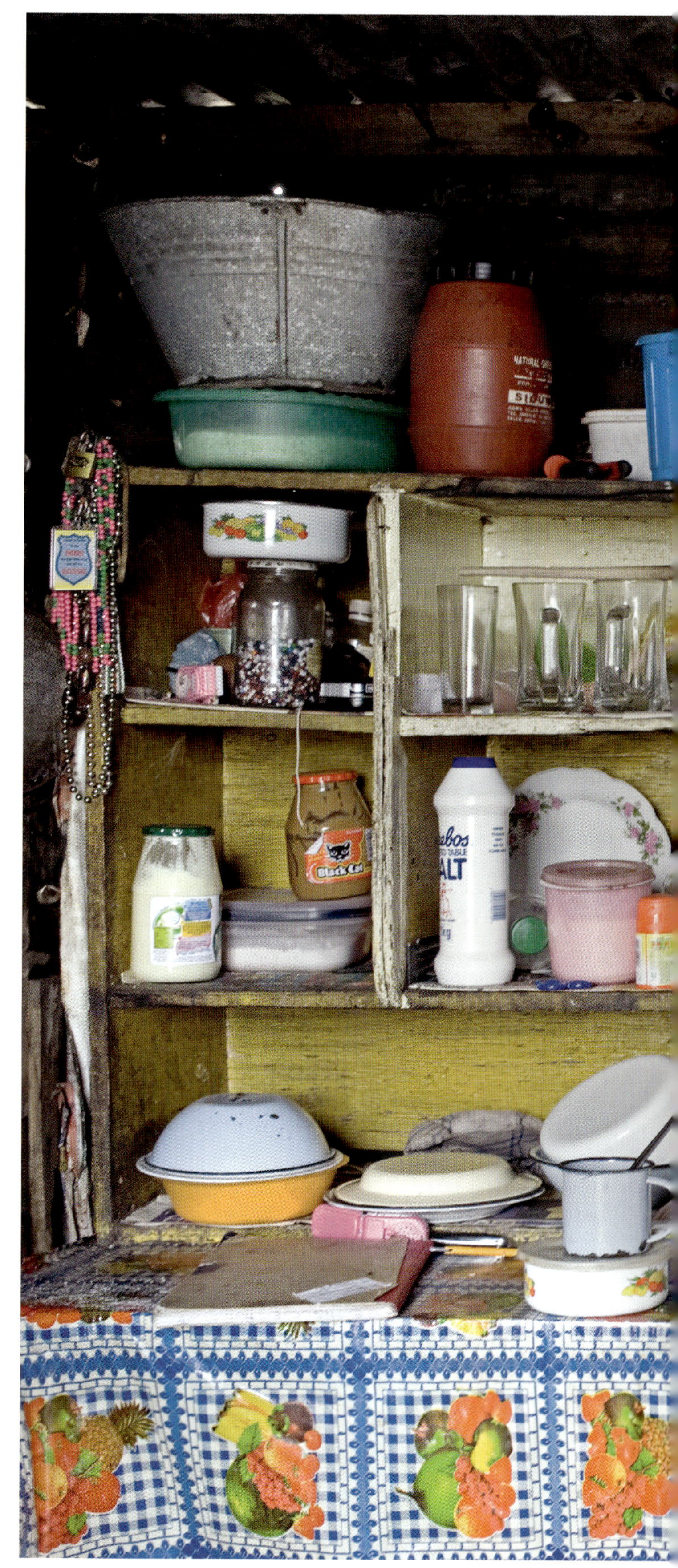

104 | Annah Nguse's home, Nomzamo Park
Informal Settlement, 2010

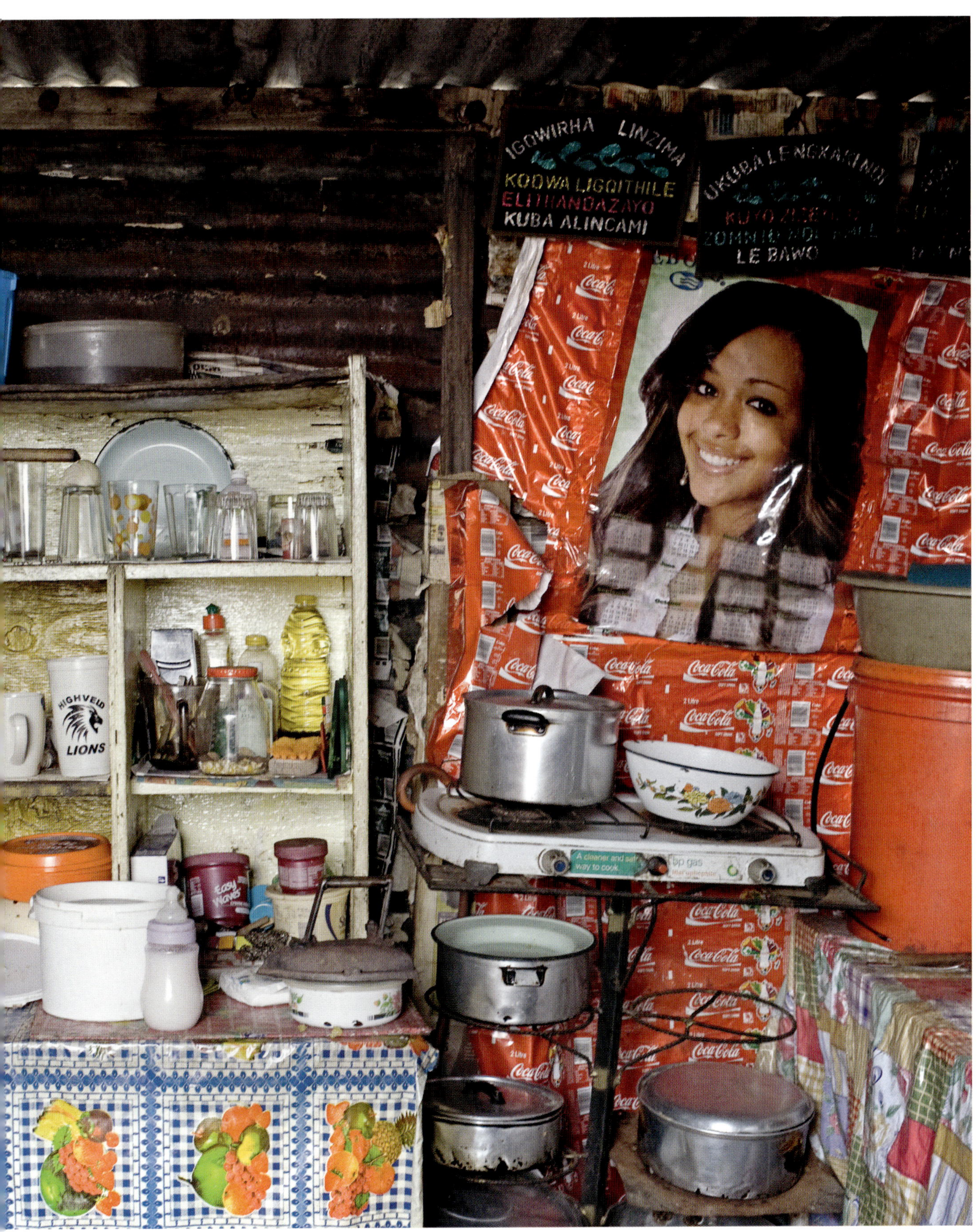
IGOWIRHA   LINZIMA
KODWA LIGQITHILE
ELITHANDAZAYO
KUBA ALINCAMI
UKUBA LENGXAKINI
KUYO ZISE
ZOMNTU NDI
LE BAWO

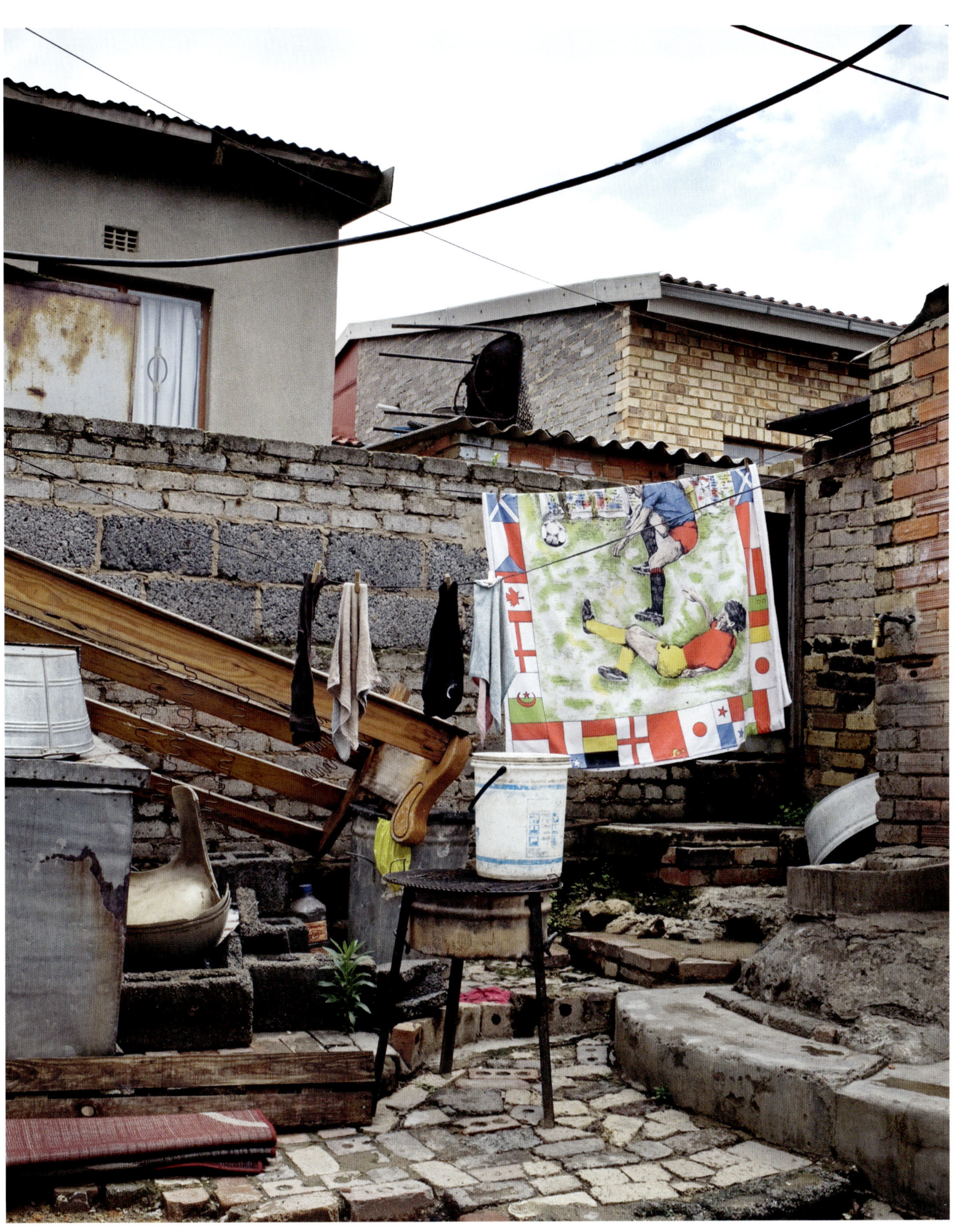

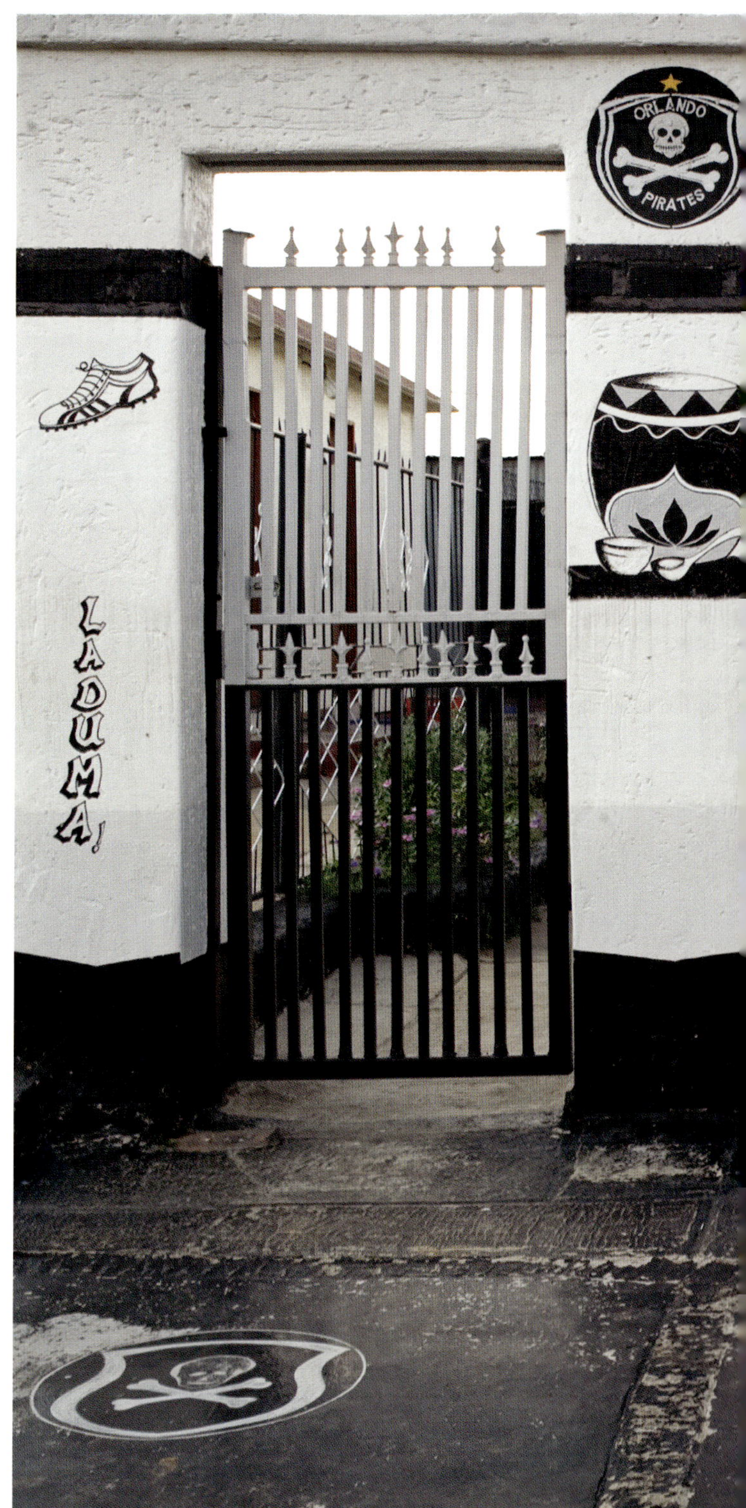

108 | Zakele Seloane's 'Orlando Pirates' house,
White City Jabavu, 2009

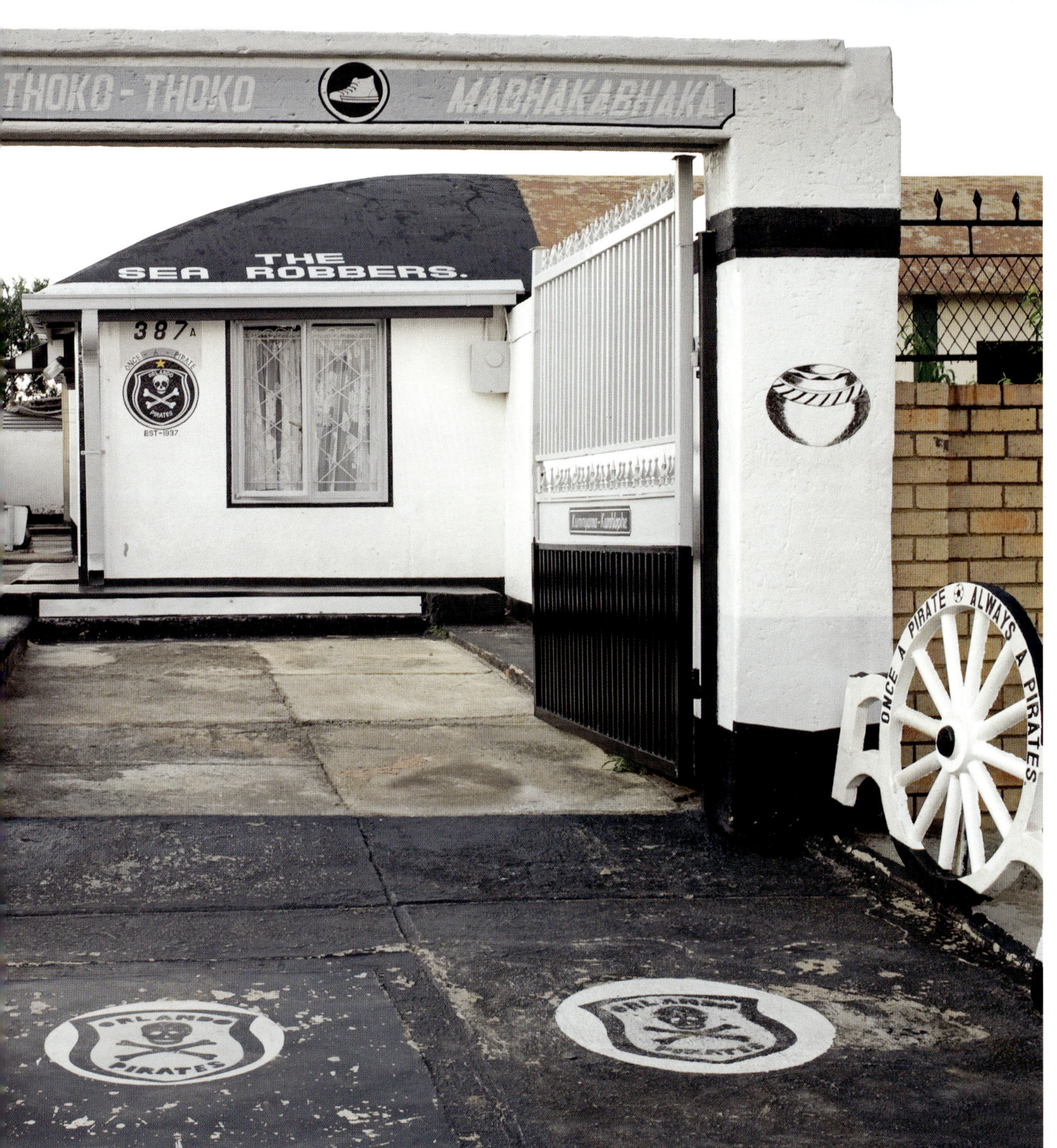
THOKO - THOKO
MABHAKABHAKA
THE
SEA ROBBERS.
387A
ORLANDO PIRATES
EST-1937
ONCE A PIRATE ALWAYS A PIRATES
ORLANDO PIRATES

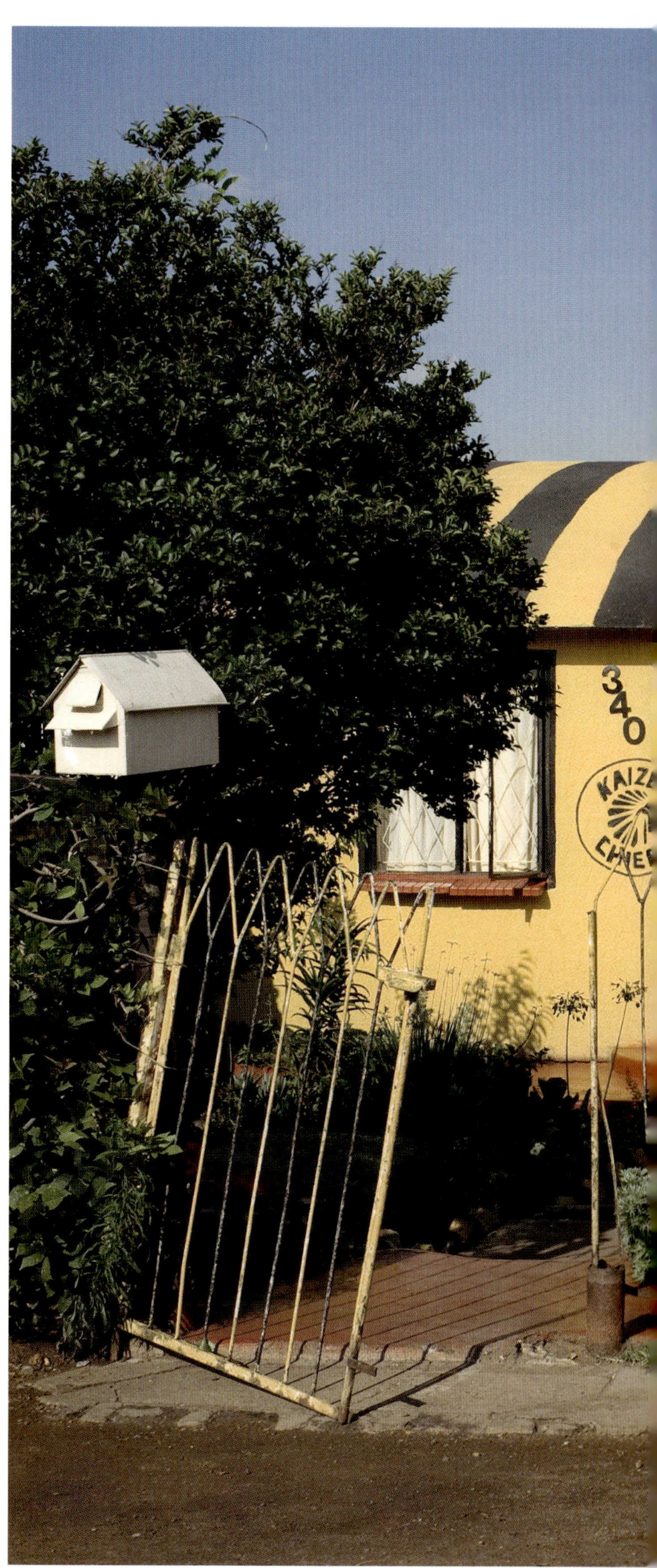

110 | Mkhonza Nichola's 'Kaizer Chiefs' house,
White City Jabavu, 2009

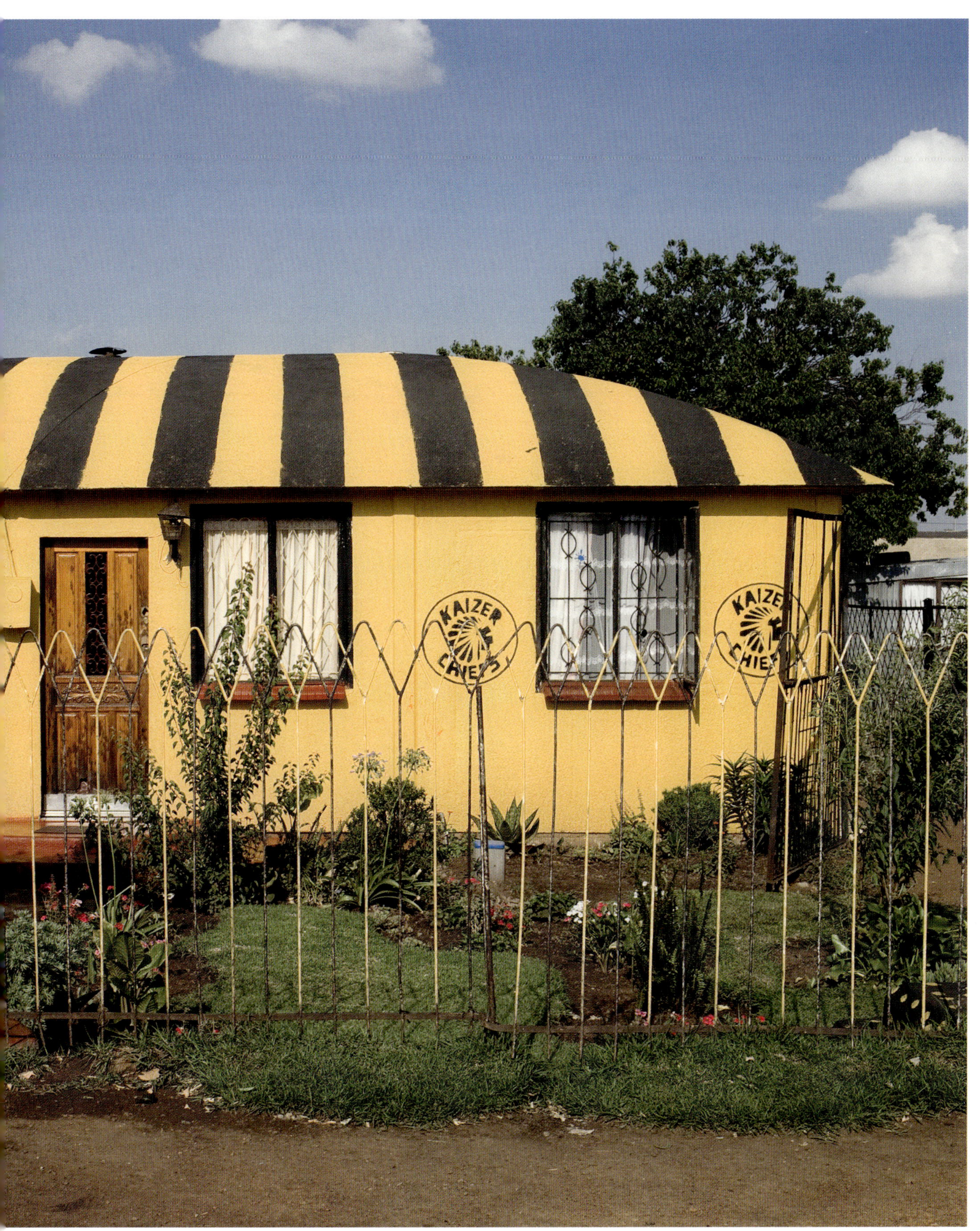

KAIZER
CHIEFS
KAIZER
CHIEFS

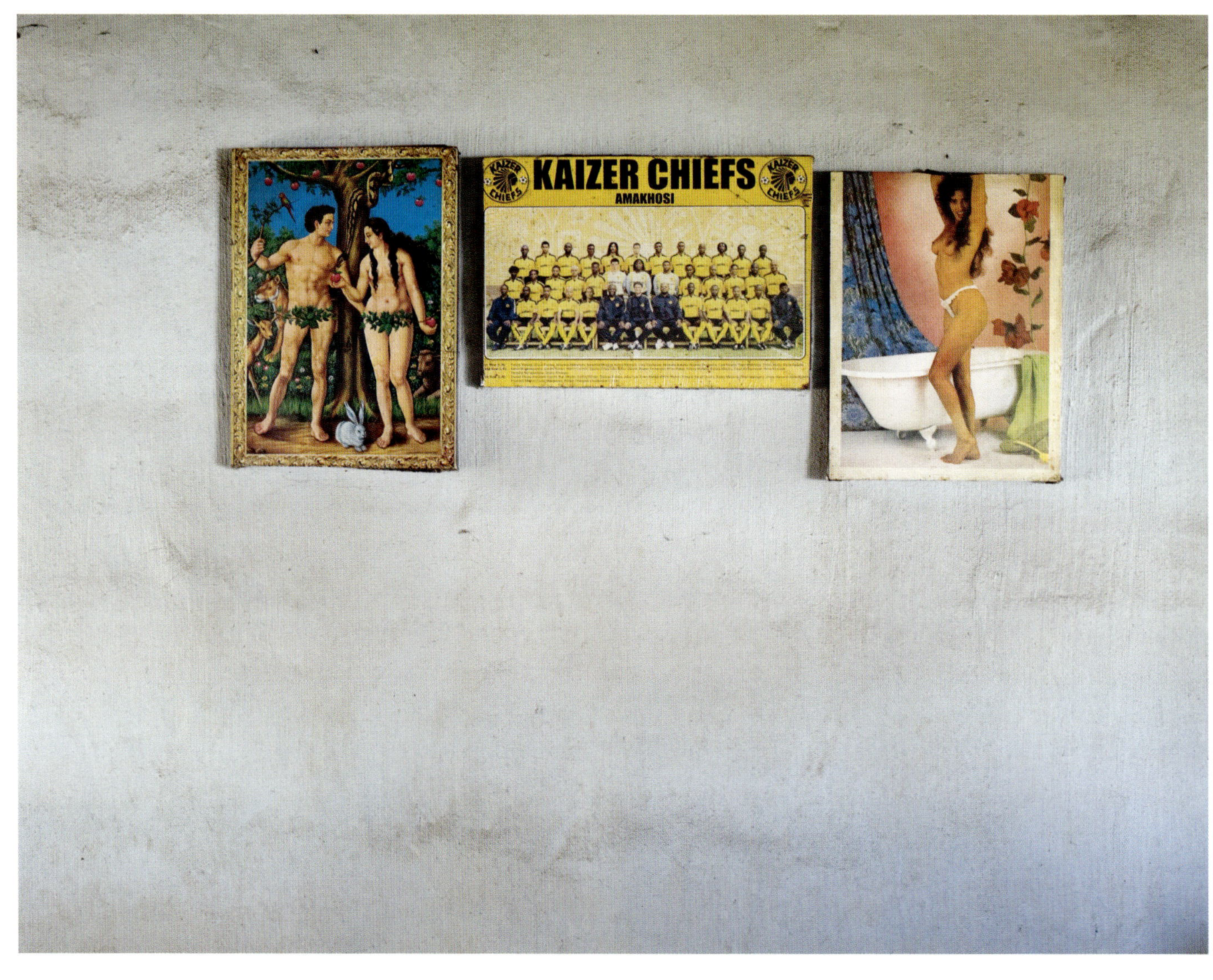

112 | Induna Thitsha Shange's House, Nancefield Hostel, Klipspruit, 2009
[Right] Nolwadle Duma and an anaconda outside her house, Mamfiso Arts
and Crafts, Vilakazi Street, Orlando West, 2009

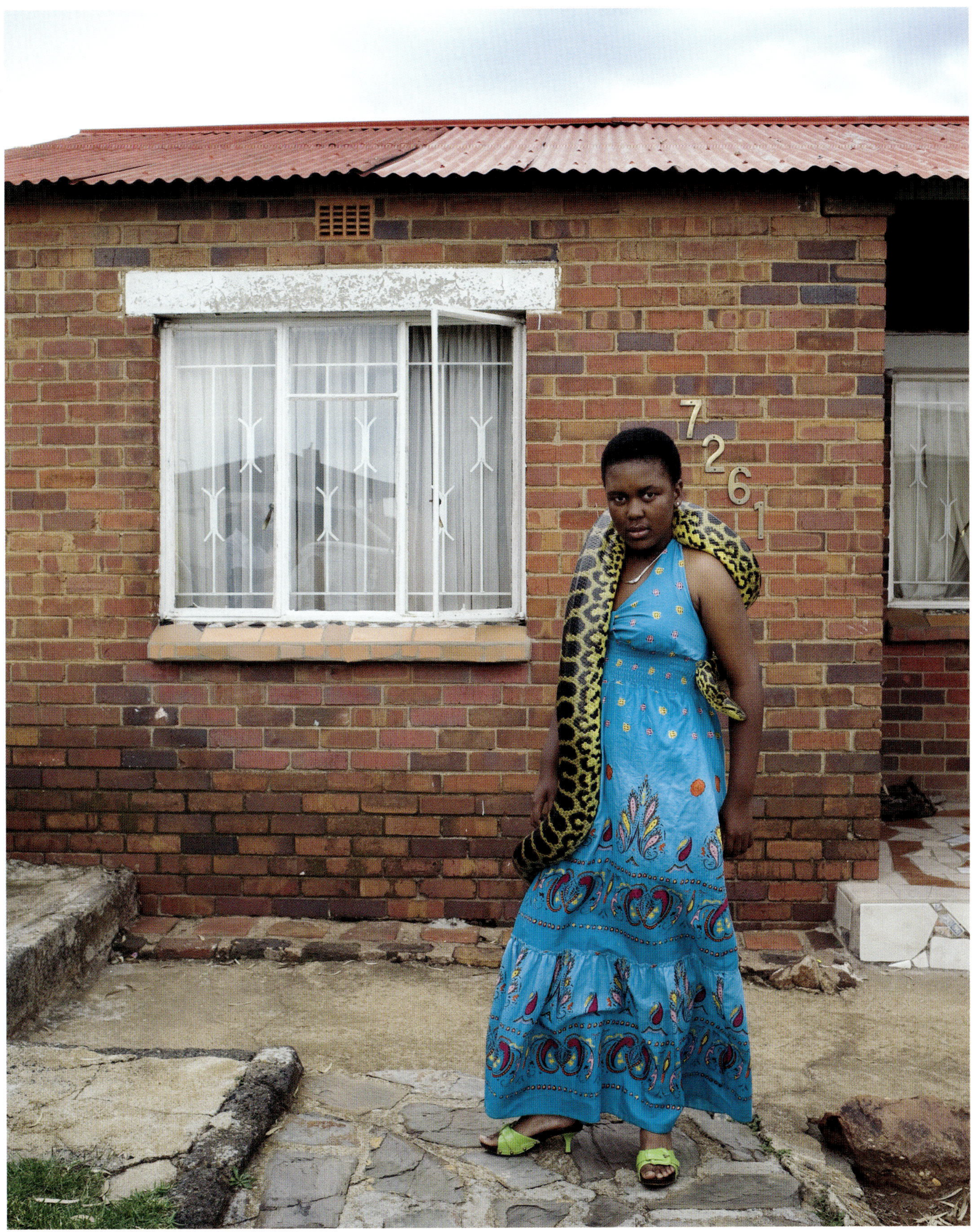

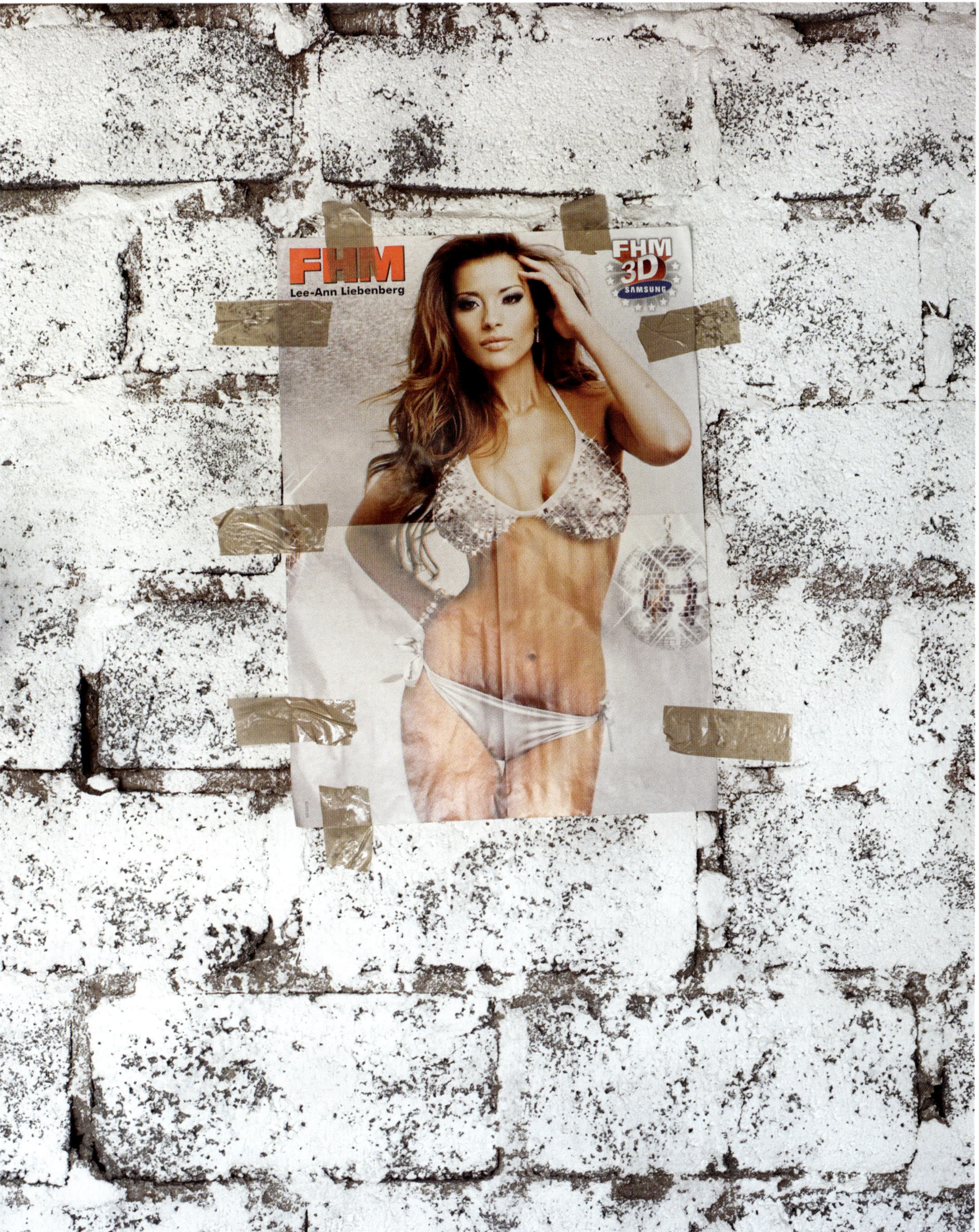

FHM
Lee-Ann Liebenberg
FHM 3D
SAMSUNG

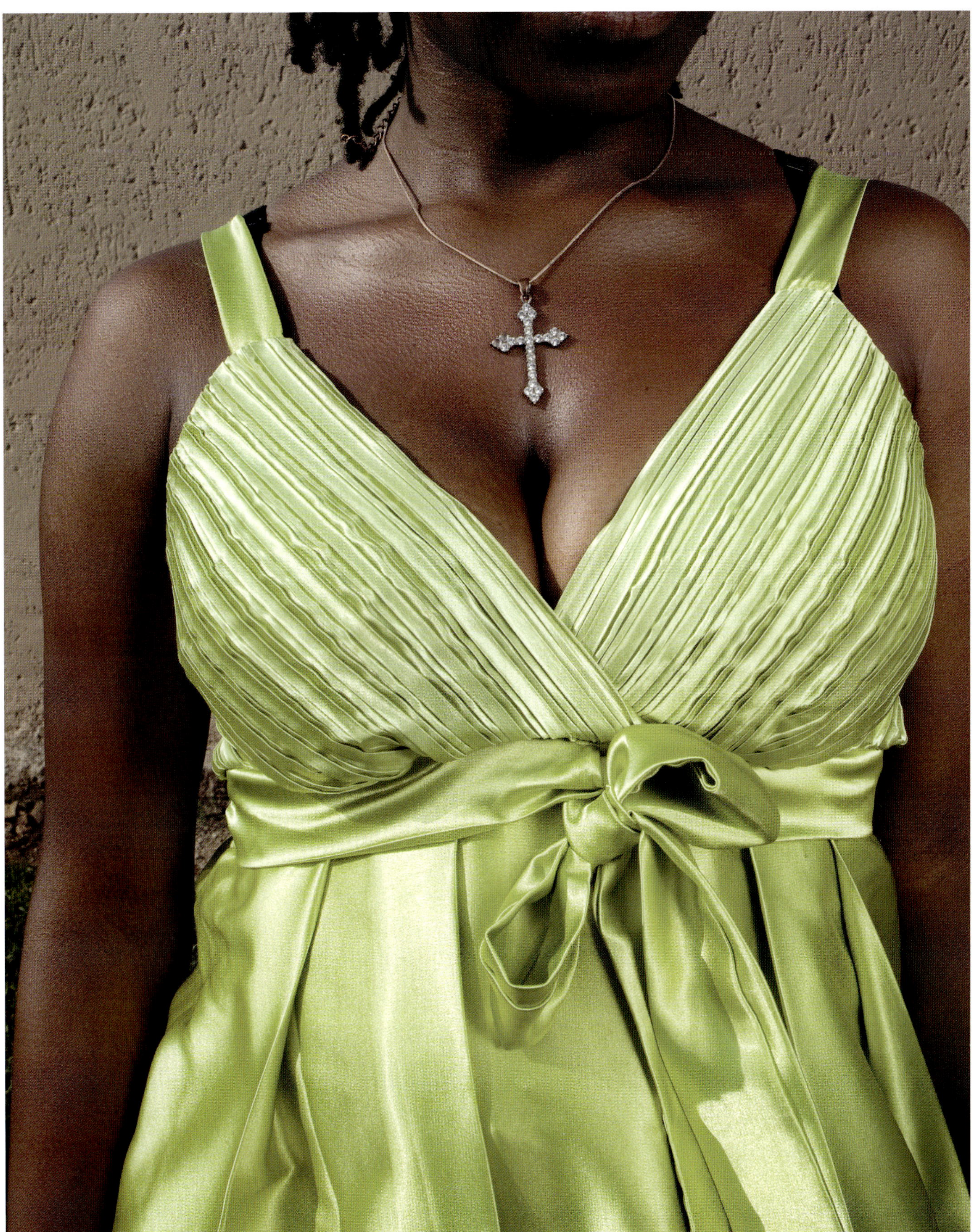

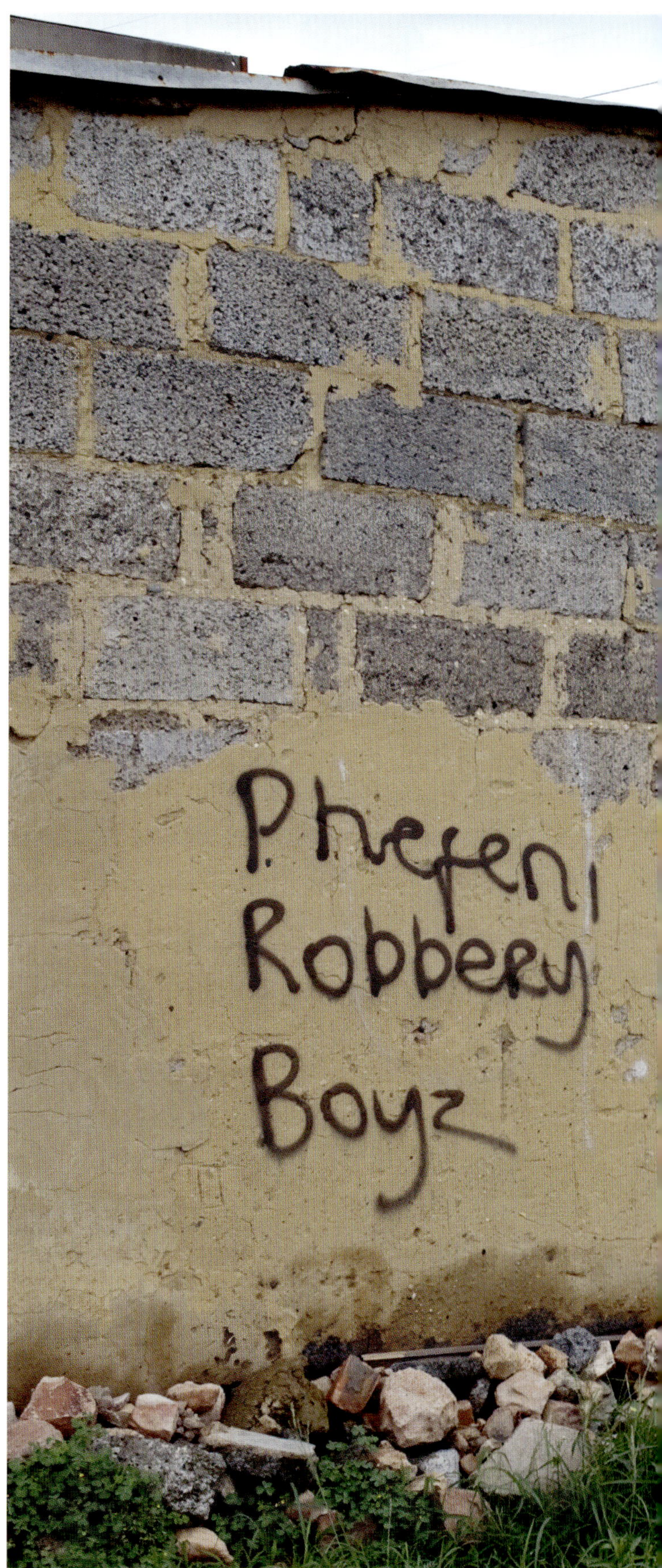

118 | Phefeni Robbery Boyz, Orlando West, 2010

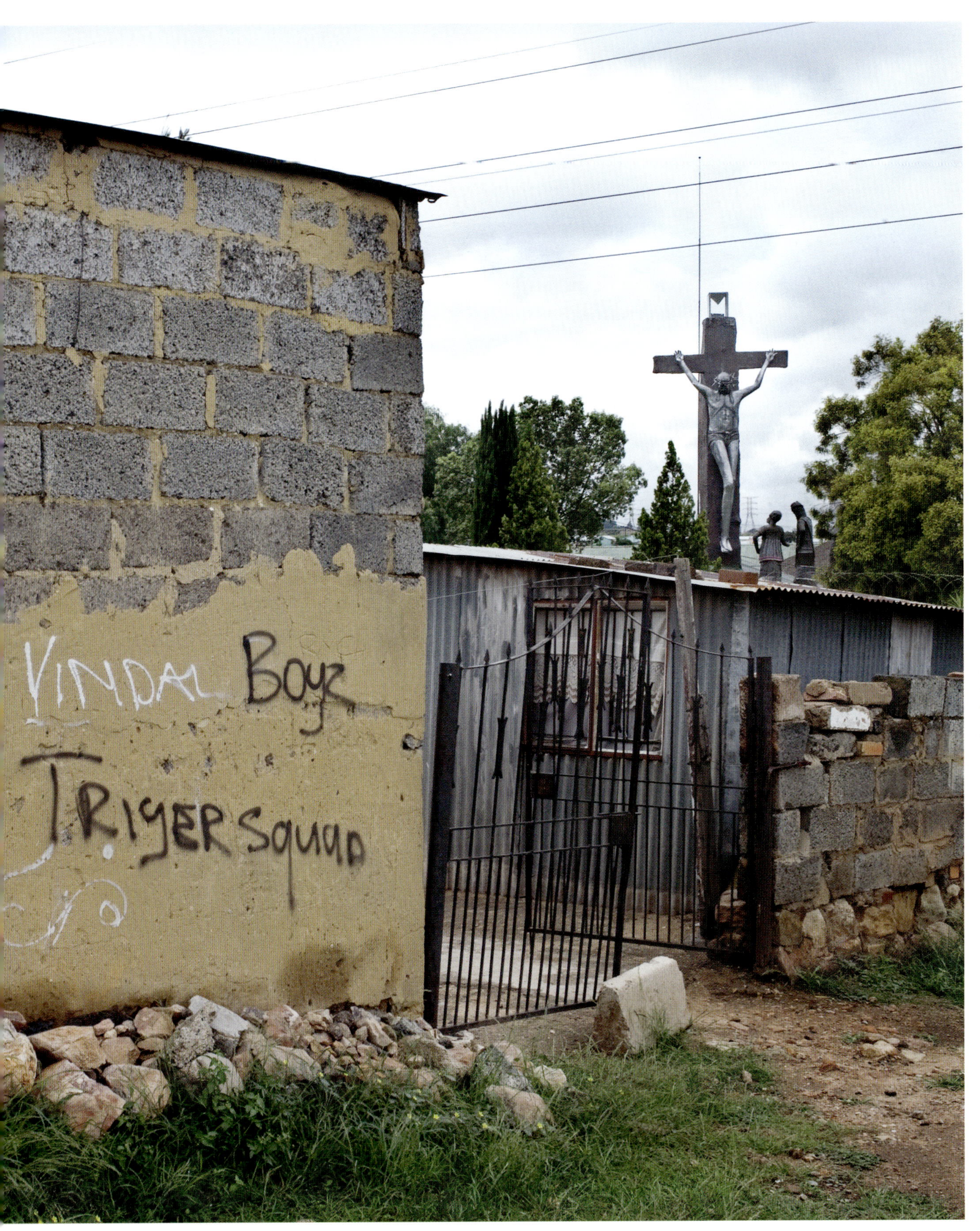
KINDAL BoyZ
TRiger squad

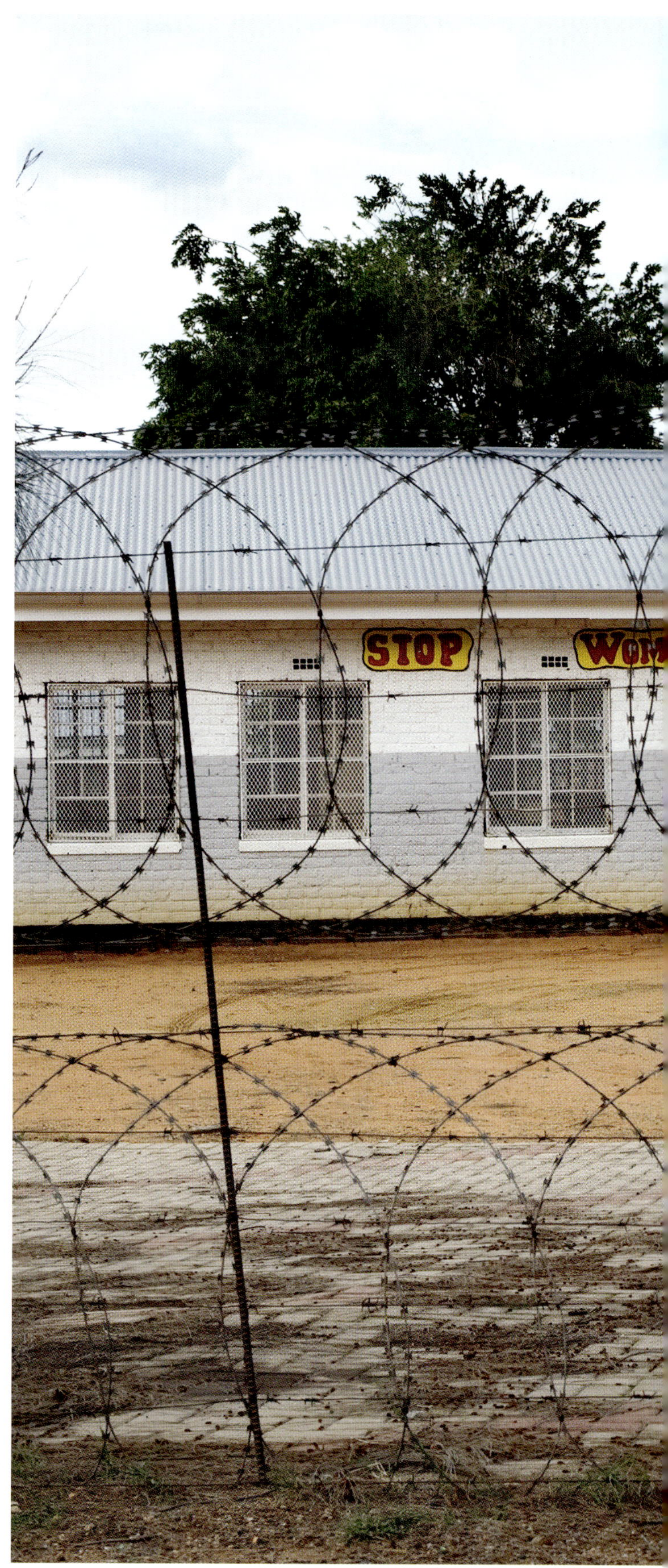

120 | "Stop Women and Child Abuse", Inkwenkwezi School
Diepkloof, Zone 6, 2010

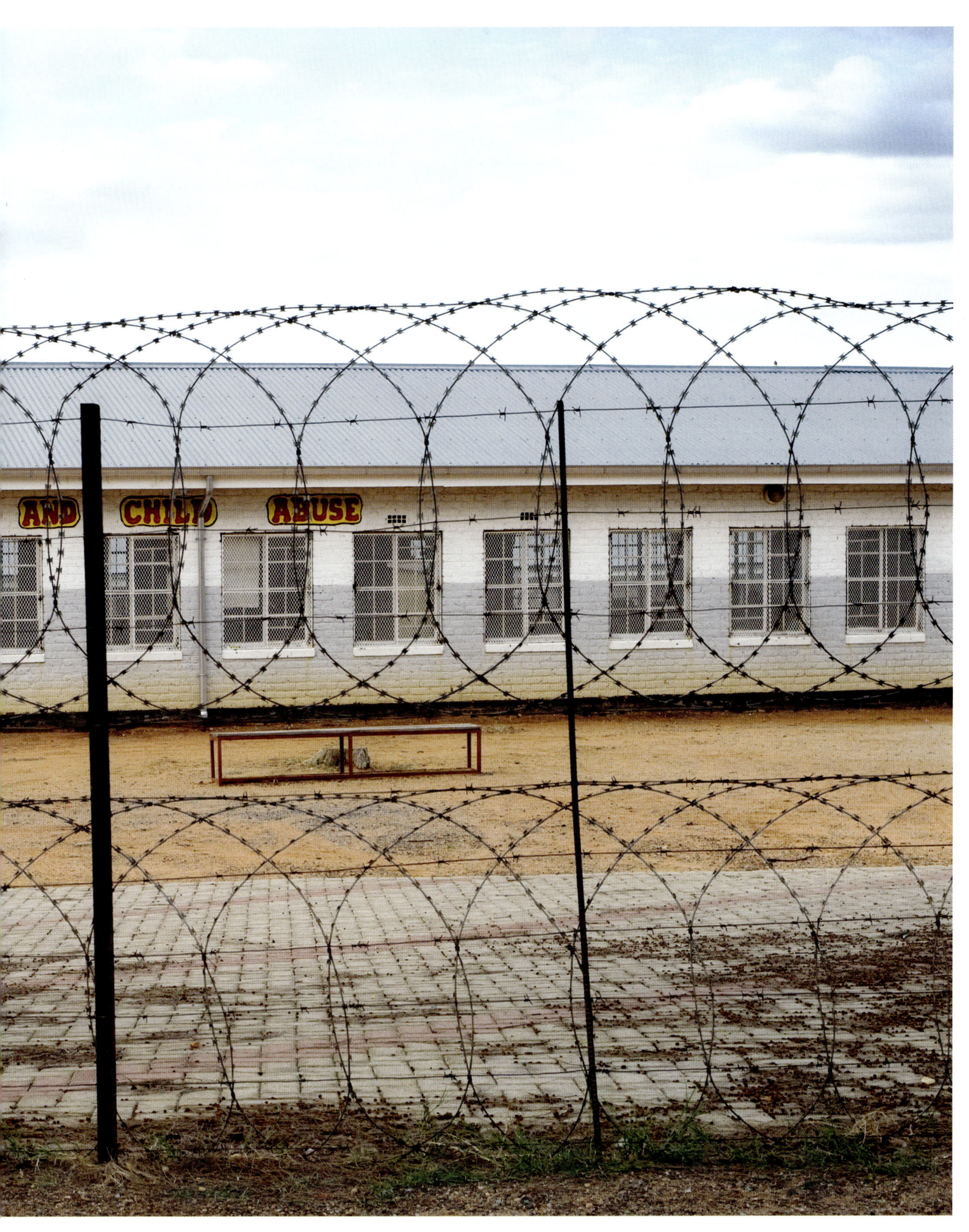

AND CHILD ABUSE

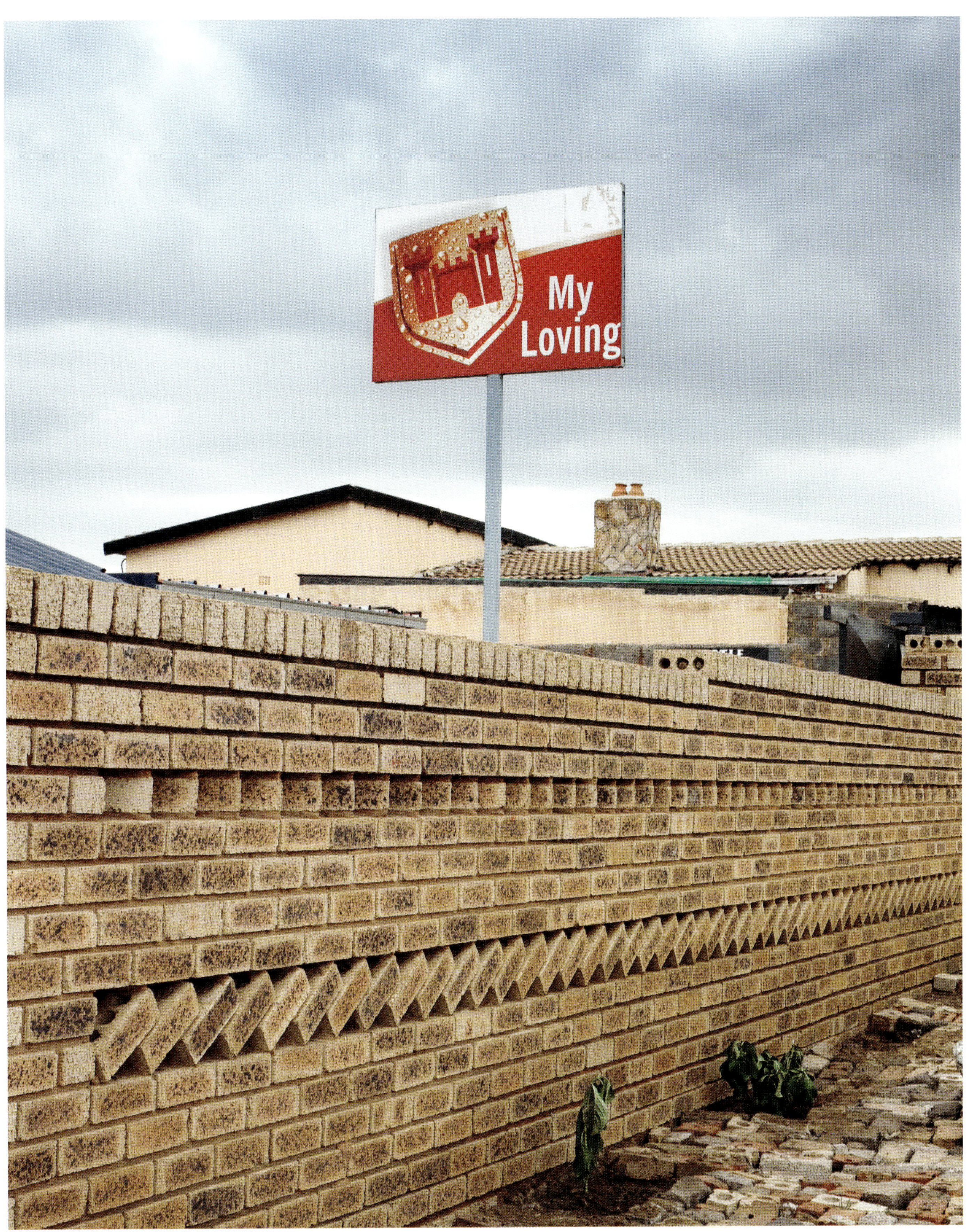
My
Loving

124 | Petros Pule Mahlahola, *JoziFM* Gospel Festival 2009, Hyundai Park, 2009

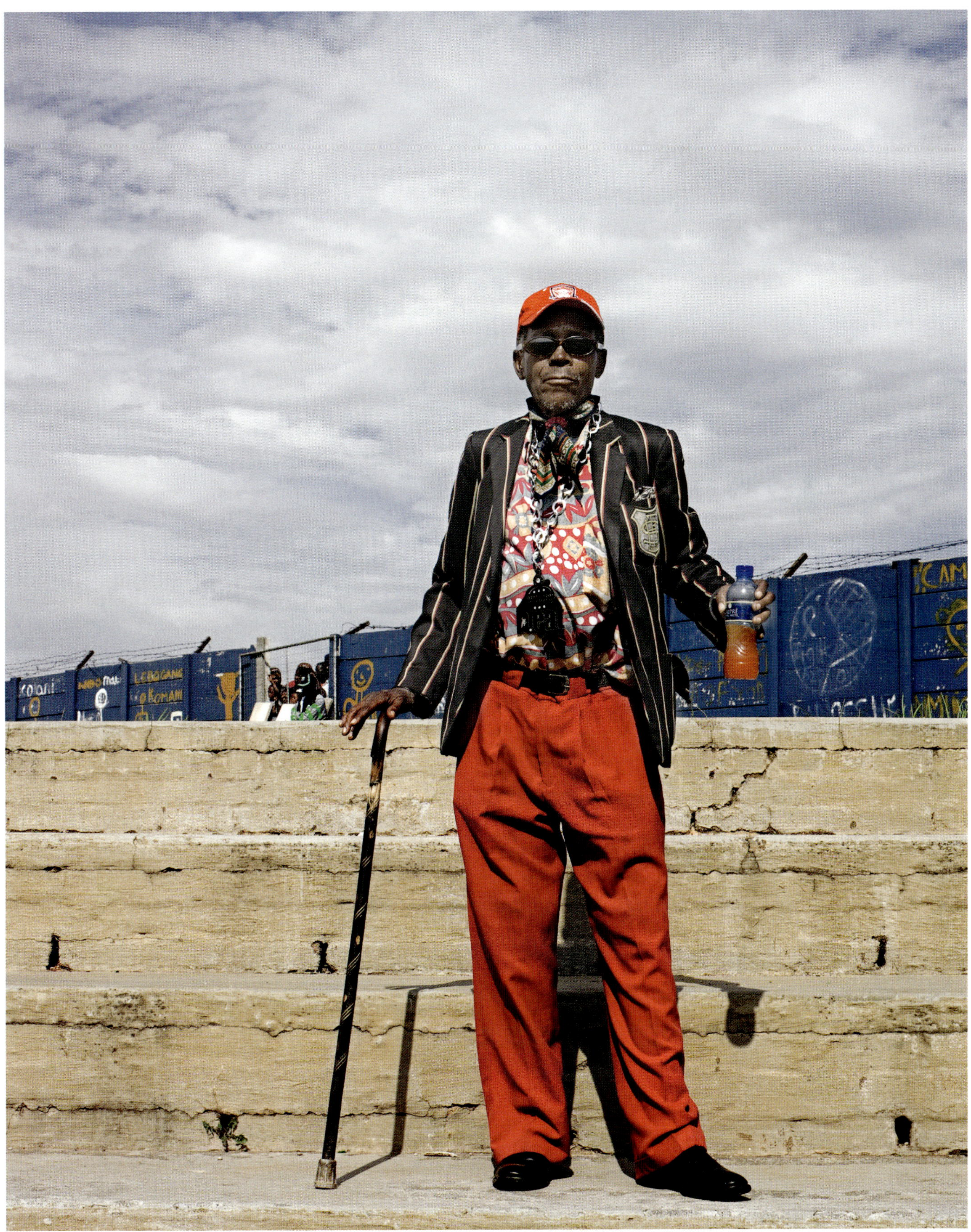

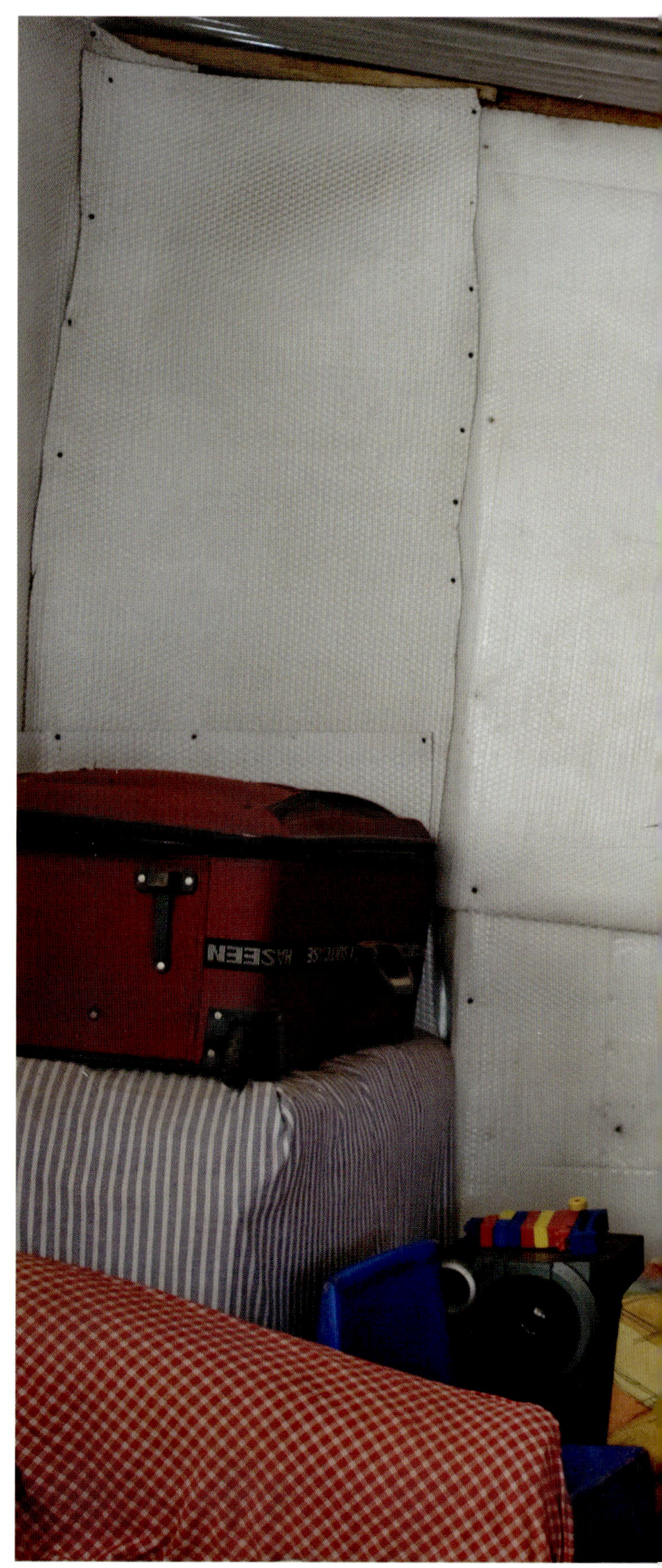

126 | Michel Unathi Madikane,
Motswaledi Informal Settlement,
Power Park 2, 2010

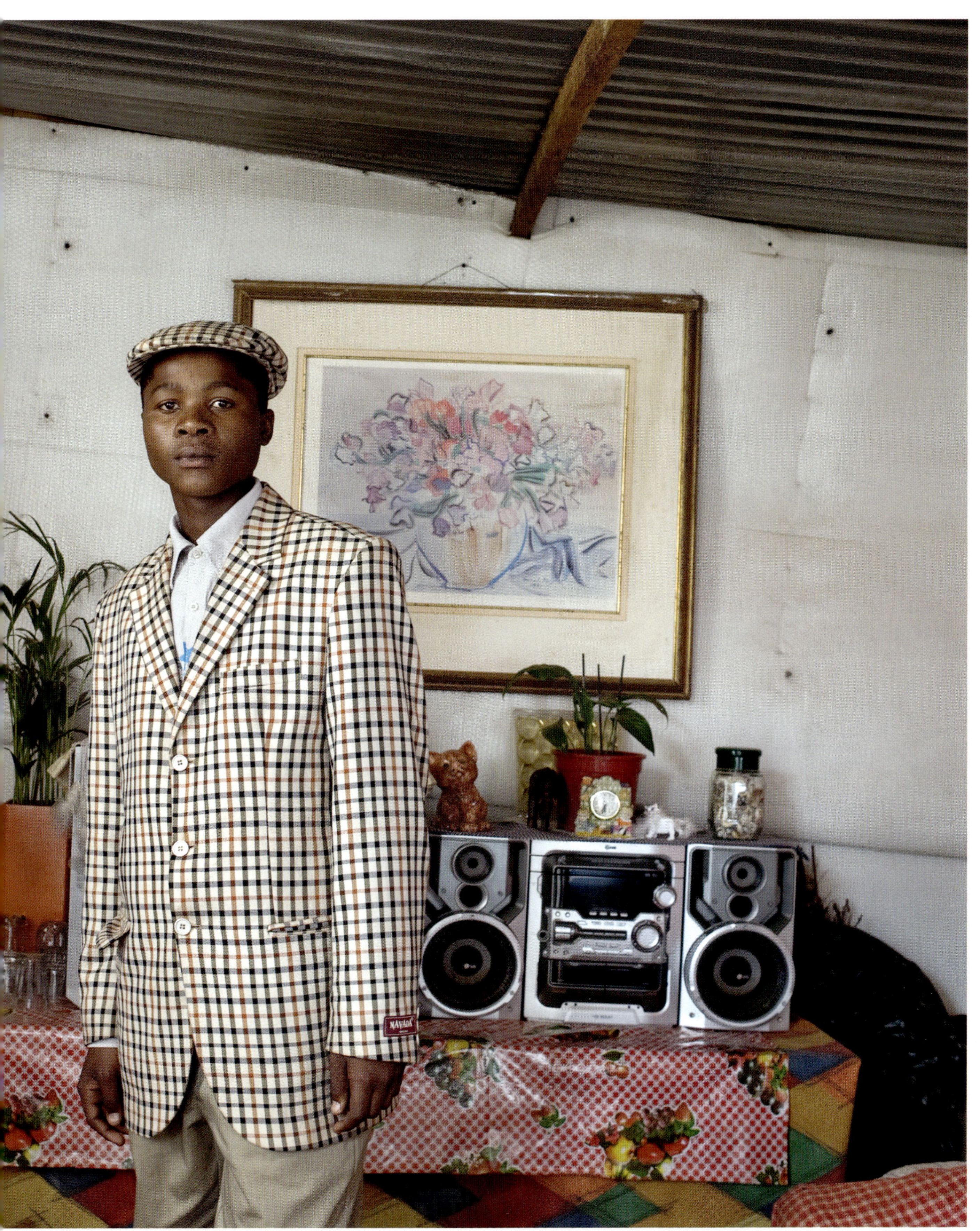

 | Andrew Sithebe 'dressed to kill', Molapo Ext, 2009

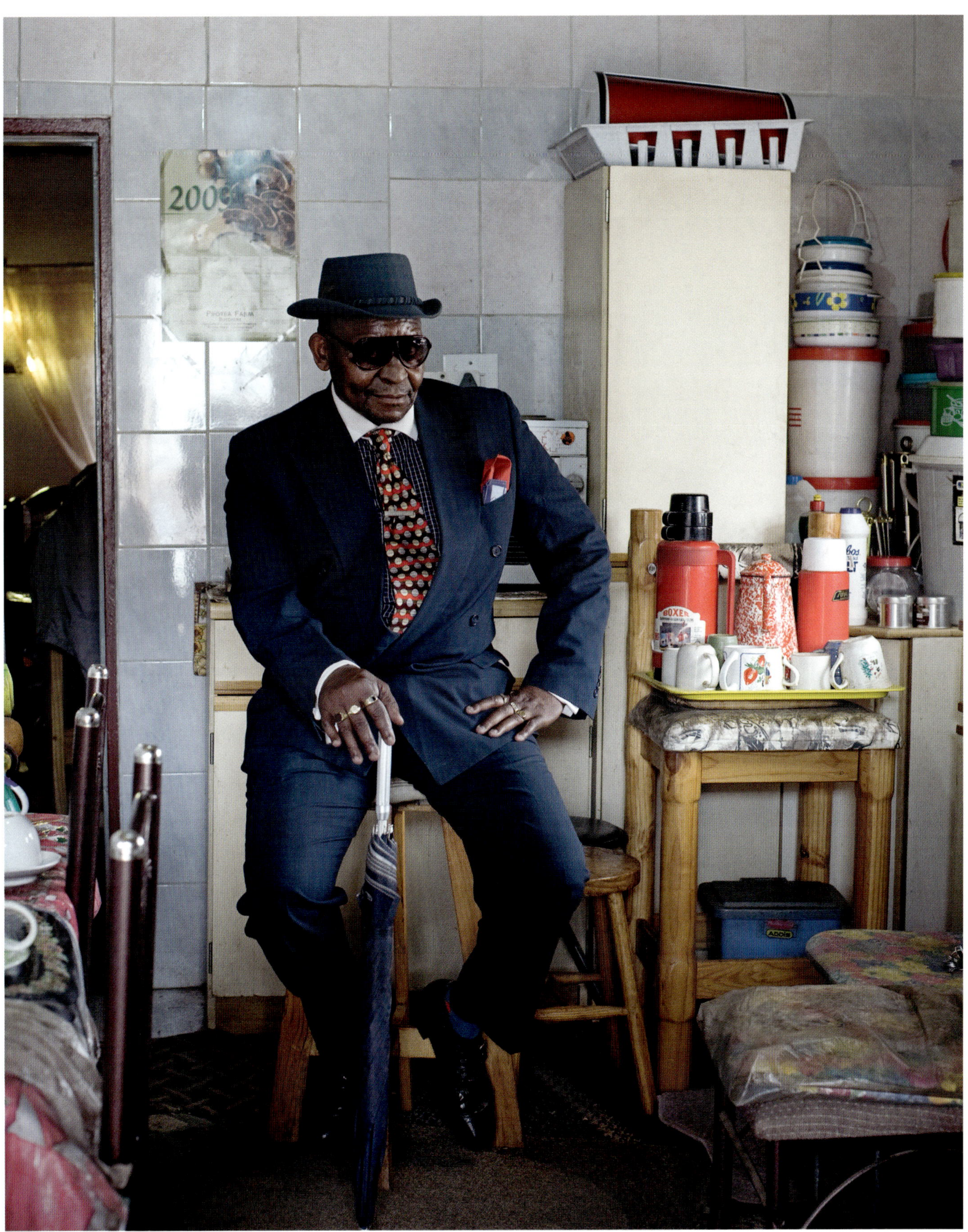

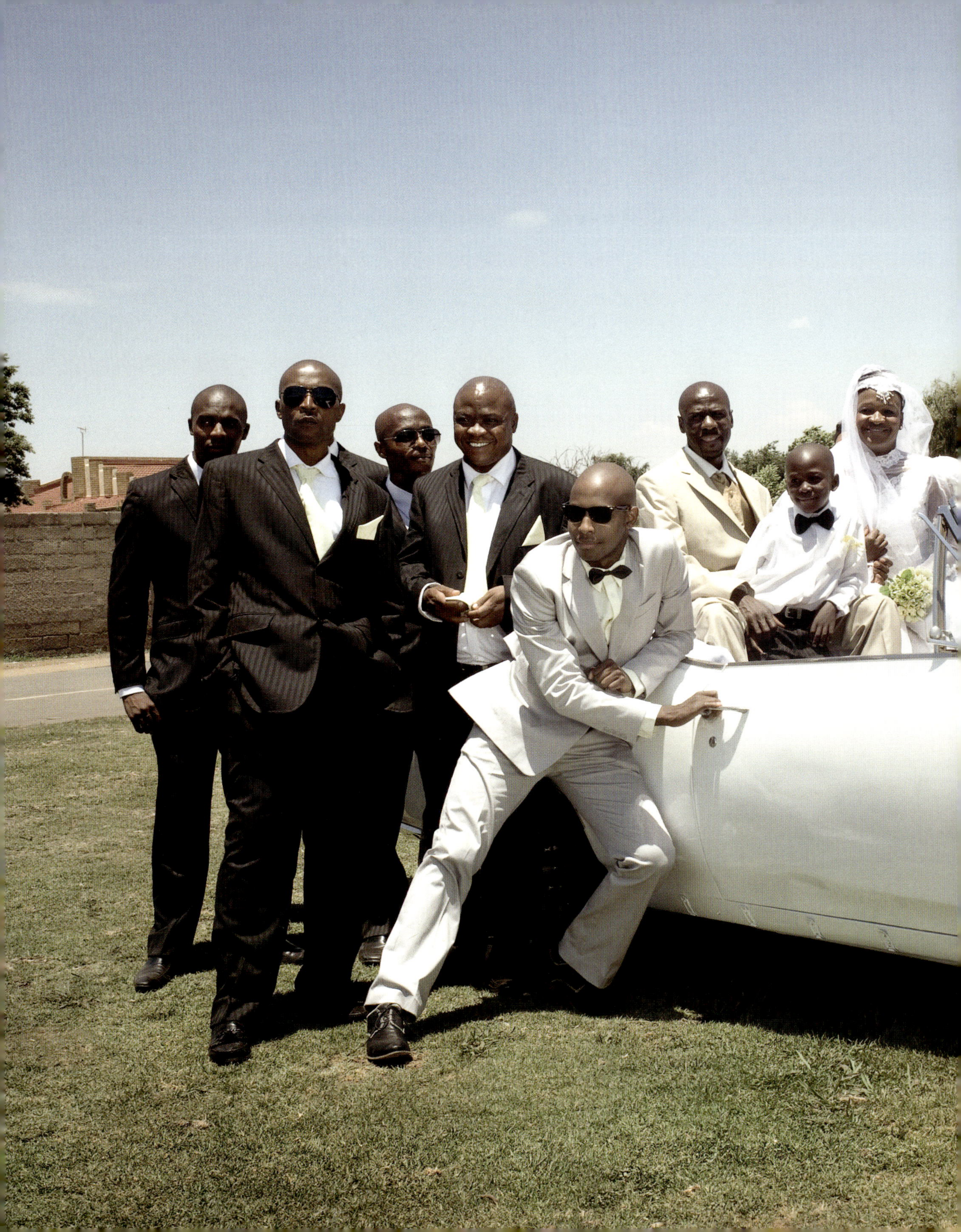

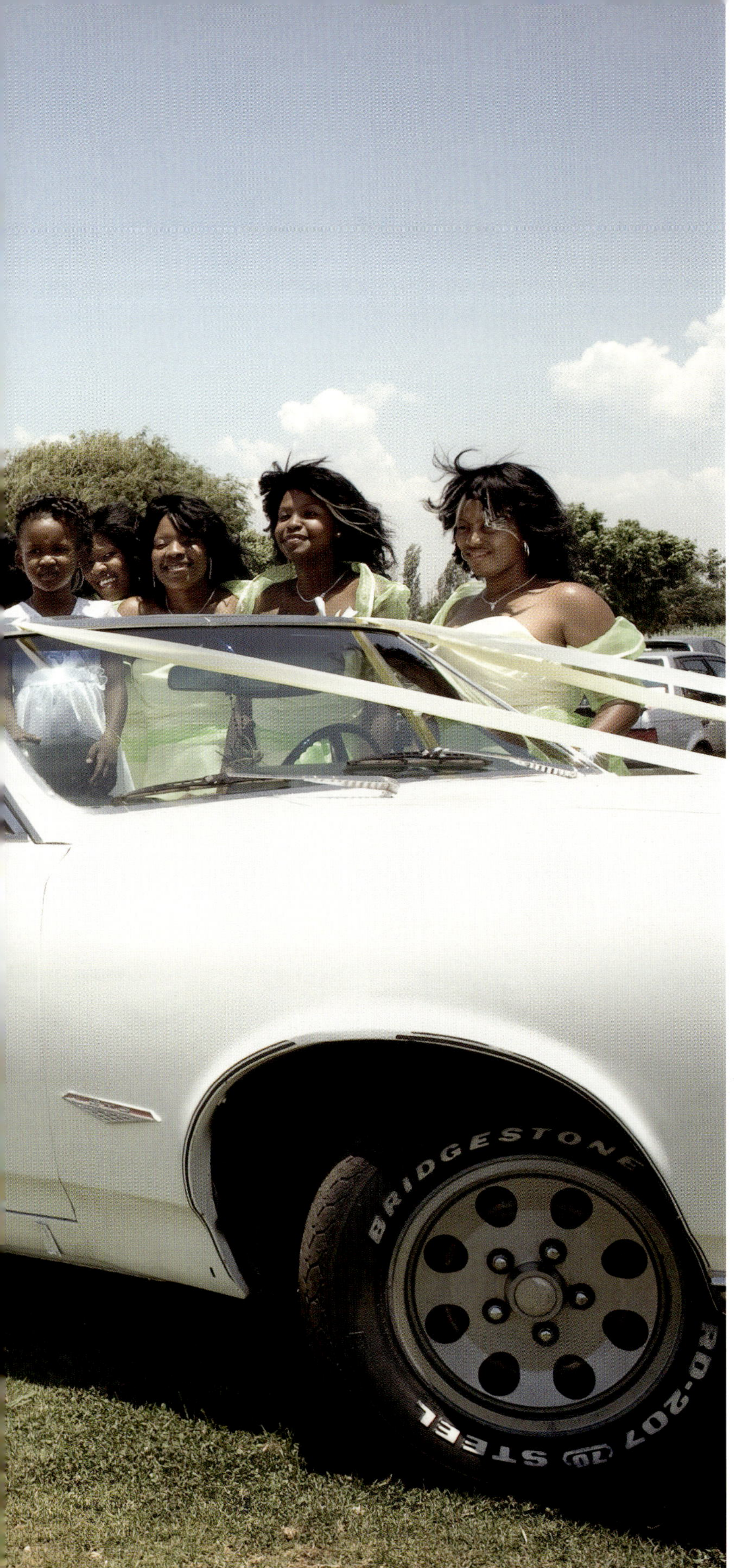

Humphrey Nkosana and Goodness Sonto Mokgokgo, along with their guests, posing for wedding photographs, Rockville, 2009 | 131

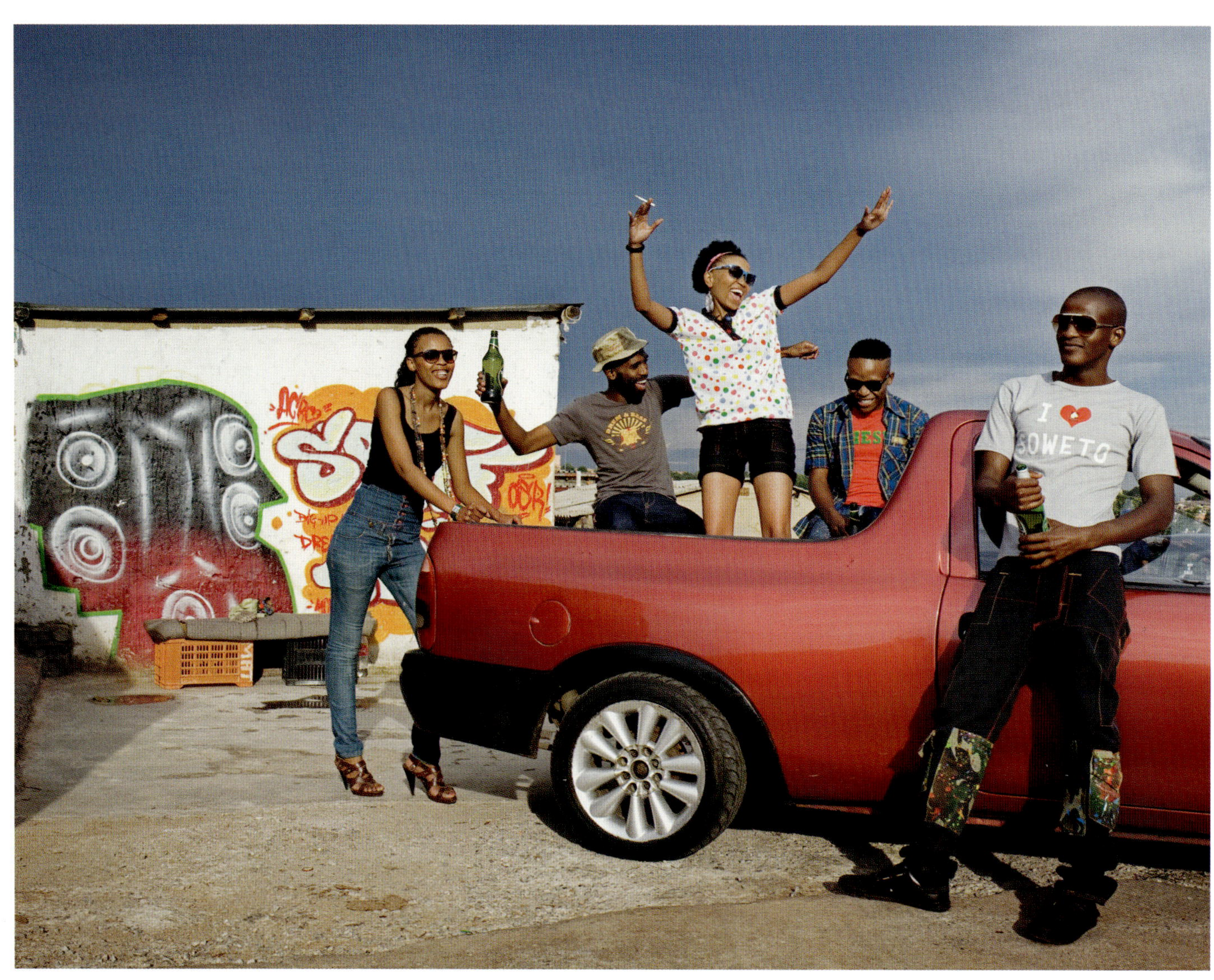

132 | Fashion shoot for Thesis clothing, Mofolo Village, 2010
[Right] Sam Kutoane and Eugene Mzila, Soul Seekers Biking Club, P&B Tuckshop, Pimville, Zone 3, 2009

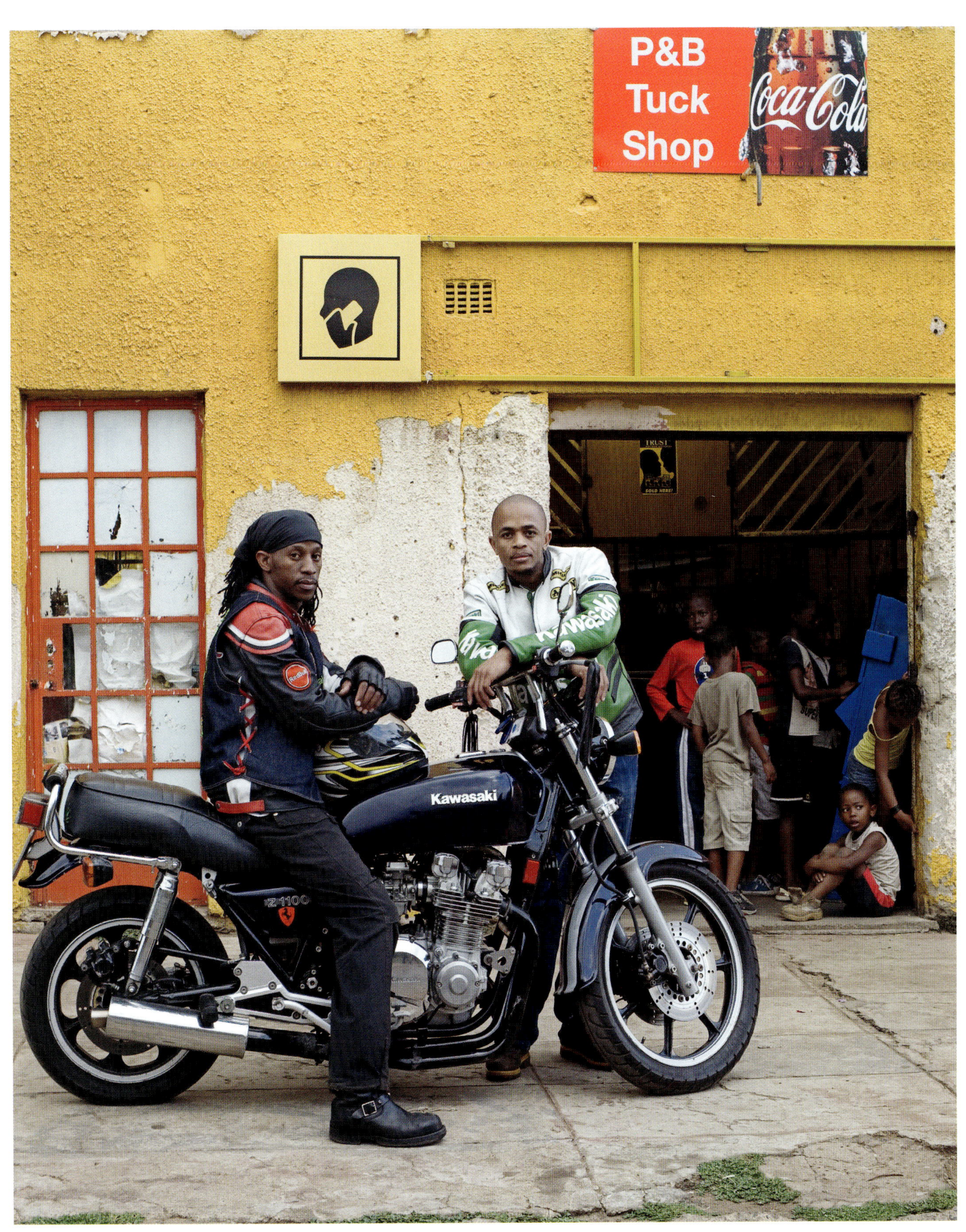

P&B
Tuck
Shop
Coca-Cola
Kawasaki
Z1100
TRUST

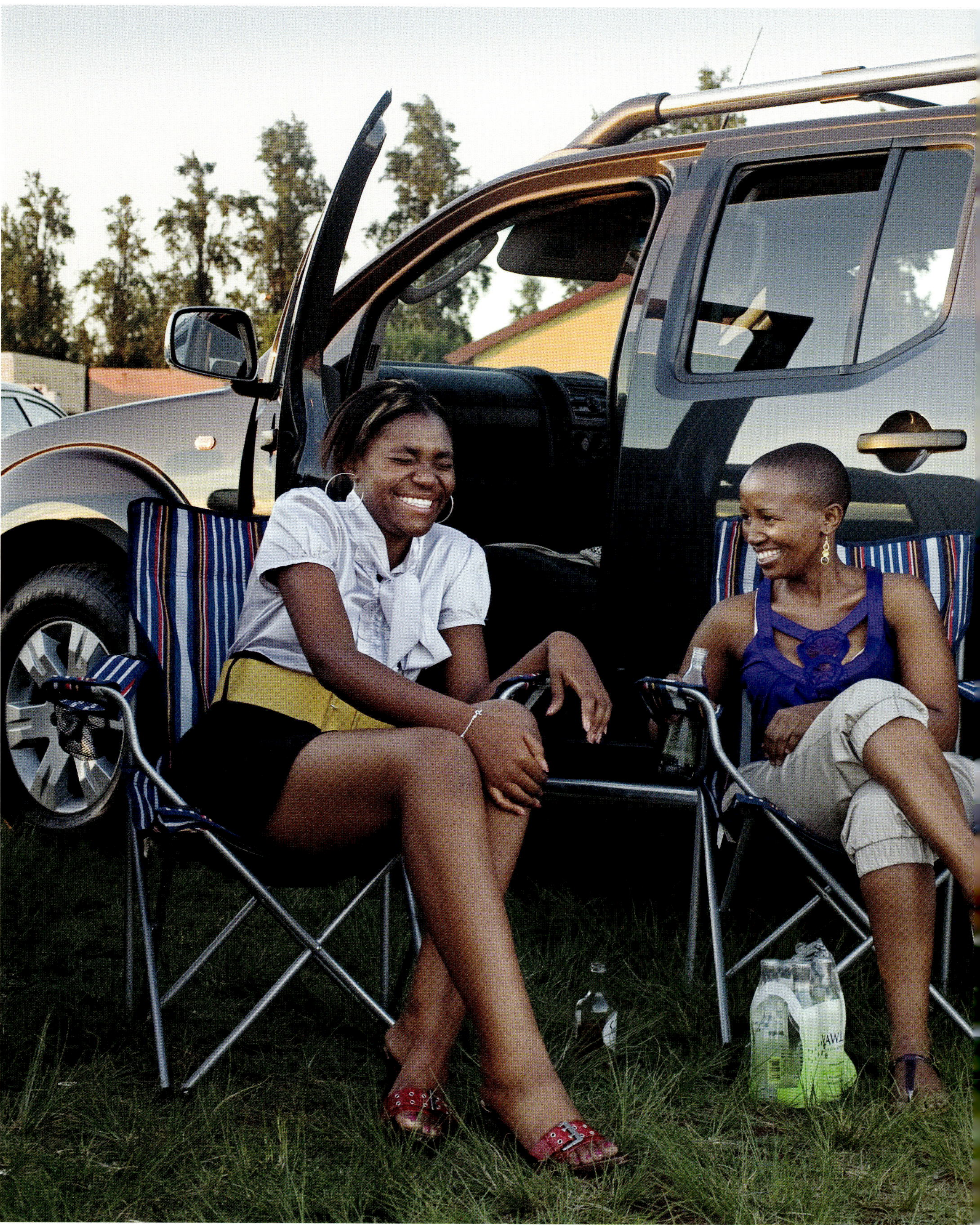

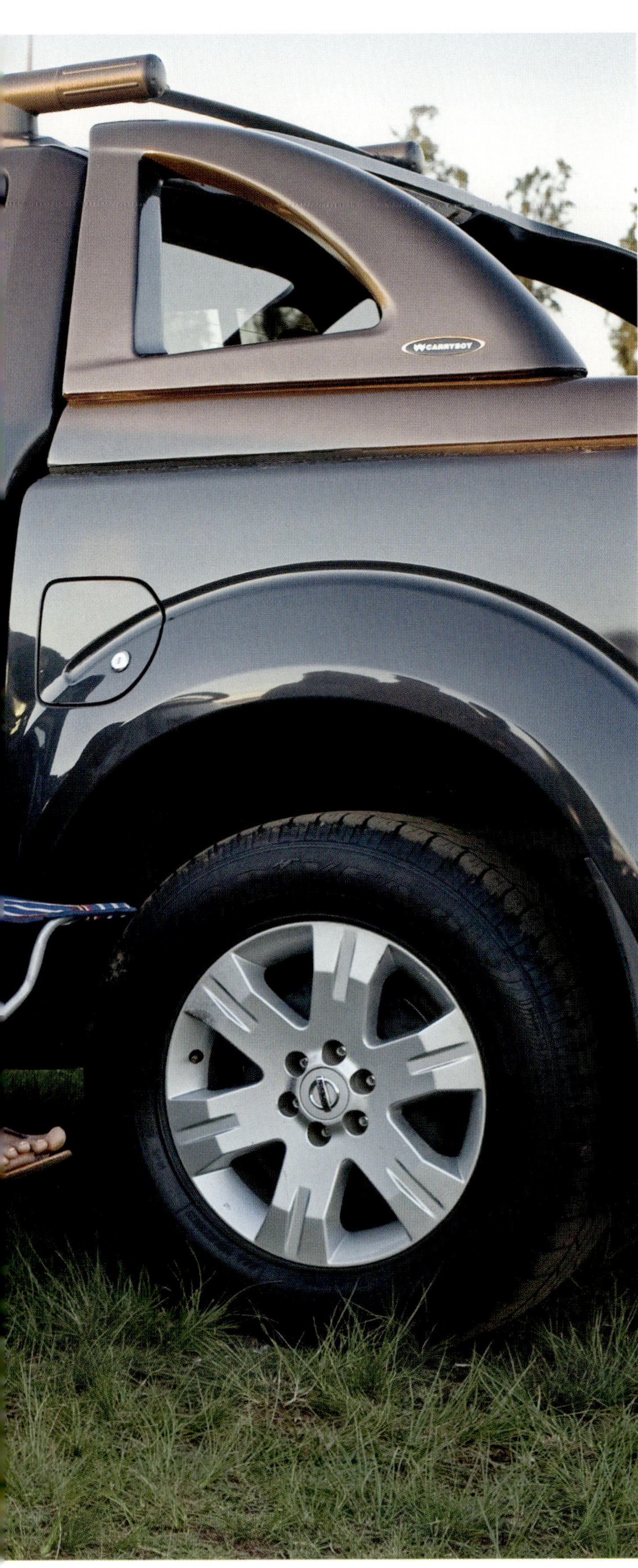

Sibongile Hlongwane and Adelinah Mofokeng outside
Panyaza's Butchery *chisa nyama* (braai or barbeque),
White City Jabavu, 2009 | 135

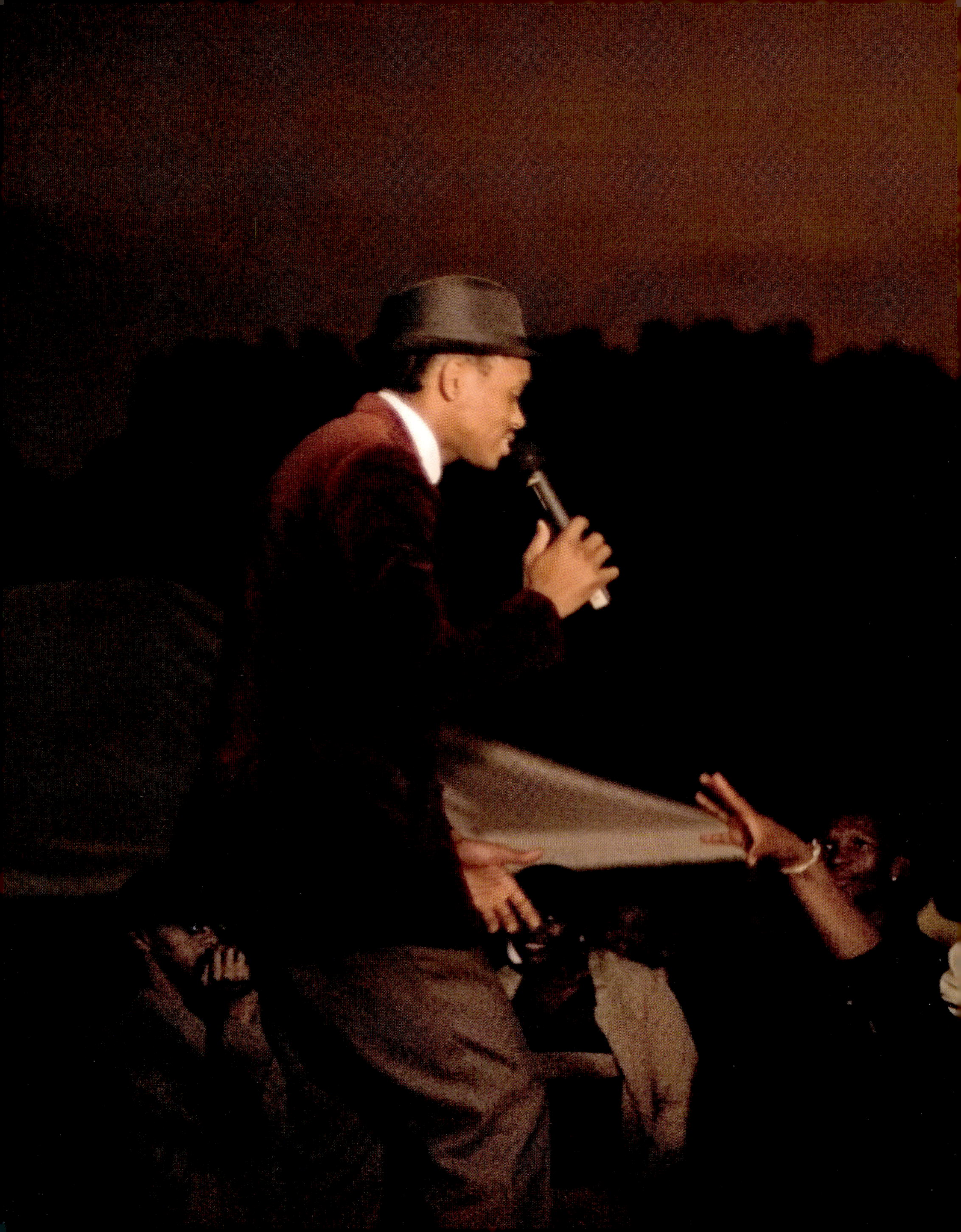

Donald performing at
DJ MacG Mukwevho's
YFM birthday party,
Godfrey Moloi's Place,
Protea Glen, 2009 | 137

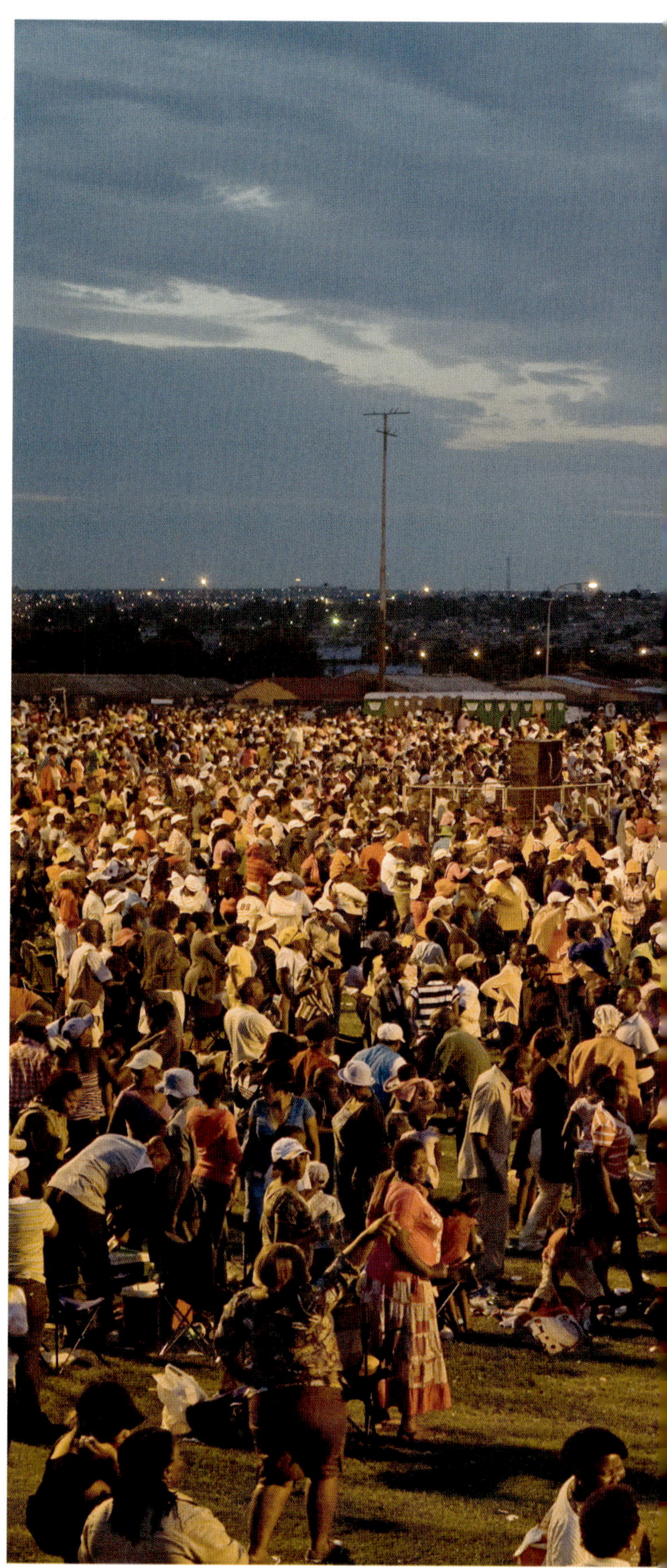

138 | *JoziFM* Gospel Festival 2009, Hyundai Park, 2009

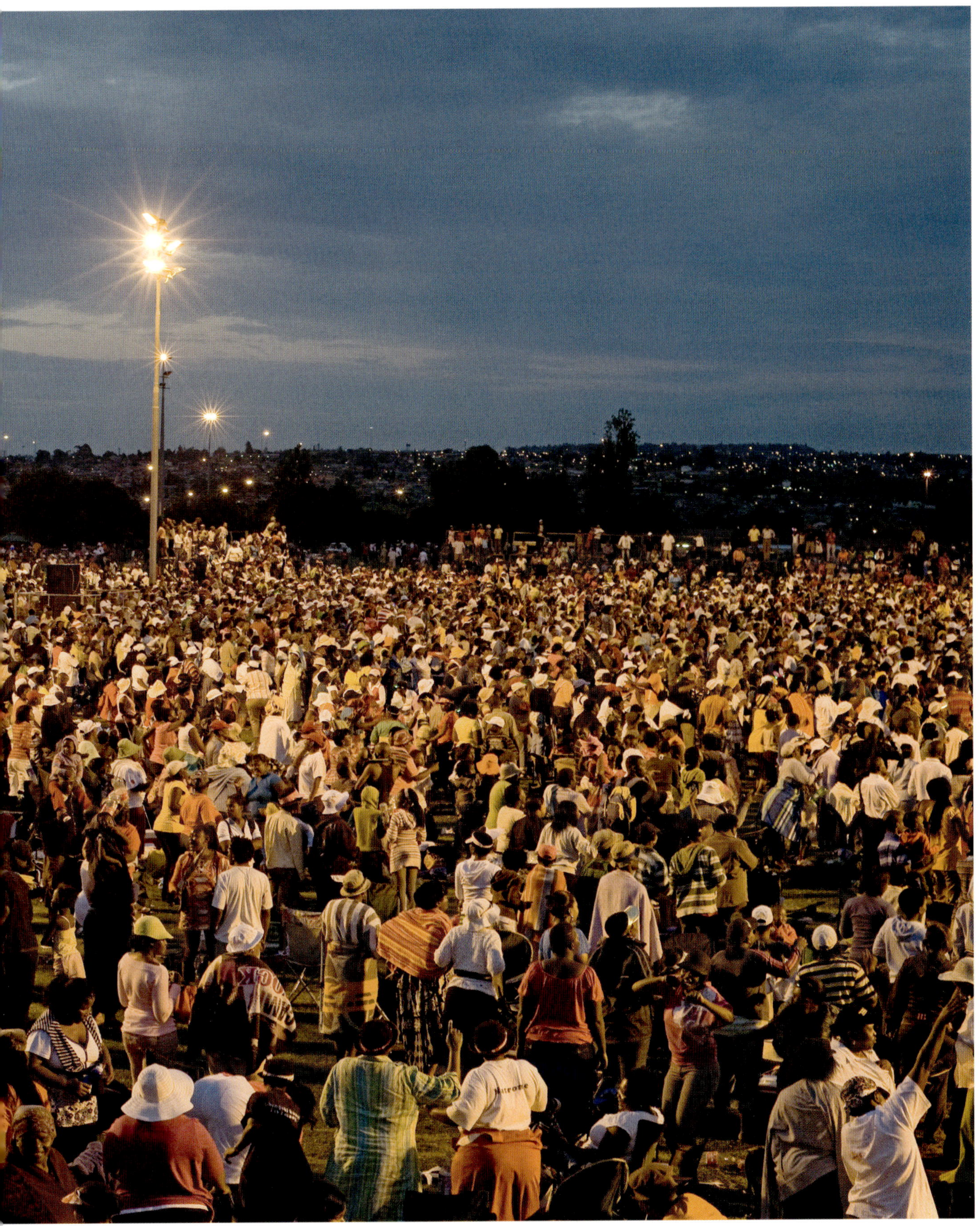

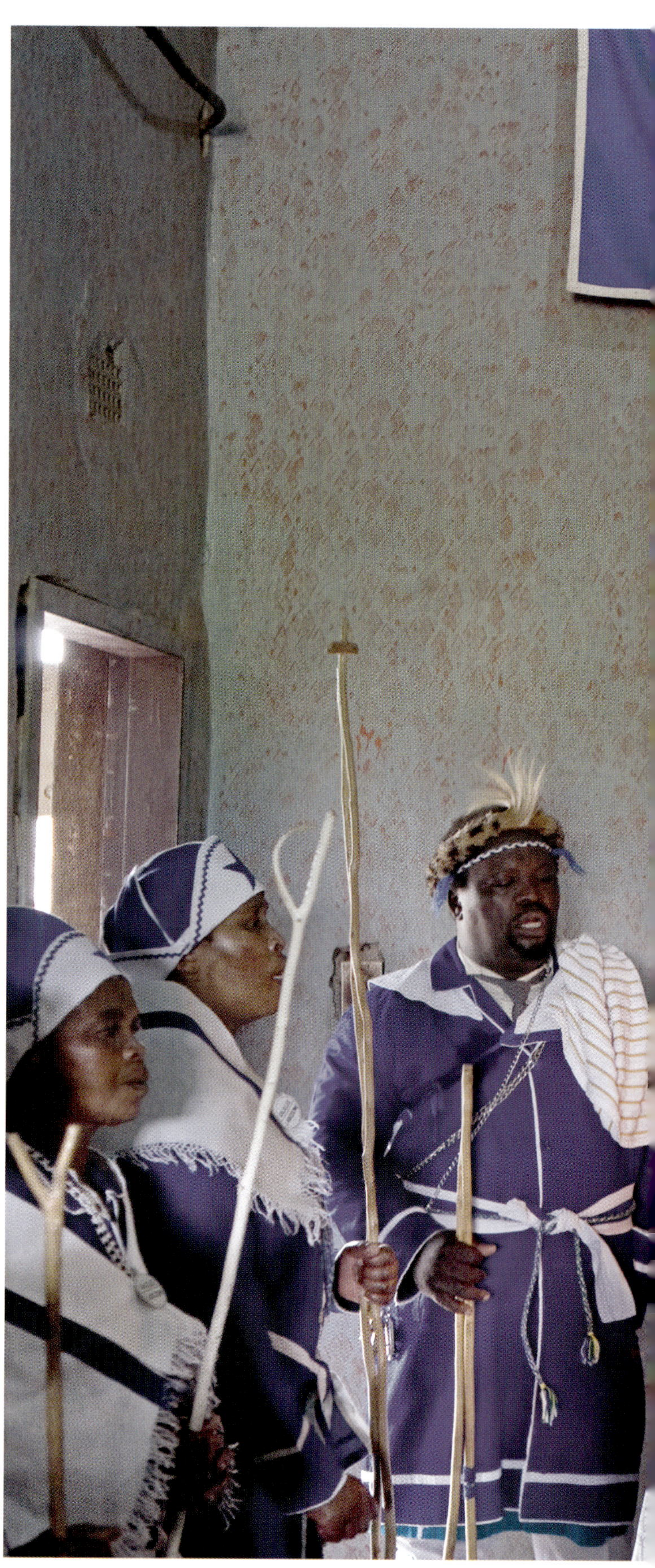

140 | Gallie of Zion Christian Church, Dlamini 2, 2009

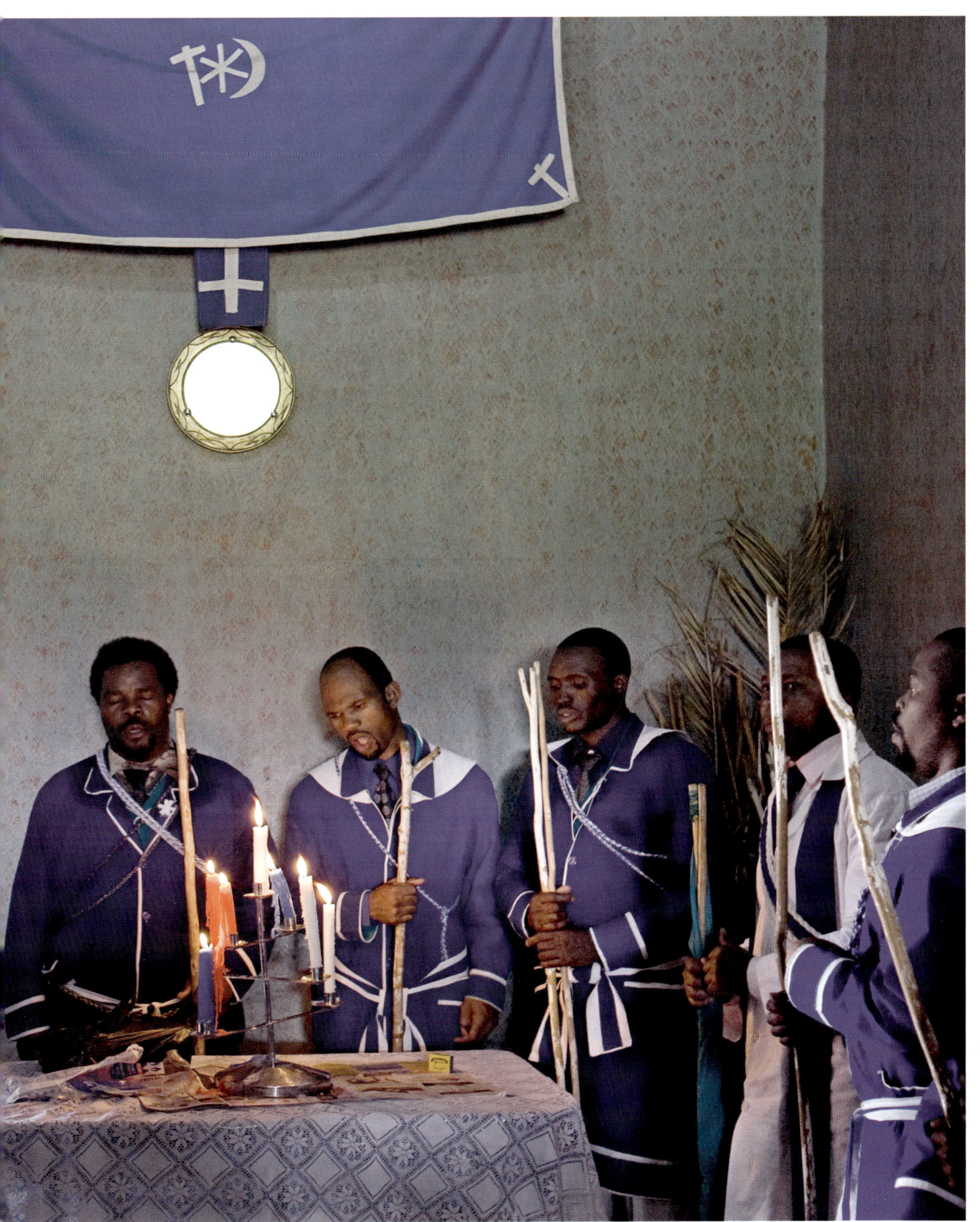

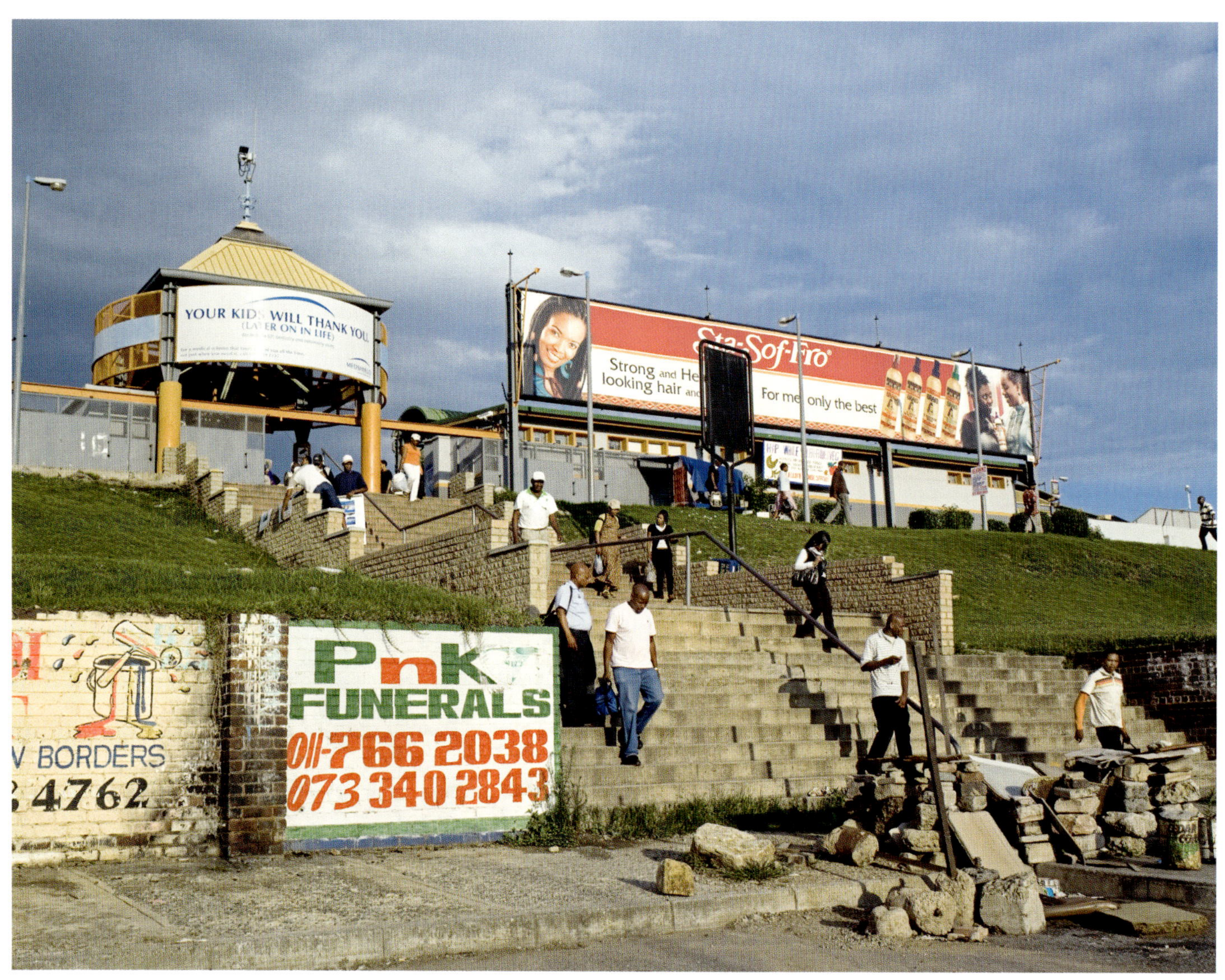

YOUR KIDS WILL THANK YOU
(LATER ON IN LIFE)
Sta-Sof-Fro
Strong and He
looking hair and
For me only the best
PnK
FUNERALS
011-766 2038
073 340 2843
BORDERS
4762

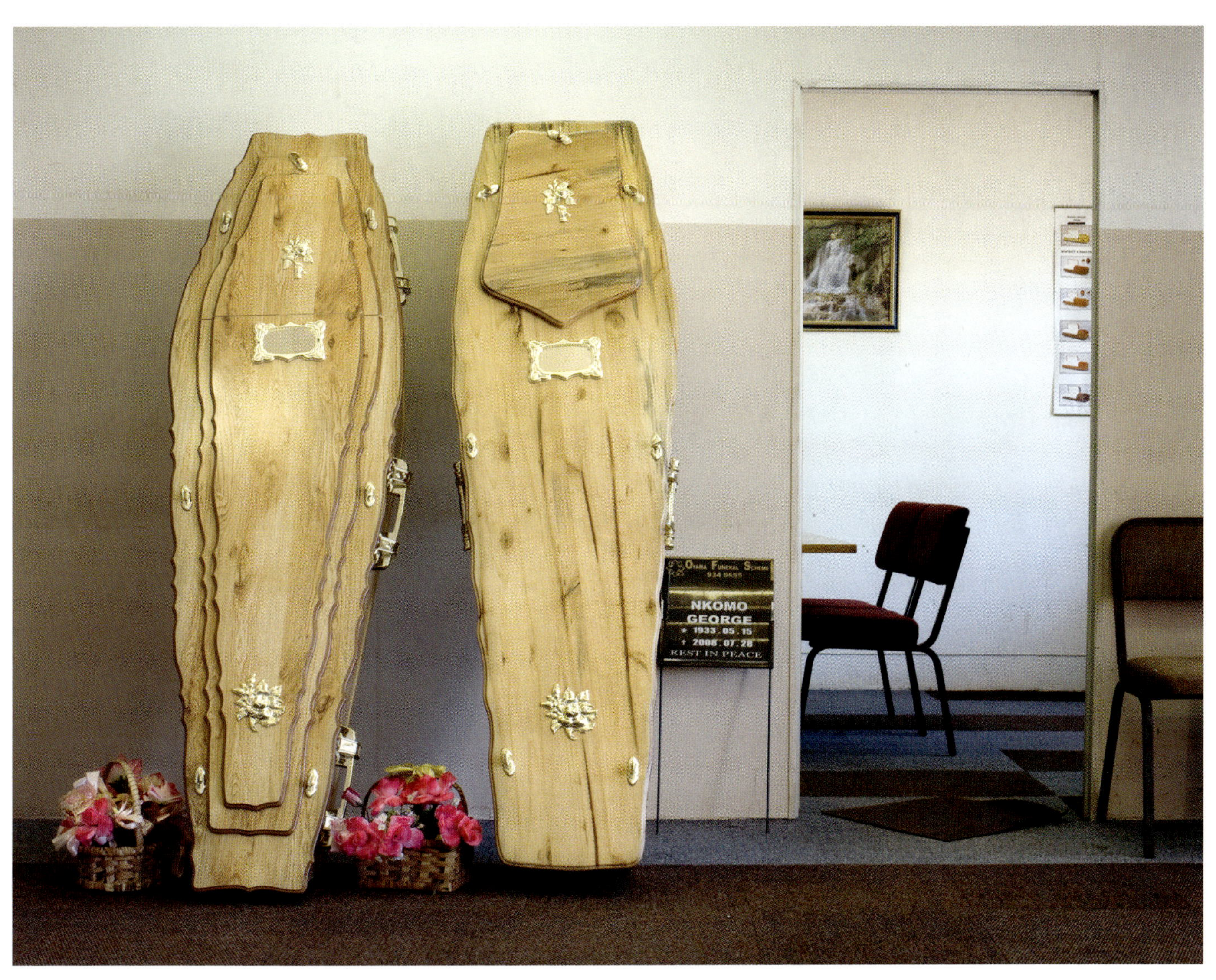

Oyama Funeral Services – "An ideal low funeral service provider", Protea Glen, 2010 | 143

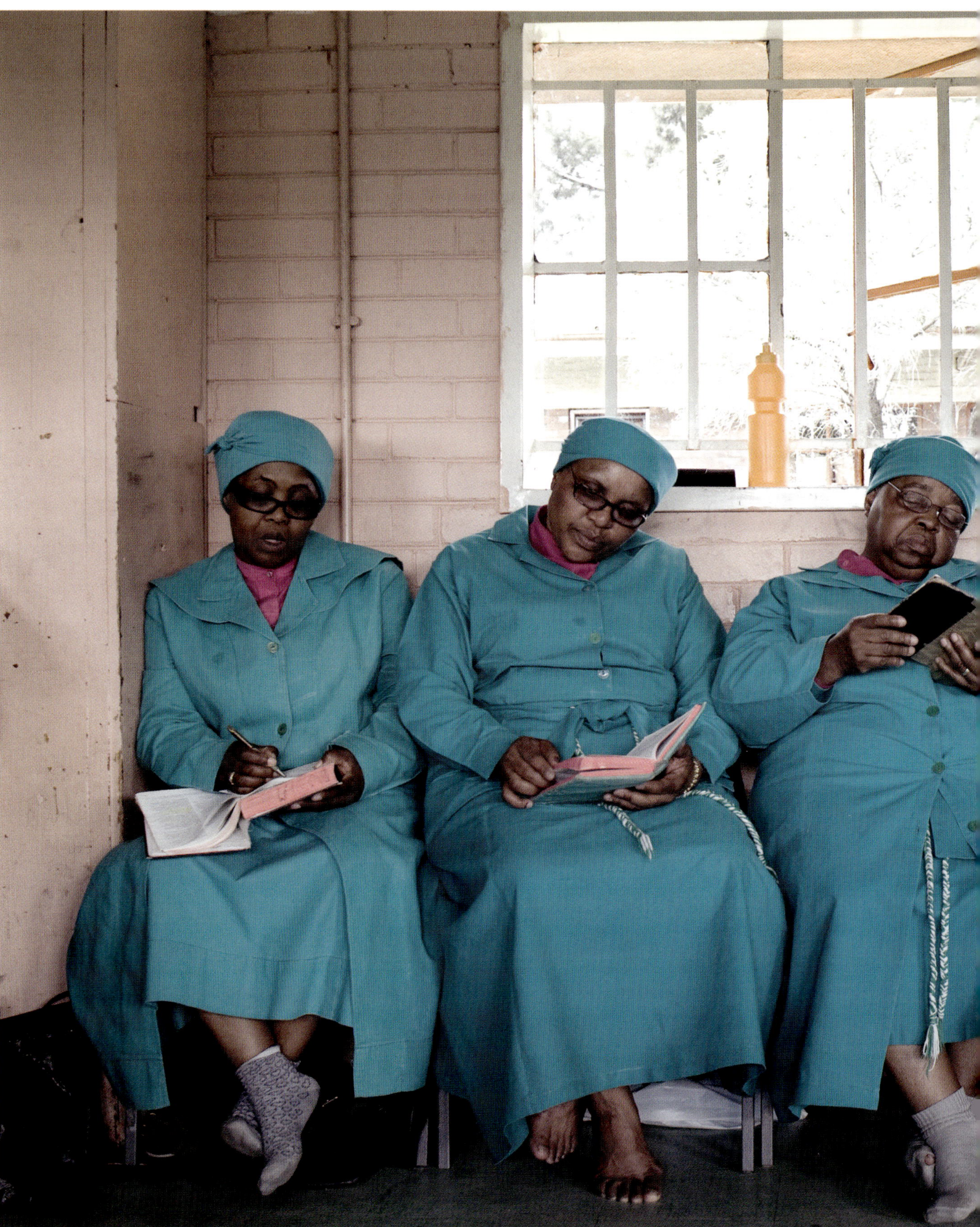

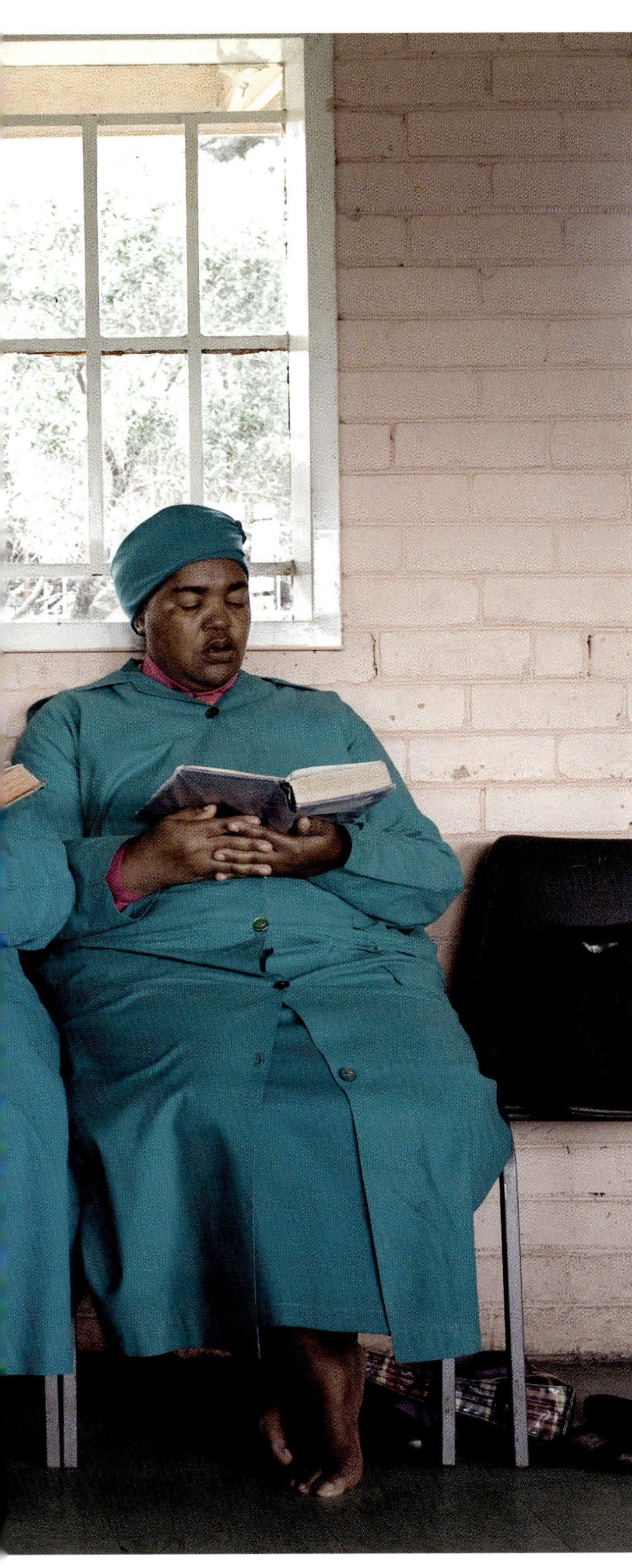

Believers in Christ, Ikhwezi Primary School,
Mofolo North, 2009 | 145

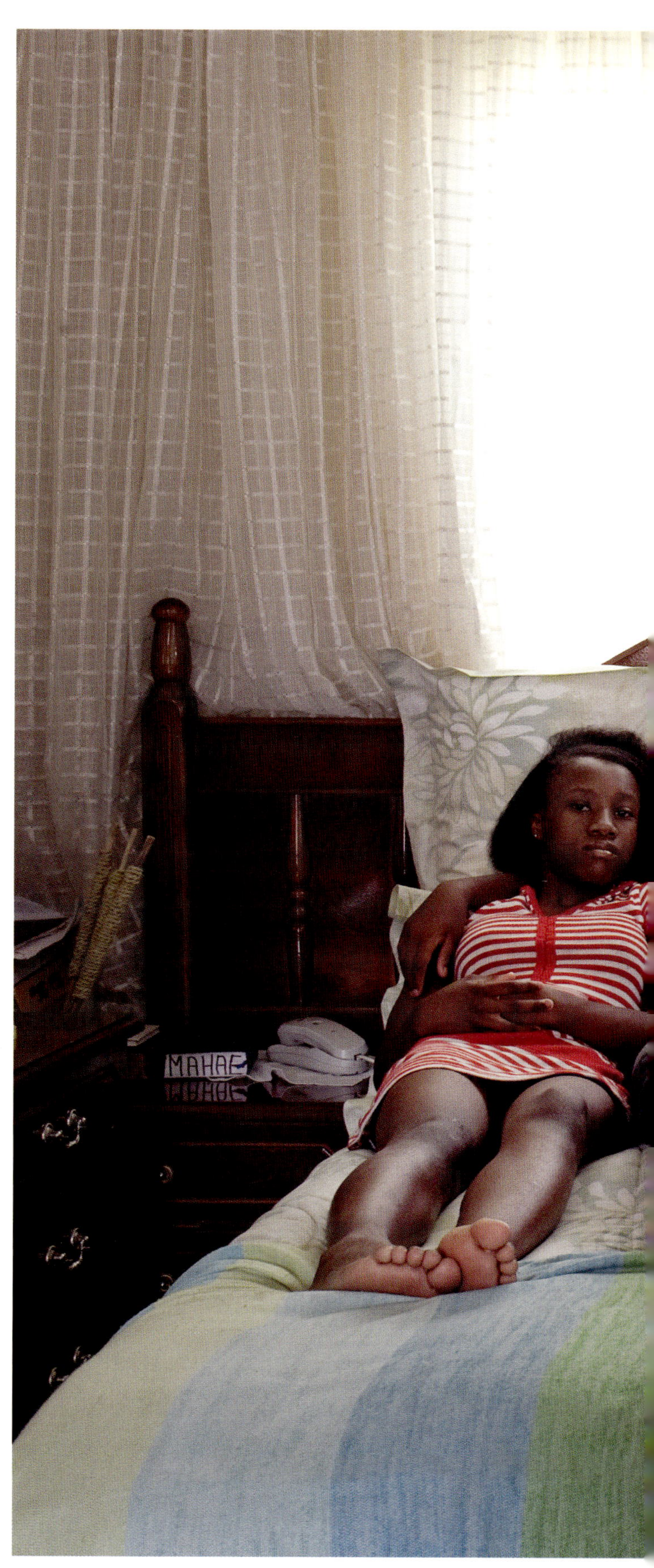

 Five girlfriends, Jabulani Flats, Jabulani, 2009

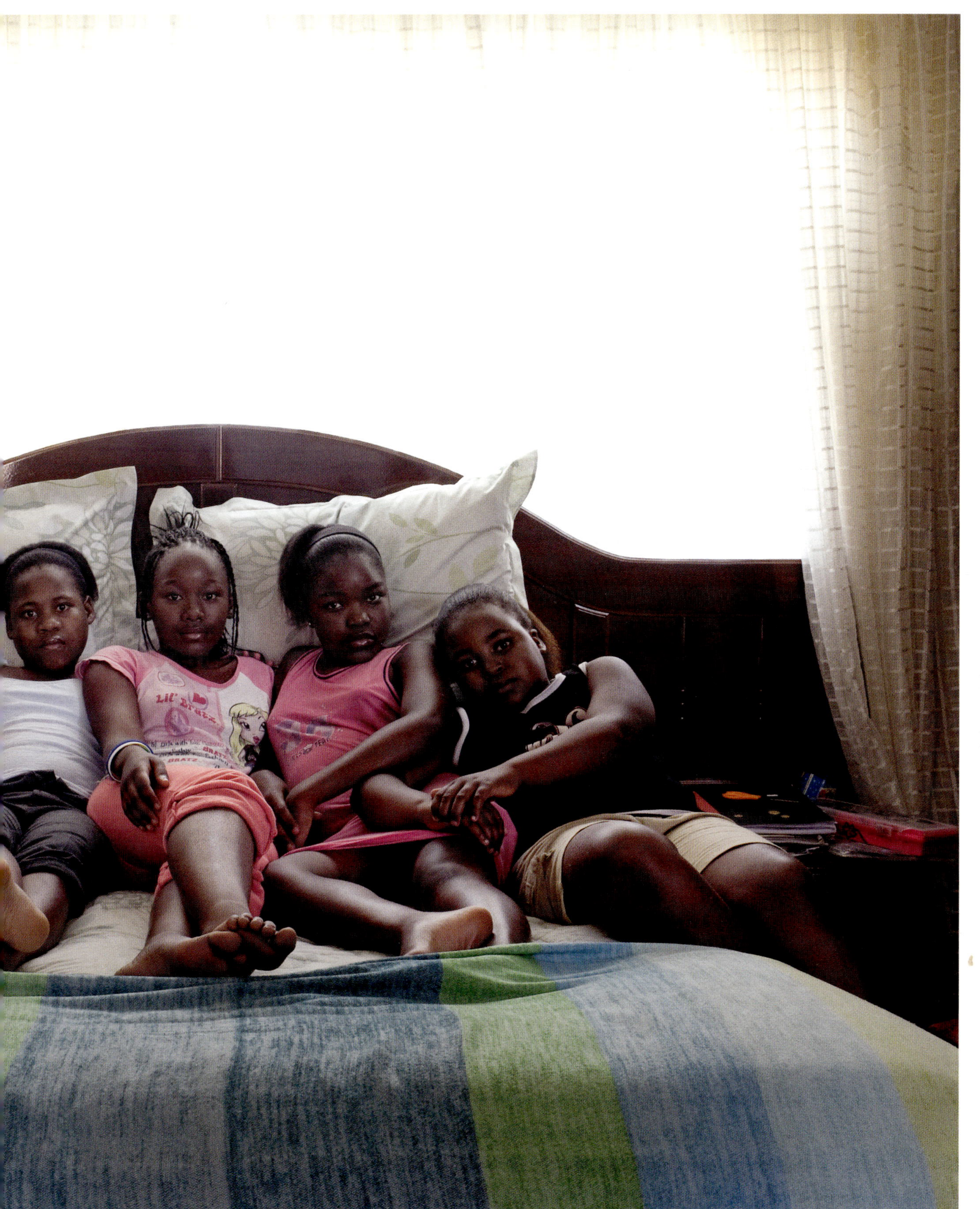

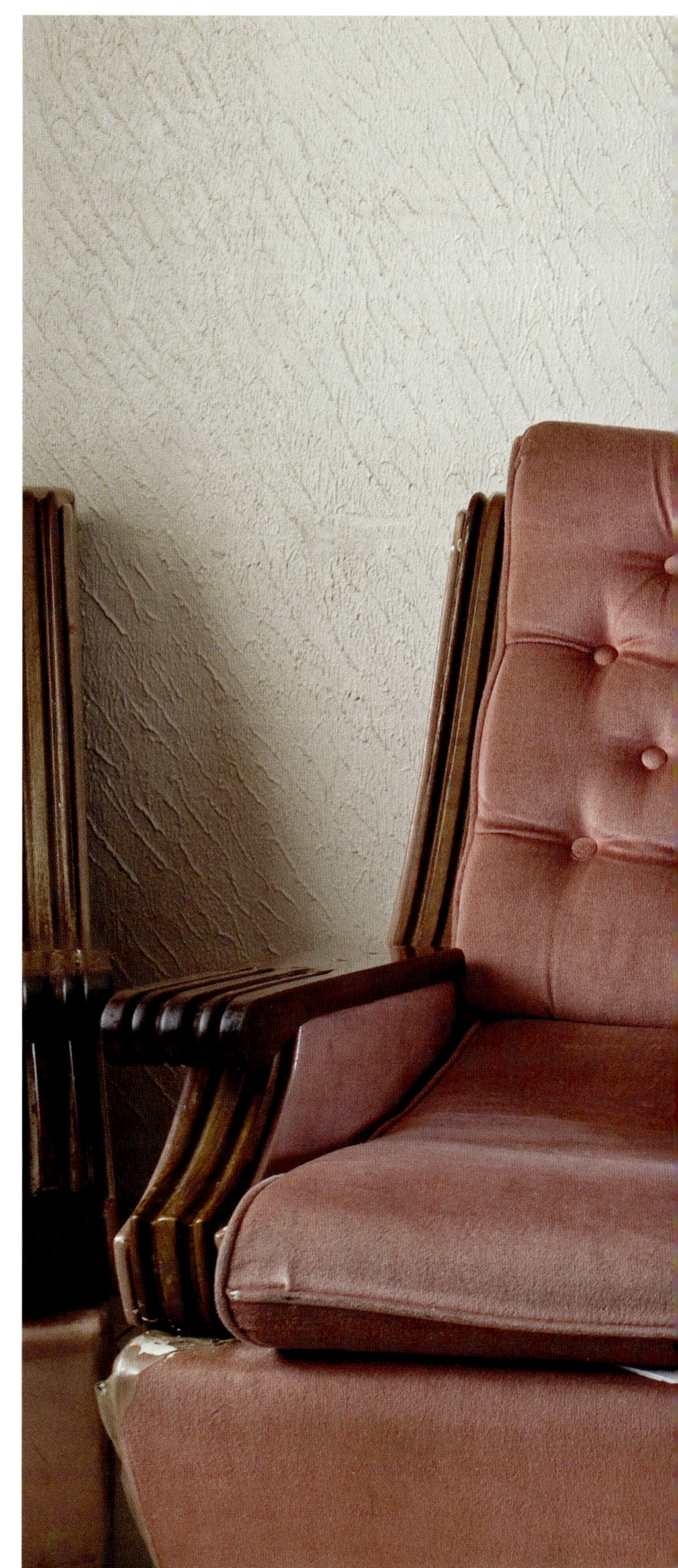

148 | Keabetsoe and Keamogetsoe Segoe,
Chiawelo Flats, Chiawelo, 2010

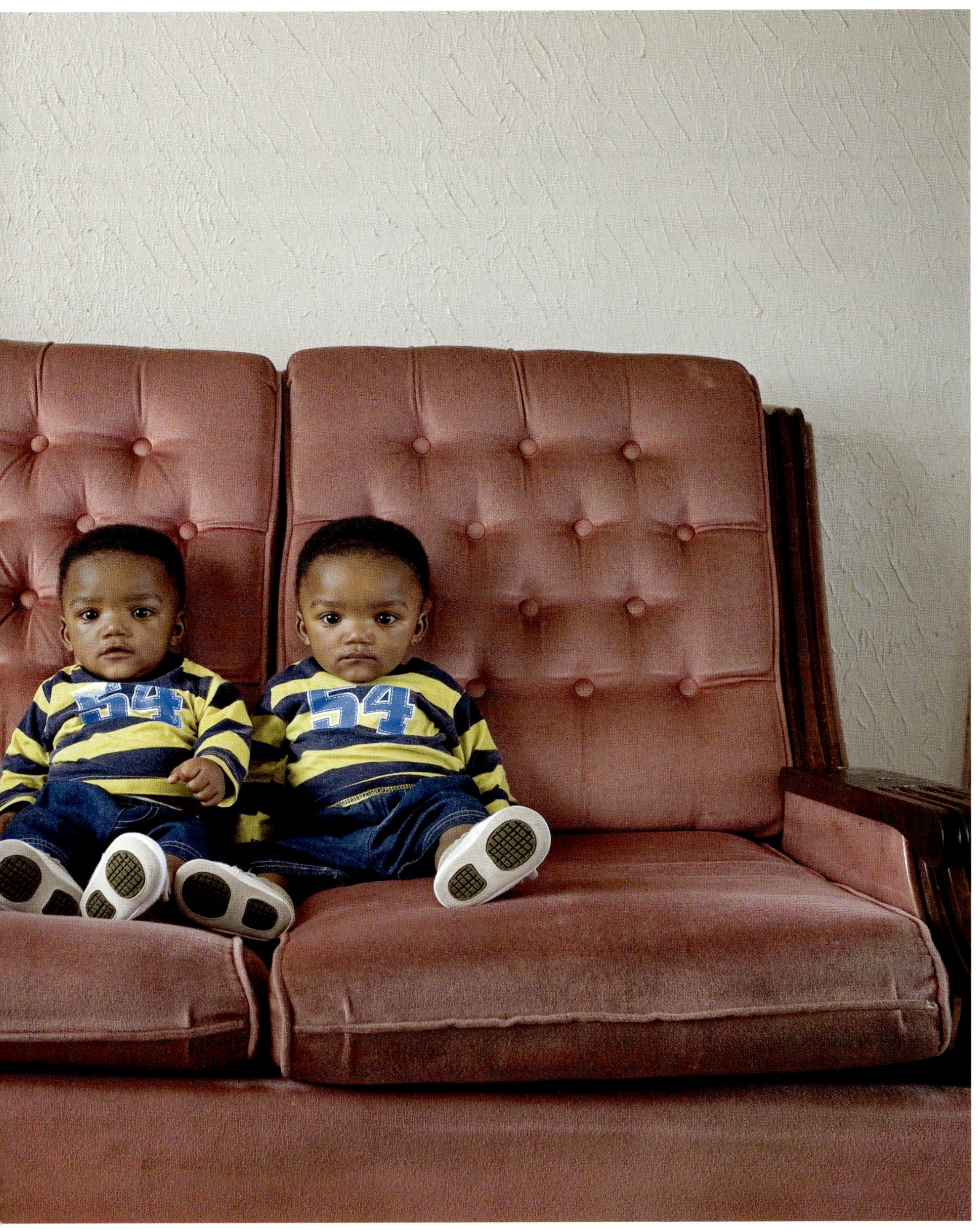

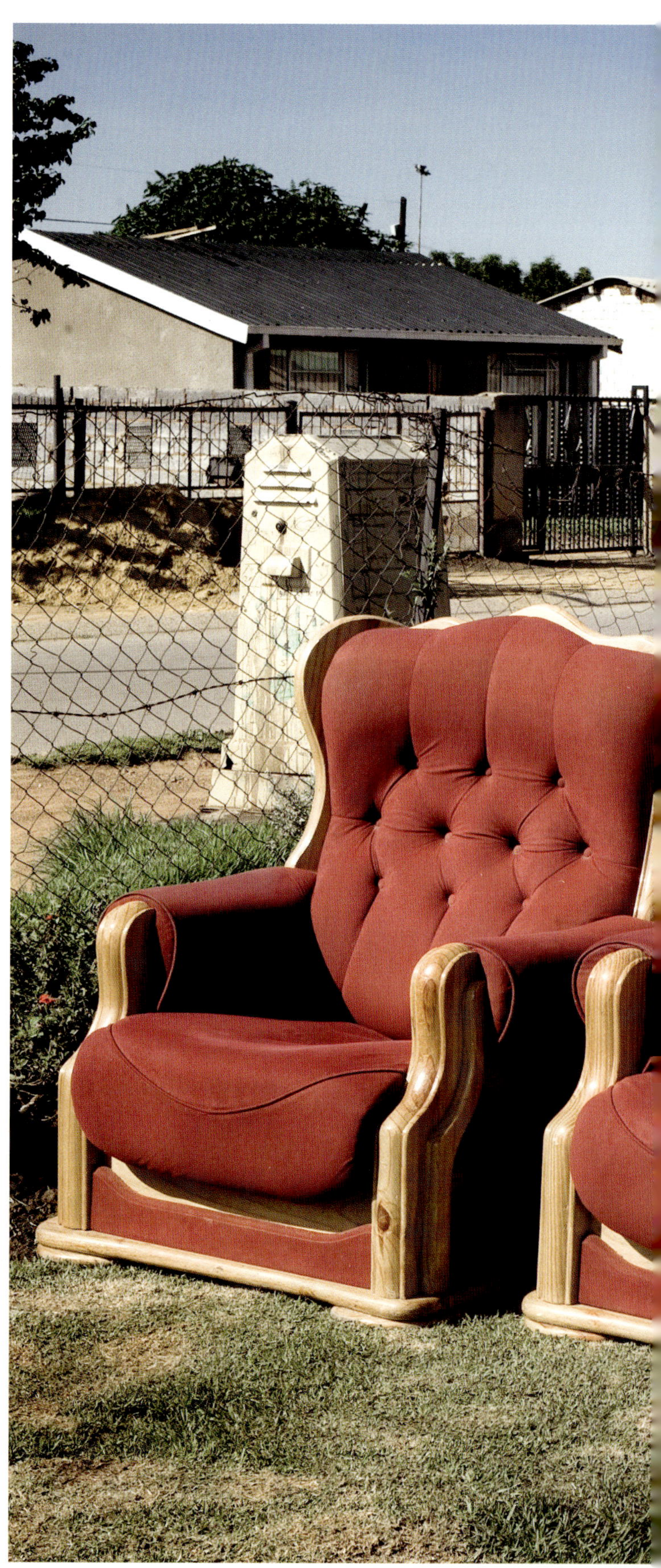

150 | Fikelephi Ngubane's home, Emdeni, 2010

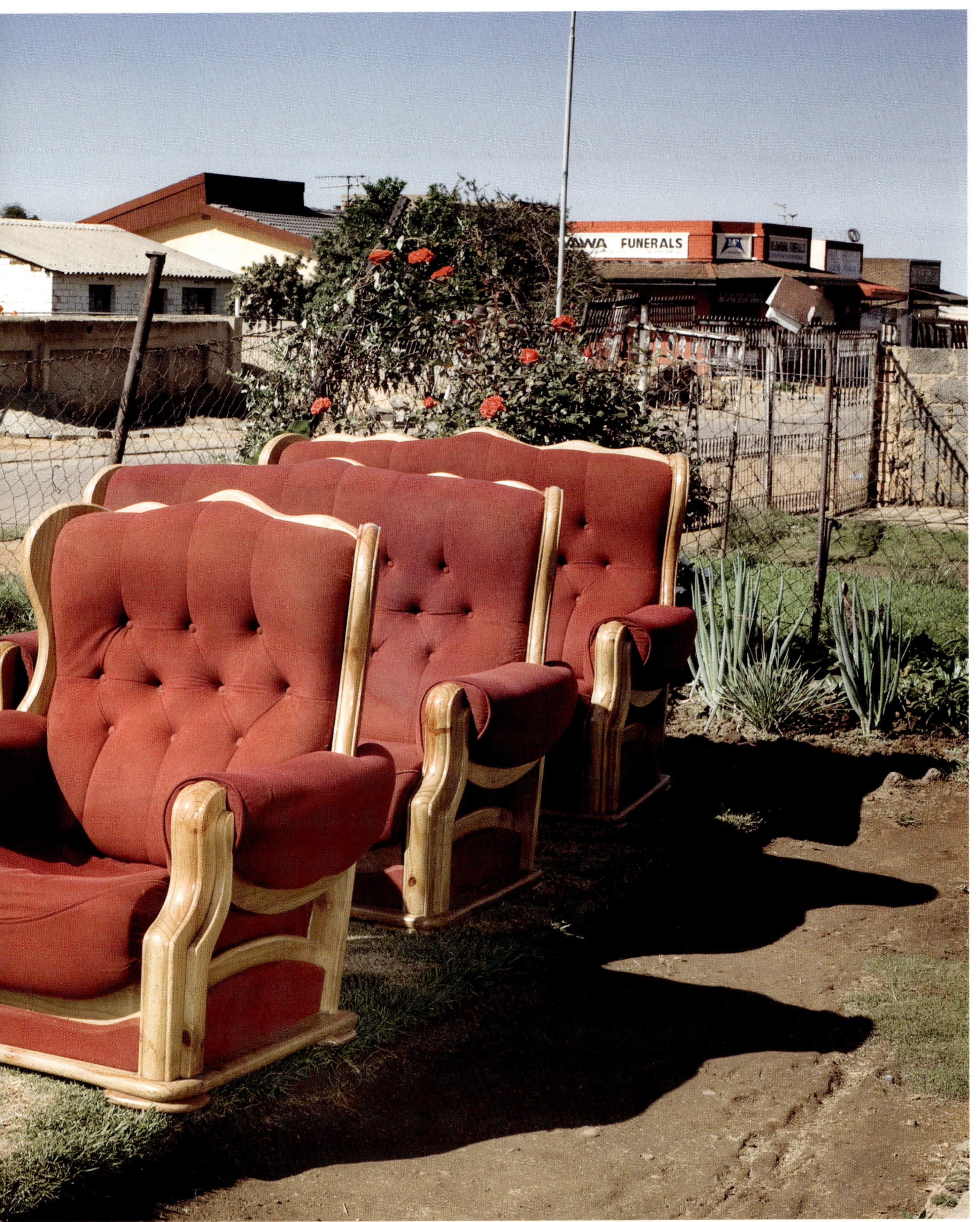
...WA   FUNERALS

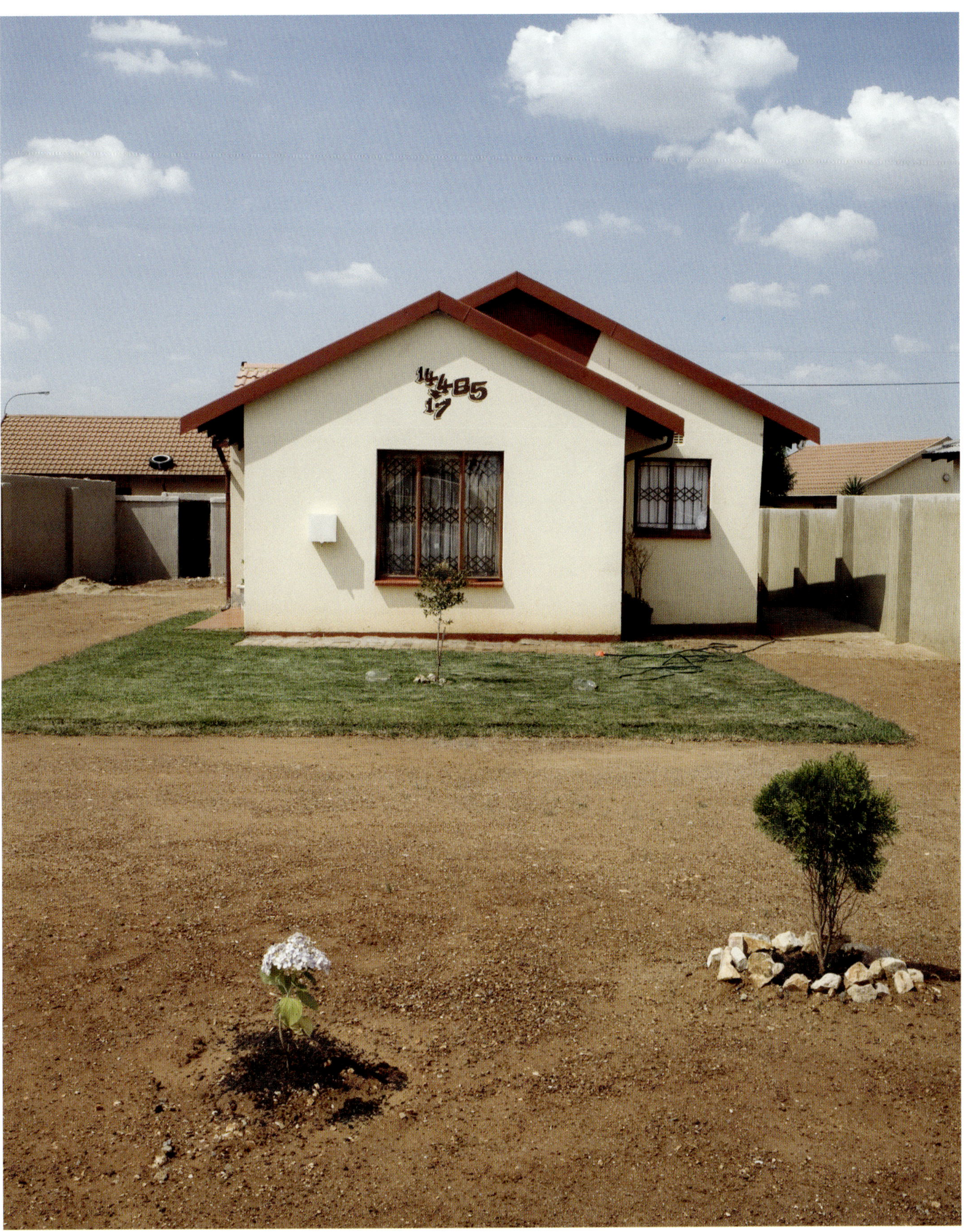
14485
17

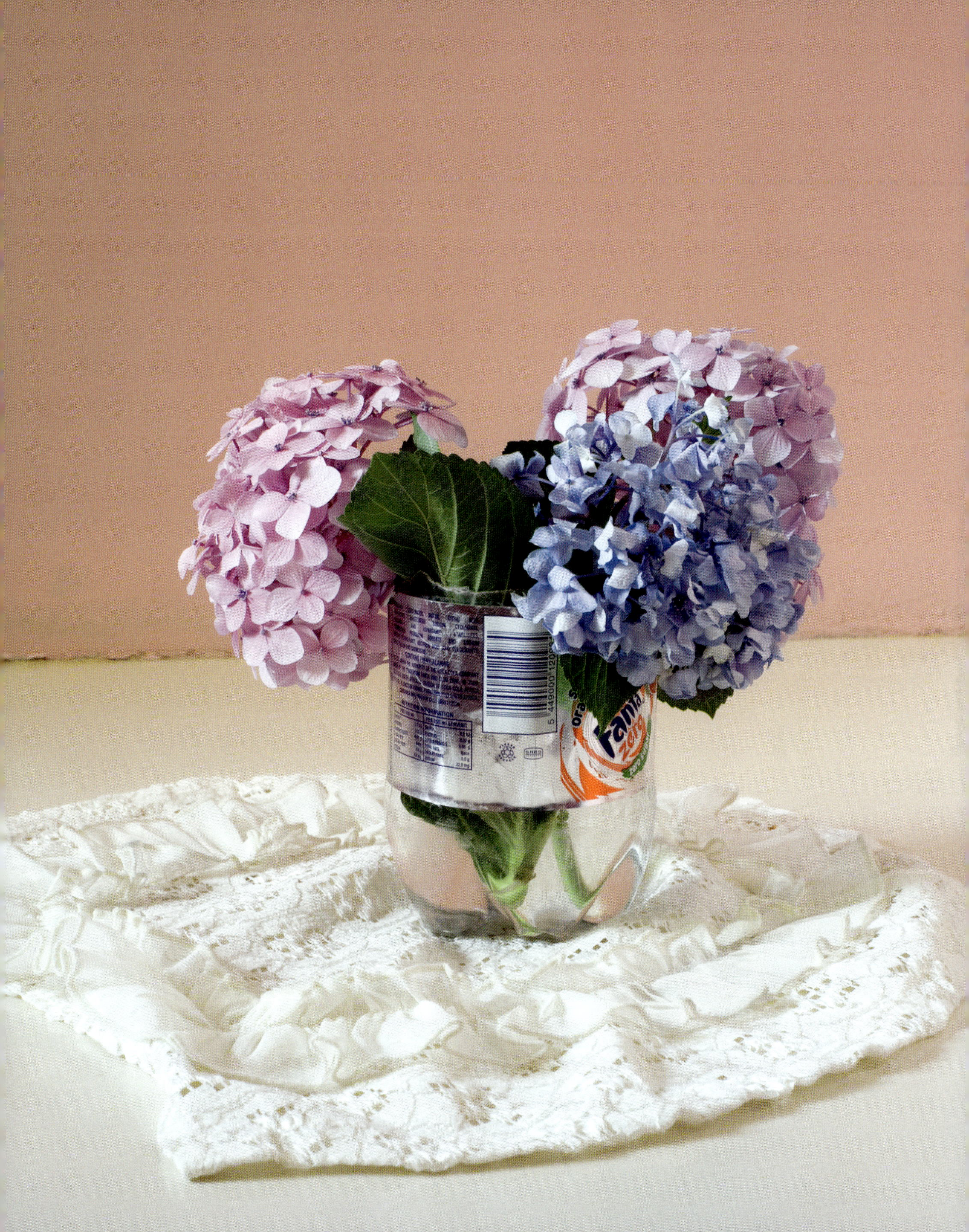

This book would not have been possible without all of your support and commitment:
Thank you to the people of Soweto who allowed this project to happen including those people whose photographs did not make the book.
Thank you to my mom Nadine, a thought for my dad Bobby, Axel Gylden who gave me the idea. Bridget Impey, Maggie Davey, Kerrie Barlow and the team at Jacana Media. Peter Anders, Cara Snyman and Dr Katharina von Ruckteschell at the Goethe-Institut, South Africa. My assistants Nigel Sibanda, Muntu Lerato Moeketsi, Simphiwe Nkomo and Sifiso Mashaba. Rory Bester who made sense of this project. Liza Essers (Goodman Gallery), Louise Gubb, Peta Hunter, David Goldblatt, Karen Coetzee, Steven Moffett, Pierre Croquet, Radhika Chalasani and Kalpesh Lathigra whose opinion helped me to move forward in my decisions. Nikki Berriman, Kirsty Wesson, Neil Dundas, Wendy McDonald and the team at the Goodman Gallery. Frank Evers and Matt Shonfeld at Institute for Artists Management who worked tiredly to get the work noticed by the international media. Francois Smit for his design at Quba Design & Motion. Dennis da Silva, Andile Komanisi, Andreas Kahlau and Boogie Dookoo at Silvertone for the photographic rendition of my images, and Niq Mhlongo.

Once again, a special thanks for the support and partnership of the Goethe-Intitut, South Africa who made this book possible, and thank you to Bridget Impey and Maggie Davey at Jacana Media who allowed me the freedom to create a book the way I saw it and who believed in the project right from the start.

Map sourced from the Corporate Geo-Informatics Directorate of the City of Johannesburg.

BIOGRAPHICAL HIGHLIGHTS

Awards

Winner of the Prix de le l'Union Européene at Recontres de Bamako Biennale Africaine de la Photographie, November 2009

1ˢᵗ Prize – Portrait Series "Real Beauty" – POYi (Picture of the Year International) USA, 2009

"Real Beauty" was one of the 10 finalists in the Leica Oskar Barnack Award, Germany, 2009

Winner at the First International Photography Biennial in The Islamic World held in Iran, May 2008

Awarded at Recontres Africaines de la Photographie in Bamako for a residency at Foundation Jean-Paul Blachère in France in Autumn, 2008

World Press Photo Awards

2005 – 2nd Prize – Contemporary Issues Story – Survivors of Domestic Violence

2002 – 1st Prize – Portrait Singles – Portrait of a young Pakistan girl.

2001 – 1st Prize – Daily Life Story – Illegality/ Repatriation – South Africa/Mozambique

3rd Prize – People in the News – Ebola Crisis in Uganda

1999 – 1st Prize – Portrait Story – People of Eksteenfontein

2nd Prize – Sports Story – Rugby in Madagascar

1998 – 1st Prize – Arts Single – Ballroom Dancers in Ennerdale

2nd Prize – Arts Picture Story – Gauteng Music Academy

Solo Exhibition

Las Canas – 2nd Thessaloniki Biennale of Contemporary Art "PRAXIS. Art in times of uncertainty"– Greece, May 2009

Las Canas – The Human Condition, Noorderlicht Photo Festival, Holland, 2009

Real Beauty – Goodman Gallery, Johannesburg, November 2008

Las Canas – Brisbane Powerhouse in Australia, Oct/Nov 2008

Between Dogs and Wolves – Growing up with South Africa – The Hereford Photographic Festival, UK, May, 2008

Las Canas – FotoFreo, Australia, April 2008

Mon Afrique du Sud 1994 – 2001 – Visa Pour L'Image – Perpignan, France, September 2002

Joint Exhibitions

Going Home – Recontres de Bamako Biennale
Africaine de la Photographie, November, 2009

Las Canas – Foundation Jean Paul Blachère – Oct
2008/Jan 2009.

Las Canas – 7th Recontres de Bamako Biennale
Africaine del la Photographie, Bamako, Mali, 2007

The ifa-Galleries Berlin and Stuttgart – Oct 2008/
Jan 2009

"I am not afraid" – The Market Photo Workshop,
Johannesburg, Dec 2007/ March 2008, CAMERA
AUSTRIA, Kunsthaus Graz

Survivors of Domestic Violence in SA – Moving
Walls – New York – The Soros Foundation,
2006/2007

Unsettled: 8 South African Photographers –
2005/2006 Reykjavík Museum of Photography,
Durban Art Gallery, The Regional Museum, Sweden
National Museum of Photography_Det Kongelige
Bibliotek_Denmark

Las Canas, Vidas en Positvo – El Museo de
la Illustracion y la Modernidad de Valencia,
November/December 2003

Survivre A L'Apartheid – Maison European de la
Photo – Paris, 2002

Democracy's Images – Photography and Visual
Arts After Apartheid Series: "Kom Blom Met
Ons" Gangsterism in Westbury, Johannesburg –
BidMuseet (Sweden) – 1998. The Johannesburg Art
Gallery (South Africa) – 2000

Blank – Architecture, Apartheid and After Series:
Corrugated Iron in Carltonville, South Africa – The
Netherlands Architecture Institute (Rotterdam,
Holland) – 1998/99; The Bensusan Museum of
Photography (Newtown, Johannesburg, South
Africa), 2000

Colours Kunst aus Suid Afrika – Haus der Kulturen
der Weldt, 1996

Under the Tropics – Permanent exhibition at
Cardiff University (United Kingdom), 1996

Collections

The Johannesburg Art Gallery, 2002

Books

*Between Dogs and Wolves – Growing up in South
Africa*, published and released in 2006 by Mets and
Schilt – Holland, Dewi Lewis – UK, Double Storey
– South Africa, Contrasto – Italy, Editions de l'Oeiel
– France

www.jodibieber.com

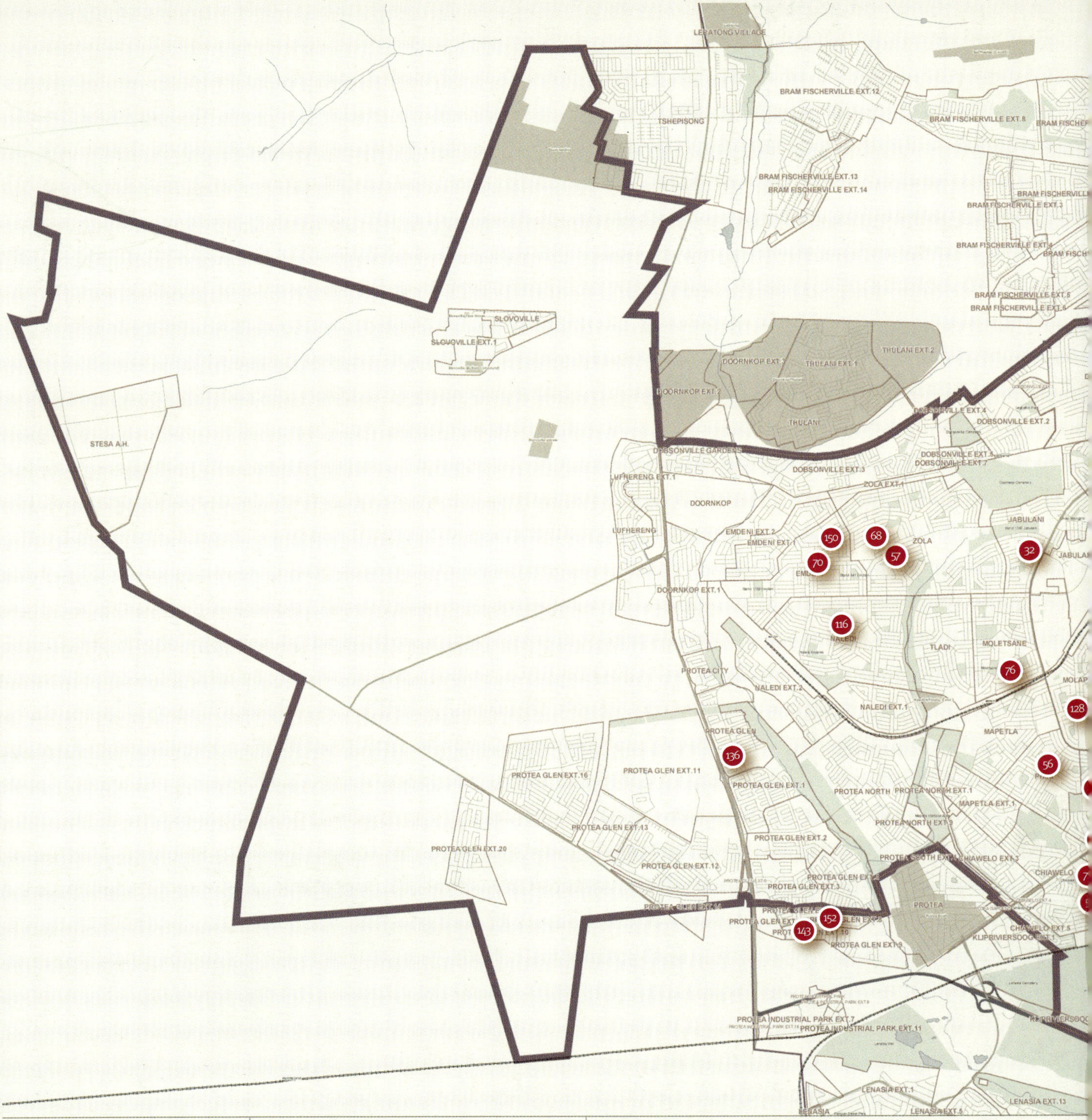

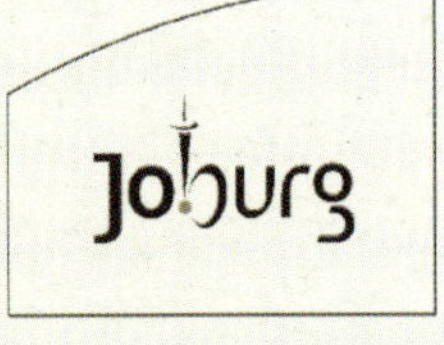

Region D

Regional Map

LEGEND

Regional Boundaries
Township Boundaries
Informal Settlements
Parks / Open Spaces
Dams
Rivers

Railway Lines
Railway Stations

ROAD TYPE

National Roads / Motorways
Provincial / Major Roads
Local Roads